Mike,

Thank you for being [?]
my Leap Year of Firsts [?] your
"fifteen minutes of fame"
article that you did on
"Saving lives and his business"
April 23, 2020.

Forever grateful
With Much Love,

Ruth

12-14-21

& 95

366 ADVENTURES TO APPRECIATE AND LEARN FROM LIFE

A LEAP YEAR OF
FIRSTS

HOW I FOUND MY "WHY"
AS A SMALL BUSINESS OWNER DURING THE
CHALLENGING YEAR OF THE PANDEMIC

KEITH L. BALDWIN
FOREWORD BY RON "JAWS" JAWORSKI
STAR NFL QUARTERBACK AND ENTREPRENEUR

A Leap Year of Firsts

© 2021 Keith L. Baldwin

ISBN 978-1-66781-296-0
eBook ISBN 978-1-66781-297-7

CONTENTS

Foreword...1

   Author's Note 2

Chapter One: Start o f A Leap Year of Firsts –
How did I get here? 4

   About the Author 12

   January 1st: Mummers Parade – Live............................... 17

   January 2nd: Daily Journal – Writing one........................ 19

Chapter Two: Learning Differently: "How to …" 20

   January 3rd: Meditate 20

   January 4th: Drive the Speed Limit to Work 21

   January 6th: Tarot card reading 24

   January 8th: CPR Certification Class 27

   January 9th: Live Portrait Model Drawing 28

   January 10th: Visit a Mosque – Attend an Islamic service 30

   January 14th: Heart Ablation 33

   January 15th: Tie a Bow Tie 35

   January 16th: Rushed to Emergency Room 36

   January 17th: Overnight Stay in a Hospital 38

   January 18th: Listen to a Podcast Series 38

   January 19th: Binge-watch a series (The Vietnam War) ... 40

   January 23rd: Wear high heels 42

   January 26th: Interview my mom for posterity 43

   January 28th: Detail interior of car 46

   January 31st: Lunch with daughter at her work 47

Chapter Three: A Quest for Understanding 49

February 2nd: Attend a Jehovah Witness service............................ 49

February 4th: iFLY Indoor Skydiving... 53

February 9th: Attend a Mormon service 56

February 11th: Work with my wife at her job 59

February 12th: Medical Marijuana Caregiver Card 61

February 14th: Dispensary with Caregiver Card 61

February 15th: Race car at Las Vegas Motor Speedway 63

February 19th: Cher Live in Vegas 65

February 21st: Bake pot brownies for mom 66

February 22nd: Home-Brewed Beer 68

February 29th: Wear Golf Knickers 72

March 6th: Dad's Ashes in My Golf Bag 73

Chapter Four: You've just crossed over into…
The Twilight Zone– Unwanted Firsts.................................75

March 9th: Business interruption claim 76

March 11th: Medical marijuana lozenges 76

March 12th: A pandemic (life changes) 78

March 13th: The Best Man (A Play) 79

March 14th: Axe Throwing 82

March 16th: Worried for the future of my business 84

March 17th: No salary – Worked for free 88

March 18th: COVID-19 exposure shut down my business 89

March 19th: Dealt with a threat to a life 90

March 20th: Laid off an employee – All 45 of them 94

March 20th: Hired back @ 4:30 – Part 2: "Manna from heaven" 96

March 21st: Became a Call Center 98

Chapter Five: WHY?...**101**

March 22nd: Gave up #1 Son status via Facebook 101

March 24th: COVID-19 "Survival Guide" 103

March 25th: Call from an employee's father 106

March 26th: A Check for No Reason Other than to Help Me 107

March 27th: Worked on another business 109

March 28th: 115 mph on I-95N to "WHY" 111

April 1st: Did NOT Achieve a Written Goal 112

Chapter Six: 15 Minutes of Fame **116**

April 2nd: Posted Selfies of Employees – My Heroes 116

April 6th: Article in Forbes Magazine 117

April 7th: Interviewed for a Podcast 118

April 8th: Passover Seder (via Zoom) 118

April 9th: PPP loan application accepted 120

April 10th: Sent "Pebble" Poem Product of Gratitude 121

April 11th: Staff Featured in the Wall Street Journal 123

April 16th: Cried on TV (6ABC) 125

April 18th: Company Facebook Page Unpublished 125

April 20th: Worked through the night with no sleep 127

April 21st: Saved 123 jobs — Answering California Unemployment calls 128

April 22nd: Lost 123 Jobs – Answering California Unemployment calls 129

April 24th: Featured as a Hero on Zoom meeting 130

April 27th: National Retail Federation's (NRF) Small Business Spotlight 131

April 28th: Cold-Called for an Interview by KYW-Radio 132

April 30th: Called a book publisher 133

Chapter Seven: "In the midst of Chaos, there is also Opportunity" — Sun Tzu 135

May 1st: Wear Tutu at Board of Directors Zoom Meeting 135

May 4th: NO Machines Running Mid-day, Mid-busy Season 136

May 5th: Margaritas at Lunch at Work 137

May 11th: Twilight Zone Edition of the Spike's Company Newsletter 138

May 13th: Started a hand sanitizer business 139

May 14th: Signed two NDAs in a day............. 140

May 30th: Canceled Nile River Cruise and Jerusalem Trip 144

May 31st: Closed showroom due to Civil Unrest in Center City, Philadelphia............. 144

June 1st: Canceled Award Associates of America's Summer Meeting........... 145

June 2nd: QVC and HSN LIVE 147

June 3rd: Slept Overnight at Work 150

June 7th: Wear a Pink Tutu on the Golf Course 153

June 16th: A Call Like No Other 154

June 17th: Sing as front man of band............. 155

June 25th: Tailgate Show for Competitors 156

June 27th: Posted an Opinion on Social Media............. 156

Chapter Eight: A Bucket List of Firsts 159

July 1st: Fly a plane 159

July 6th: Questions for Uncomfortable Conversations with a Black Man 163

July 10th: Listen to an audio book (The Fire Next Time) 166

July 17th: Moon a Friend on the Golf Course 167

July 20th: Juggle 169

July 24th: Play Pickle Ball 170

July 29th: Golf 18 Holes with Three Clubs............. 171

July 30th: Father and son fishing trip... 172

July 31st: Catch a King Salmon 173

Chapter Nine: Fun(ny) Firsts 175

August 1st: Kayak – alone 175

August 4th: Flood at One of the Showrooms 176

August 5th: A 7-figure sale (Sneeze Guards) 176

August 8th: Listen to a Classical Music station
(Sirius 76 – Symphony Hall) 177

August 9th: Today's Trendy Hits station (Sirius 3 – Pandora) 177

August 10th: PHISH station (Sirius 29 – PHISH Radio) 178

August 11th: Hip-Hop station (Sirius 44 – Hip-Hop Nation) 178

August 13th: Electro Dance station
(Sirius 51 – BPM – Beats Per Minute) 178

August 14th: Bluegrass station (Sirius 62 – Bluegrass Junction) 179

August 15th: Southern Gospel station (Sirius 65 – enLighten) 180

August 16th: 1st Grandchild's First Birthday Party 180

August 17th: Real Jazz station (Sirius 67 – Classic Jazz) 181

August 19th: Blues station (Sirius 70 – BB King's Blues) 181

August 20th: Opera station (Sirius 74 – Met Opera Radio) 182

August 21st: Joel Olsteen Radio (Sirius 128) 182

August 23rd: Comedy station (Sirius 98 – Laugh USA) 183

August 25th: Agribusiness and Western Lifestyle station
(Sirius 147 – Rural Radio) 183

August 31st: Sent invitation to fill a restaurant 184

September 5th: Horseshoe Bend Park Hike 186

September 8th: Filled a restaurant 187

September 17th: Picked up a million-dollar check 187

September 23rd: Visit the Vietnam War Memorial 188

Chapter Ten: Getting back to normal?..**190**

October 2nd: Acquired a company due to COVID-19 190

October 12th: Watched Collateral Beauty 191

October 16th: Rent Abatement 192

October 20th: Mail-in Vote for President 193

October 22nd: Skyline Drive, Virginia 195

October 23rd: Blue Ridge Parkway 196

October 24th: Stargazing App 196

October 28th: Isle of Palms Sunrise 197

October 29th: Lying next to a live Alligator on a golf course 198

November 2nd: Smoke a Cigarette 200

November 3rd: Acupuncture 201

November 5th: Virtual Cooking Class 202

November 6th: Disc Golf 204

November 10th: Multiple Staff Test Positive for COVID-19 206

November 16th: Visit my grandparents' gravesite 207

November 17th: Call with Warren Buffett 208

November 20th: Played Hooky from Work to Play with Grandson 209

November 22nd: The Opera – Falstaff (virtually) 211

November 24th: COVID-19 Test – Four-Hour Line 212

November 26th: Communicated Thanksgiving Gratitude and Love 213

Chapter Eleven: Lessons Learned...**215**

December 3rd: Birding 215

December 4th: Nitrile (medical) glove order 217

December 5th: Slept on the streets with the homeless 219

December 7th: Assemble Bikes for Charity 223

December 8th: Watch a movie with subtitles 224

December 9th: Guitar Lesson 225

December 11th: Write a Song (Twenty-Twenty) 226

December 12th: Free-Form Watercolor Painting 228

December 13th: Perform a magic trick 230

December 18th: Write a speech 231

December 19th: Trap Shooting 234

December 21st: Gave Money to a Homeless Person at a Stoplight 237

December 25th (Christmas Day): Watched It's a Wonderful Life 238

December 26th: Kwanzaa (learn about) 239

December 27th: Cast a Spell 242

December 29th: Being blind (simulated) 245

December 30th: Fly a Drone 248

December 31st: Write a book (finish manuscript outline) 250

What I Learned from 2020 253

Chapter Twelve: Epilogue – How It Changed Me 257

Postscript – Twilight Zone: Part 2 259

Acknowledgments – *It Takes a Village* 261

List of 366 Firsts and 10 Core Values 266

Our Core Values 282

Contact 284

Giving Back: 285

FOREWORD

As a quarterback in the National Football League for seventeen years the ability to adapt, adjust, and pivot were a requirement of the job. During the pandemic of 2020 those abilities were essential if you wanted to remain a viable enterprise in the business world.

COVID-19 sidelined everyone when it hit our world. In the midst of a global pandemic we had a choice with which attitude we would move forward.

Keith Baldwin, — an incredibly selfless, highly respected business owner and good friend — began 2020 with an idea to broaden his world and add to his lifelong quest for learning. His idea was to do something every day that he had never done before and carry it through for a year; a fun project that, someday, he could share with his grandkids.

March 20, 2020 rocked Keith's world as he had to walk into work, a 90-year-old company that he had built up for the last 44 years, and tell all of his employees that the company was closing. For most people, that would have put an end to this *year of firsts* — **but n**ot Keith. He called an audible: his *firsts* became more intentional and meaningful. His drive to lift other people up *and* save his company was paramount in his quest to complete his project, as his *firsts* became selfless acts of kindness and heroism. Not surprising for a man whose company walls proclaim their core values with words like: care, dependability, respect, integrity, and hustle.

As you read about Keith's *Leap Year of Firsts*, you'll laugh about when he took his 85-year-old mother — suffering from intractable pain — on a trip to the cannabis store. Or the day when he drove the speed limit for the whole day.

You'll cry as Keith writes about the night he slept on the streets with other homeless men, or the unemployment calls he fielded with suicidal individuals who couldn't feed their families.

What you won't do is regret learning how he was able to *flip the switch* and turn adversities into opportunities. That is what amazing people do. Thank you, Keith!

Ron Jaworski

.   .   .

AUTHOR'S NOTE

This book is a combination of some actual journal entries, with minor spelling and grammar edits. They were cut and pasted from the day and moment they happened and were written. I'll let you know this by including *"unedited journal entry"* prior to the entry for that day's *first*. Some have been rewritten from emailed entries or from the handwritten place markers from my desk calendar from the day. I've deleted some names and places for various reasons. I also spare you the details of many of my *firsts*. I provide my full list of *firsts* at the end of the book to save you from boredom and conserve the number of pages in the book.

If I have any after-the-fact comments to add, I address them at the end of that day's *first*. I wrote these at the time of putting the book together in 2021, as I reflected with the knowledge of a Monday morning quarterback.

Finally, I may have a question or two for you throughout, for you to think about. Maybe the question will challenge you. Maybe it will spur you into action, to take a chance, to be spontaneous, to be curious. Maybe it will get you to live a little more. Maybe it will ask you to take your own adventure. Who knows? Maybe you'll put your own list of *firsts* together to experience. These questions are marked with bold question marks: "**???**"

. . .

CHAPTER ONE:
START OF A LEAP YEAR OF FIRSTS – HOW DID I GET HERE?

It's midnight on December 5, 2020, and I'm horizontal on hard, wet ground, on a slightly sloped hill between two large boulders, strategically positioned to block the breeze. I'm tucked in a worn, beaten-up sleeping bag. A rolled-up old towel is my pillow. It's in the 30s, with a biting wind — COLD. I didn't shower, and my clothes are war-torn and old. My location is Sixth Street, between Callowhill & Race Streets in Center City, Philly, just blocks from where the business I currently own started almost a century ago. It is blocks from where I walked through the door of that business as an ignorant, wet-behind-the-ears teenage employee 40-plus years ago. My head is on a swivel, keeping a constant eye out for danger. The din from the nearby highways is distracting. There is a half-moon with a few stars above. The nearby streetlights provide a minimal amount of illumination. I am trying to catch a bit of shut-eye, despite having one eye open. I'm spending the night among the homeless on the streets, with mini tent-cities on either side of me that reside under the adjacent highway overpasses. How did I get here? Why do I find myself here for the *first* time in my life sleeping on the streets of Philadelphia, Pennsylvania on a bitter December night as a homeless person…voluntarily?

The answer to this question started exactly one year ago to this day, less than ten miles away, at my *first* Human Resources Management Association breakfast meeting on the morning of December 5, 2019, at a local South Jersey eating establishment. I was one of the few guests in the crowd of close to a hundred members. The guest speaker was LuAnn Cahn, a veteran Emmy Award-winning journalist and cancer survivor who wrote a book called *I Dare Me: How I Rebooted and Recharged My Life by Doing*

Something New Every Day. It was fate that the speaker that day hit on a topic that inspired me to pursue my very own unique journey. A year-long adventure of sorts. During her 20-minute presentation, she asked the attendees to write on an index card one thing they would commit to in the upcoming year, which would be a *first* for them. I wrote "fly a plane." (This was an idea I gave up on many years ago because of the assumed cost and time commitment.) She had us turn to the person on our right and make this commitment. She wanted it to be a goal, a written one we were committed to. She asked for volunteers in the audience to stand and share their commitments. I was one of the few guinea pigs selected to share. I was honestly somewhat embarrassed and self-skeptical when I stood and said, "fly a plane." I'm sure, like most in the room, I thought we would commit and forget about it once we walked out of the door and back into our busy lives. My goal seemed far-fetched, self-important, and rather unachievable, especially at my advanced age. I'm old — I'm over 60! Would I do it? I really wasn't sure that morning.

I hung around after the presentation to acquire a signed copy of the speaker's book. I also wanted to personally tell her that she had inspired me that morning. The story she recounted of sitting down next to a homeless person in Rittenhouse Square touched me. It was the *first* time she had a conversation with a homeless person. Her curiosity and dare to herself had pushed her out of her comfort zone. The room was silent, as people wiped away tears as she recounted it. It still moved and affected her to that day. It moved me! She planted a seed that day within me that would grow into a life-changing experience, one that would place me on the Philly streets, homeless for an evening, a year later.

I received a signed copy of the book that morning. I disclosed to the author that I was going to take her dare and do my own *year of firsts* starting on January 1, 2020. There you go. I was committed. I was all in. I'm sure she heard this commitment often. I wondered how many would follow through. I wasn't sure if I would after the high of the morning wore off.

Did I have the staying power to see it through once punched in the mouth by the fist of everyday life?

As I walked to my car, I started to think, *"every day?"* It seemed like a lot of work, but I have never been afraid of hard work. I opened *I Dare Me* and skimmed the list of her 365 *firsts* at the end of the book. I was intrigued. That day I started to read the book to wrap my head around what my firsts might look like. The author's *first* of her year was the Polar Bear Plunge in Atlantic City on New Year's Day. I decided that was a good start for me, too. I had never taken a Polar Bear Plunge in freezing cold water before. I Googled the event, signed up, ordered, paid for a commemorative t-shirt, and awaited my *first* on the 1st. I was on my way.

I am fortunate that 2020 was a leap year. It would make my year of *firsts* unique in a way; 366 versus 365 — I'd have one extra first. In the weeks leading up to my first, I started to write a list of other possible firsts. I pilfered a few from her book and started to come up with several of them on my own. I sorted them into *firsts* I would need to plan for and others I could do at a moment's notice as filler. I also searched my upcoming calendar of firsts that were already booked for the year that I could count on.

As part of this, I wanted to start a daily journal for the *first* time in my life to document these firsts. On January 2, I would start my journal. My intent was to turn it into a book, this book, another *first*. I would do this for me, for posterity, by self-publishing a few copies for my family. I was planning to call the book *A Leap Year of Firsts — 366 of Them*. Here is the list I compiled and headed into my year with:

IDEAS I NEED TO PLAN FOR

- *Fly a plane*
- *Speech – Write & perform one*
- *Watercolor class – Paint my wife*
- *Walk to work*
- *Magic trick – Learn*
- *Song – Write*

- *Unplugged – A day without a cell phone, Outlook, Facebook, etc.*
- *Edit a video – Learn*
- *Serve dinner at a homeless shelter*
- *Work with my wife (Carter's)*
- *Fly in an air tunnel*
- *Karaoke*
- *Fenway/visit Boston*
- *Rock climbing – Indoors*
- *Skydive*
- *Sign language – Learn to say: "I Love You" and "Forgiveness"*
- *Surf*
- *Limoncello – Make*
- *Row on Schuylkill River*
- *Drum lesson – Learn a song*
- *Guitar lesson*
- *Race car – Drive*
- *Wheelchair – Spend a day in one*
- *"Blind" – Spend an hour/day*
- *Yom Kippur service – Attend*
- *Video interviewed by my kids (my life)*
- *Shoot 78 – Lowest round of golf in my life*
- *Reconcile longtime feud – To forgive*
- *Acupuncture*
- *Piano – Learn to play a song*
- *Pickle Ball – Play*
- *High heels – Walk in*
- *Poetry reading – Attend one*
- *Shoot a gun*
- *No TV for a week*
- *Mud run*
- *Snowboard*
- *Zoo – First time with my first grandson*

- *Grandson firsts throughout the year*
- *Virtual reality – Try it*
- *Book – Write one*
- *Wire an electrical outlet (or something electrical)*
- *Speedo – Wear one*
- *Radio show – Call in*
- *Mummers Parade – Live*
- *Fantasy Football – Participate*

IDEAS – SAME DAY/FAST

- *Engrave holloware (mug or bowl) on computer*
- *Make a vinyl sign*
- *Tweet*
- *Juggle*
- *Skype someone*
- *Joke – Learn to tell*
- *Speed limit – Drive all day*
- *Red Bull – Drink one*
- *Bow tie – Tie one*
- *Mosque – Visit*
- *Poem – Write*
- *Medical marijuana with mom*
- *"Moon" – Old neighborhood friends*
- *Teeter – Hang upside down*
- *Socks – Wear wild/crazy socks for a day*
- *Tarot card reading*
- *Tattoo – Henna or real?*
- *Rap – Create & perform*
- *Stranger – Talk to*
- *Amazon – Order*
- *Dance – Learn a new one*
- *Shave head*

- *Medical Marijuana Caregiver card – Obtain*
- *Meditate – Learn/for 20 minutes*
- It's a Wonderful Life – *Watch the movie*

BOOKED ALREADY – IN CALENDAR

- *Daily Journal – Start Jan. 2*
- *Heart ablation – Jan. 14*
- *A Woman of No Importance (Play) – Jan. 17*
- *Tri-state HRMA partner event – Jan. 21*
- *PAPPA Winter Showcase – Jan. 28*
- *76ers game with son – Feb. 9*
- *Hammock Beach Resort – Feb. 27*
- *Las Vegas Cher Show – Feb. 16*
- *Bike City-to-Shore Cancer Ride – June 14*
- *Father/Son Great Lakes fishing trip – June 20*
- *Host national industry group in new building – Sept. 11*
- *Jerusalem & Egypt River Cruise – October*
- *Black Friday – Shop at midnight*

When I first started to document my *firsts*, I was writing my journal entries with detail, without thought to the overall length as a book. My *leap year of firsts* turned upside down and eventually, quickly, took a new direction, a new meaning, and a new purpose. I not only had trouble finding time to write, I had trouble having a second to think of and do a *first*. I barely had time to sleep. My job, career, and life were about to blow up in my face. But somehow, some way, I did it. Up until that point in March when the pandemic hit, I was documenting each *first* with a photo. I had planned to create a photo book for my family — those plans got scrapped. I went into 24/7 work mode for the next several months after March to not only save my business and my life's work, but more importantly to save the jobs associated with the business. This book turned into a documentary of *the* most challenging and unique year in probably not just my life, but in many others — maybe ever? A worldwide pandemic caused by COVID-19 showed up amid my *leap year of firsts*. I am sure it provided several of you many firsts during the year, as well. I kept referring to it as the Twilight Zone. Each day, hour, or minute, something bizarre, crazy, and unimaginable happened (or so it seemed). Each day became a new episode. Each episode seemed to have plot twists, some unimaginable. We had a pandemic like 1918, civil unrest like the 1960s, and a business downturn and unemployment like the Great Depression of 1929. Place on top of that a divisive election that brought back thoughts of our Civil War. Are you kidding me? And there was more thrown at all of us throughout the year with a record number of hurricanes, historic wildfires on the west coast, and much more; I can't remember it all. My business endured floods and blackouts caused by an EF2 tornado that struck the Northeastern Philadelphia suburbs. An EF2 tornado has wind speeds of 111 to 135 miles per hour. It was a *first* for our area. We do not have tornadoes. We are not Kansas! Well in 2020, we did. I kept waiting for the locusts to descend upon us, or for an asteroid to hit. We didn't get the locusts or an asteroid, but we did experience the 17-year swarm of cicadas and the murder hornets in the Pacific Northwest. At times, there were no words.

I now have a list of planned *firsts* that unfortunately, for one reason or another, I did not accomplish. I have included this list in the Epilogue. I ran out of days in the year, or the pandemic and the inability to congregate as a group prevented my best-laid plans. Man plans and God laughs. I had no idea when I started this year of firsts that by attending my *first* live Mummers Parade on Broad Street what the year had in store for me. My *first* of the year was to participate in the Polar Bear Plunge, but as you will see, I needed to modify my plans. Things change and you roll with it.

I hope you learn a little something in the following pages of what a small business owner endured on the wrong side of the shutdowns caused by the pandemic. The pandemic created a dichotomy for organizations and people. Depending on what side of the divide you fell on it determined if you thrived, while the other side struggled to survive, and businesses struggled to keep people employed. I will pull the curtain back on the "glamour" of being your own boss and a business owner during this global crisis. If you were part of the tech, real estate, logistics, or various businesses that befitted people staying home, you thrived. If you or your business depended on gatherings, you struggled to survive. The travel, event, school, catering, restaurant, and award industries were hit the hardest due to no fault of their own. My business — an awards and sign manufacturer in addition to being a promotional products distributor — revolved around events. During the busiest time of my industry's year, those events which included meetings, award ceremonies, trade shows, athletic gatherings, community and school activities, etc., were canceled, stopped, or placed on hold. It was our "busy season." In a seasonal business, that is when we make our profits to keep the business going and to keep our people employed.

We would have no busy season. Our three showrooms were ordered to close because we were a non-essential business. We were basically out of business. Quite honestly, we should be out of business, but we aren't. As you will see, it is not so glamorous. You will get a glimpse of the hard work needed and how I, along with many others, "worked the problem" every day to survive. Half of my work when the pandemic hit seemed to be devoted to providing and promoting hope to others. Hope to my family, friends, employees, and business colleagues. I don't know how that happened; it just did. My wish is that this book provides a little bit of just that: hope.

Some of the year's *firsts* just "happened" because of these challenging circumstances. I just went with it and did my best. I counted some of these happenings as my firsts, which they were. I could have never planned for some of these firsts; they were some of the most inspirational and emotional. At least they were to me.

To this day, when I retell some of these *firsts*, I find the emotions are still there, very close to the surface and strong. I'm embarrassed at times by the welling of tears as I choke up and take a breath to compose myself in recalling that specific *first*. As I pulled all this together to share in these pages, it hits me at times, reliving these *firsts*, sometimes unexpectedly. This book is my feeble attempt to toss a pebble into your pond in the hope that it spreads a ripple or two in your life and maybe the lives of others. This is my attempt in some small way to pay it forward. The actions of some individuals affected me this past year, and in turn, impacted many lives. The pandemic made this book more than for just my family. *Amazing. Blessed.* My wish for you is to enjoy the read as much as I savored the journey.

I look forward to taking you on the adventures of my *firsts*. Like life, some of these *firsts* are not exciting while others are. It is the ebb and flow of life. My first finished manuscript was in chronological order writing of every first. The first draft was over four hundred pages. The second re-write was not in chronological order and grouped in themes. With the help of my beta readers and editor I went through a few rewrites over the months and ended up with this book back in chronological order. It was one *wild* unexpected ride. I hope you will join me in enjoying this journey in the following pages.

ABOUT THE AUTHOR

Please don't let this book fool you. I am nobody special; just a hard worker from humble beginnings. I was born at Sixth Street & Indiana Avenue in North Philly, now affectionately called "the badlands," to a lower middle-class family. Sixth & Indiana is currently an "outdoor pharmacy," better known as a drug corner. No one in my family had ever owned a business. I was the *first* one, as my dad told me proudly shortly before his departure from this Earth.

I come from a union family. Growing up I was a derelict of sorts, drinking and venturing into drugs in the sixth grade. I turned into a college drop-out in my late teens. I started work at 14 as a dishwasher at a local seafood establishment. I had to clean bushels of crabs weekly for all-you-could-eat crab nights. After cleaning the crabs, with the spices in the open wounds of my carved-up hands, I would plunge them into scorching hot water to begin my dishwasher duties. I can still feel the pain almost fifty years later. It is etched in my bad memory banks. I can remember going to high school and falling asleep in class because I didn't get home until well after midnight from work. I could never seem to wash out the residual fish stink that would travel with me. All for $1.25 an hour! Hell of a resume, huh? What I'm trying to say, as I sit on the side of the road typing this part of my first book for the past hour, is that I'm no better than anyone else. Did I forget to mention that I am follicle and waistline challenged with a face made for radio? My memory and IQ are not doing so well, either. So, confidence does not come naturally. I must work at it. If I had been told when I was younger that I would write a book, I never would have thought it would be this one about *firsts*. I would have guessed it would be about the long, hard work necessary to climb out of these humble beginnings. I was not born with a silver spoon in my mouth. But I was lucky in birth, as I have come to better understand this past year. I was not born with a headwind of race, gender, religion, or ethnicity. I had the tailwind of being born a white male straight Christian child in the U.S.A.

I can proudly say that my grandparents lived in a rented broken down "pink house," as we called it, because it was painted pink. It did not have interior plumbing. I grew up in that dilapidated house with my cousins during the summers. It was a Tom Sawyer-like existence in Kratz, Pennsylvania. We affectionately called it *"The* Country." We had an out-house (outdoor bathroom), horseshoe pits, plenty of land to play ball, and a cold dank basement. We filled that basement with "critters" (snakes, frogs, lizards, turtles, and a raccoon) we caught during the day along the Perkiomen Creek. We had an old barn and a "cement pond" across the way at a "rich" aunt's home. We could use this luxury swimming hole only because my grandmother cleaned their home. Our access to this luxury was her pay. Our fishing spot was under the now non-existent old-school "bridge," the same bridge from which my father's ashes were spread. The same bridge whose painting and photos hang in my home and my office.

The same bridge my own ashes will hopefully someday be spread under. We fished under that bridge and walked the rails along the property with holes in our shoes and pants. *The Best* times of my life. And we had no money. It didn't matter. This experience wasn't lost on me. Money is nice, but it ain't everything; family, friends, shared experiences, and fun thrown in with love is. It was a kid's paradise and my own Citizen Kane's Rosebud.

I only had one other job besides my dishwasher days. I was still employed as that dishwasher when I walked into a local mom and pop sporting goods store. They were looking for help and offered me a job as their tennis racket stringer and skate sharpener for a raise to $1.50 an hour. Sign me up! I never looked back.

From that glorious beginning I worked *very* hard. In my mind, it was the only value I thought I could bring to the table. I was a shy, lost kid with a lack of confidence in myself, like many kids. I worked to be promoted to stock boy! I then traveled into the office — retail sales — and onto an assistant manager position as they expanded. When the opportunity to take over a floundering local trophy company came, they needed a sucker to help run it. I was their boy. At the time, I was putting myself through Temple University and was in my sophomore year. I was only mildly interested in school and just going through the motions. I was more interested in work and making some money. I dropped out to run this awards division. Or, I should say, have it run me. My parents were not exactly thrilled. I was young enough and dumb enough not to know any better. To show you how smart I was, I would work one hundred plus hour weeks and only report forty. I knew the parent company couldn't afford to pay me due to their financial issues. The job required more.

The reason that the awards company had become available was due to my predecessor having run it into the ground. He was selling items below cost and pocketing the proceeds. He was living the high life. When the sale became apparent, he absconded with the inventory and the orders to open as a competitor. He later ended up getting arrested, convicted and went to rehab. I ended up buying back the stolen inventory years later for cents on the dollar. This story alone could be another book. I distinctly remember sitting at my desk late one Sunday night, after another twelve hours plus day, crying. I was thinking, "*No WAY am I going to make a go of this*." I should have failed; I didn't. I learned the business through osmosis afforded by hard labor as a scared teenager. I worked on my diploma from the school of hard knocks for a dozen years. I eventually grew and made the awards division profitable. This allowed for it to eventually be sold off to an investor, with me included in the deal. The sporting goods company took the proceeds to expand, but eventuality went bankrupt a few years later. The investor was a new venture capital firm, and we were their first deal. I worked as the general manager for the absentee owner. They held on to the company for a dozen years until I started begging for help in achieving my *first* written goal.

The *first* goal I ever wrote was as that eighteen-year-old kid who walked into this left-for-dead awards company with a dream of owning it with my friends someday. That goal was realized twenty-five plus years later, fifteen years ago, due in large part to that hard work. I, along with four other long-term employees, broke our piggybanks to realize this audaciously written goal.

I was fortunate to have had a few mentors along the way that provided opportunities that I was able to take advantage of due to my hard work. These mentors exposed me to a worldly education of some exotic destinations (Hawaii, Caribbean Islands, cruises, and many other adventures). I was taken to gourmet restaurants and the most expensive clothing stores in Philly. I learned to become a gourmet cook, with the advantage of testing my dishes on other young up-and-comers as my guinea pigs. Later, multiple trips to China sourcing product at the behest of my national industry cooperative gave me knowledge that came in extraordinarily handy during the business crisis I was headed into. So culturally, through work, I was presented a world I would have never known existed. A world at times I was hoping to tap into to survive. But I always remembered where I came from. Hopefully, I never became too self-important and stayed grounded.

Once my partners and I had achieved our goal of ownership, we turned our sights to owning our own home for the business. I'd sit around and listen to other owners' counsel when I was still just a hired hand. I'd listen to tales that the business would pay your day-to-day expenses, but your wealth and retirement would come from your real estate. I listened intently. It became a second written goal for when the opportunity presented itself. Eight years after purchasing the business, after a two-year search, we found our home. Not having deep pockets (read NO money), we had to get resourceful. Through the help of the Philadelphia Industrial Development Corporation, in coordination with the state and our bank, we were able to one hundred percent finance the deal at a favorable rate. Yep, no money down! (Because we didn't have any!) My house and the business as collateral would have to do. As someone that kept his head down and focused on the business, I was ignorant to the ways and pitfalls of buying and rehabbing a building in the city. We soon got an unwanted education that almost put us out of business. That story will go unwritten. I'll spare you.

Suffice it to say we put a lot of sweat equity into the project to save it. I literally lived at the location for the better part of a year during the building's rehab. 2020 was not our first run through the survival gauntlet. These past experiences provided me with the scars, thick skin, experience, perspective, and perseverance needed to get through this year in one piece. I know I am not alone as a small businessperson with these scars. Many of us have similar tales to tell. I also think the expression "ignorance is bliss" fits here. At times I had my doubts. We just kept working it as we persevered.

On January 1st, 2020, I was headed on a unique journey of wanted firsts. A bucket list of them! This was before the unwanted firsts appeared in March. Why a "Leap Year of Firsts?" How did it start? What was it that grabbed me about this idea? Why did I do it? How did I come up with my list? What were my rules? What counted as a first? I'm glad you asked.

JANUARY 1ST: MUMMERS PARADE – LIVE

If you are not from Philly – What's a "Mummer?"

As defined by Wikipedia: *"The Mummers are a group of local clubs that compete in one of five categories: Comics; Wench Brigades; Fancies; String bands; and Fancy Brigades. They prepare elaborate costumes, performance routines, and movable scenery, which take months to complete. This is all done in clubhouses — many of which are on or near 2nd Street (called "Two Street" by some residents) of the city's South Philadelphia section. The parade starts at 9 a.m. with the Comics and Wench Brigades and runs all day until 6 p.m. with the String Bands being the featured acts of this tradition. The Mummers Parade travels down the central street (Broad Street) in Center City, Philly between South Philly and City Hall."*

As defined by the locals it is a reason to drink, party, and dress up like Mardi Gras in the winter with some very talented musicians in string bands as the headliners. It is a 120-plus-year-old Philly New Year's tradition. Although having the Mummers as customers and having seen them on TV every New Year's Day, I am ashamed to say I never saw them live, in person, on Broad Street. It seemed an appropriate *first* as a born and raised Philly boy. My son and I arrived around 2 p.m., parked in South Philly and walked to Broad and Bainbridge Streets to watch. For a few hours, we observed a few string bands (Woodland and South Philly) along with a Comic and Fancy Brigade club. Those watching were such an array of humanity that it was part of the experience. It went from barely standing painted inebriated drunks who had not slept in days to wide-eyed kids seeing the parade for the *first* time and everything in-between. The disappointing part, that I had not anticipated, was the long wait in between each group of performers. There was no flow to the parade at all. The bands would sit at an intersection for a half-hour or so, talking with each other, as they waited for the street in front of them to clear for them to parade on. It was too sporadic for our liking.

I can now say I experienced the Mummer's Parade live and in person. It only took me over 60 years. I had my first *first*! Day one down.

P.S. Looking back: *I had initially signed up for the Polar Bear Plunge in Atlantic City, but my doctor, a friend, caught wind of this from a little birdie, my concerned wife. With my upcoming scheduled first heart ablation on January 14, for an atrial fibrillation, I was persuaded to select another* first. *AFib (or Atrial Fibrillation) is a quivering or irregular heartbeat (arrhythmia) that can lead to blood clots, stroke, heart failure, and other heart-related complications. As my friend said, "You could die from the shock of the cold water with AFib." Since I like life, I chose to see the Mummers Parade instead.*

??? – Is there something that you have grown up around, that you have taken for granted – that you have not experienced yet? There is no time like NOW – will you?

JANUARY 2ND: DAILY JOURNAL – WRITING ONE

I had never written a personal daily journal before. I didn't think I had the time, or I didn't have the inclination, or maybe I was afraid of putting personal thoughts down on paper for fear of someone finding them and reading it? I knew I wanted to write a daily personal journal for a *first* to document the hopeful 300-plus *firsts* to come. I just wasn't sure how I was going to do it. Would I really have time to write it longhand in a journal book? Nope! I decided my process would be to set up a sub-file in Outlook on my computer where I could dump the daily happenings as my journal. I would type at my desk, or heavy thumbed on my iPhone to email myself the details of the *firsts* of the day. Then I'd drag these emails into my new subfile named *2020 FIRSTS. So as not to not miss a day, I would jot in longhand the first of that day on my monthly 17"×22" desk calendar. It was like marking each day with a big "X". This would come in handy later in the year, when the shit hit the fan, which I did not foresee. I wrote my *first* official daily journal entry today about yesterday.

P.S. – Looking back: *Many of my journal entries were admittedly not good writing. They were hurried at times and flat without color.*

??? – Have you ever written a daily journal? Would it help capture your thoughts? Would it provide future memories and a perspective in looking back?

. . .

CHAPTER TWO:
LEARNING DIFFERENTLY:
"HOW TO ..."

Merriam-Webster dictionary defines learning as: "The act or experience of one that learns," and "knowledge or skill acquired by instruction or study." Google reads, "The acquisition of knowledge or skills through experience, study, or by being taught."

The dictionary says nothing about typing "How to ..." into YouTube to learn how to do something. Google doesn't mention downloading an app to provide knowledge, and they left out listening to podcasts to gain comprehension on a subject. I used all these tools and numerous others to learn this past year. When you are doing something for the *first* time, you must learn. I even did some traditional learning by taking a few classes either live or virtually. I learned a lot this past year and found an assortment of ways to learn differently. The following are a few these *firsts*.

JANUARY 3RD: MEDITATE

Today was the *first* of many times throughout the year I typed "how to" into YouTube to learn how to do something for the *first* time. This morning I typed "How to meditate." I went through a half-dozen videos on the subject. I learned that the key was focusing on my breathing. I also downloaded some soothing background audio to listen to: ocean waves, rain with thunder in the distance, birds chirping. I was learning a new way to use technology.

I descended into my basement, turned out the lights, and sat upright with my hands out and ankles crossed. I turned on the app to the ocean waves, closed my eyes, and focused on my breathing. The sound of waves seemed to transport me to a place and time on a St. Maarten beach long ago. I found myself watching a full moon over the Caribbean, listening to the water lapping in the distance. Time melted. When I "came back," seven-and-a-half minutes had passed. I had my first meditation experience. I tried again for another five minutes, this time listening to the sounds of rain. The rain placed me on the porch of my grandparents' beaten down shack in Perkiomenville, Pennsylvania; the "pink house" in "the country" of my youth. I was seven or eight years old again. I breathed in the smell of a fresh rain. I could hear the drops hit the porch roof as I steadily breathed in and then out again. I was immersed — pretty cool.

*P.S. - **Looking back:** I would use what I learned by meditating sporadically throughout the year and beyond. It has helped at times by slowing me down and helping me to be more in the now.*

??? – Have you ever typed "How to ..." into YouTube to learn how do something you have never done before?

JANUARY 4TH: DRIVE THE SPEED LIMIT TO WORK

I guess I wanted a challenge today — that or I went temporarily insane; it is a toss-up. I chose to drive to work at *the* speed limit — PERIOD — not a single mile per hour over! Anyone that knows me or has ridden in a car when I was driving is aware that I *have never* done this. One could say that I have a heavy foot. Ask my wife, or the state for that matter. Unfortunately, I have the speeding tickets to prove this. I'm not proud, just shamefully telling the truth. To defend myself, I have gotten better, or should I say slower with age. My wife would beg to differ. To make matters worse, my car is fast.

As I pulled out of the driveway for my rush hour commute to work, I started to think, "*what am I doing?*" For someone who drives 25 miles per hour *in my driveway*, driving my neighborhood's 25-mile per hour speed limit is a challenge for just a block. So today's *first* was a BIG challenge for me. I pulled up the app Waze on my phone so I could tell the speed limits along my route to work in case they were not posted. Geez, just driving the speed limit out of my neighborhood was enough for me to start pulling whatever hair I had left out of my head. My morning commute is 25 miles, which normally takes 45 minutes or so. I was only driving for a few minutes, less than a mile in, and I was starting to have doubts, but I was committed. I was not folding my hand now. I pushed on … *very slowly*. It felt like the car was standing still. I made my way, about halfway to work, to the bridge that crossed from New Jersey to Pennsylvania over the Delaware River. The normal speed limit on the bridge is 45; of course the day I picked to do this it had been reduced to 25 miles per hour! So, over the Betsy Ross Bridge I traveled on this windy day with a mix of rain and sleet. I had to put on my emergency flashers so people would stop beeping and flipping me off. In my panic, my mind was screaming … *NEVER AGAIN!*

I made it to the other side of the bridge, only to encounter the on-ramp to Route I-95N, with a speed limit of 15 miles per hour due to construction. I was crying (figuratively) at this point, as the cars behind me were getting more aggressive and riding my bumper. Onto I-95 North at 55 miles per hour, are you friggin' kidding me? I pulled into the far-right lane the SLOW lane, with my emergency flashers still on. I felt inadequate; like EVERY car traveling north was running over me. The off-ramp was 25 miles per hour, followed by 15 miles per hour through a school zone, and onto Academy Road at 30 miles per hour, and finally onto Grant Avenue. Grant Avenue, where my business is located. Grant Avenue is also 30 miles per hour. Both Academy and Grant are main thoroughfares. Cars passed me on every street, except the ramps, with beeping and finger-waving "fans." If they could have passed me on the ramps, they would have. My fans kept letting me know that I was #1 with their middle fingers raised. They flashed their high-beams and mouthed words I was glad my virgin ears could not hear. I'm pretty sure they weren't telling me how wonderful I was for my adherence to the law.

I made it, but I was *FRIED*! My stress level was worse than any challenging business deal I have ever endured. One of my partners came into my office and asked, "Why are your emergency lights on in your car?" I obliviously forgot to turn them off (another *first?*). I was totally rattled. I'd *never* adhered to the speed limit before, and I can guarantee you I will never, ever do it again! My initial goal was to drive the speed limit for the whole day. But it was so stressful driving into work, I figured for the same reason that I did not do the Polar Bear Plunge, I was NOT going to drive home at the speed limit. My heart couldn't take it — for real!

When I went down to my car to turn off the emergency lights I'd left on, I noticed I had also left my keys in the car and left the car running! Do I have to say any more? I think I set the Guinness Book of World Record this morning for receiving the most "You're #1" signs from fellow drivers. My conclusion is that observing and driving the real, official, speed limit is dangerous! Oh, and NO ONE does it.

P.S. - *Looking back:* *When people ask me, "What was the most difficult first you did this year?" I always answer, "Driving the actual speed limit!" I'm dead serious, try it sometime. Even the slowest drivers drift five to 10 miles over the limit. My police friends tell me they generally allow for a 10-mile-per-hour cushion before thinking about pulling someone over for a ticket.*

??? – Do you drive the actual speed limit? Could you drive the actual speed limit for a day? An hour?

JANUARY 6TH: TAROT CARD READING

I was sitting in front of a stranger on the back porch of her house. The lighting was subdued. It was after work, and we had just met moments ago. Her name was Virginia. She seemed very nice, spiritual, middle-aged, shapely, and blond — pretty. We got acquainted and she told me that she had two kids. We were alone. We proceeded with some small talk. She asked why I was there and if this was my first time doing something like this. She wanted to know if I was nervous. I let on that indeed it was my *first* time doing something like this, which was the reason I was there, for my *year of firsts*. She commented that others had come for the same reason. If not for the title of this *first* listed for this day, what would you be thinking? Shame on you! No, I'm not about to have an extra marital affair for the first time and she was not a lady of the night. She was a professional tarot card reader and I'm here for my *first* reading.

She spread the tarot cards on the table and was preparing to tell me what lay ahead for me. Full disclosure, I don't believe in this kind of thing, but in fairness I'd never had a reading before. I had Googled "tarot card reading near me." I settled on this one, as it had the most five-star ratings.

I'd called and arranged for a ten-card half-hour reading, which would run $60. It was a half-hour from work. I scheduled the reading for after work at 6:30 p.m.

Virginia had prefaced the reading by stating, "The reading you are getting is for just today!" My skepticism immediately led me to believe this was her out in case anything turned out to be wrong. The reason it was just for today, she explained, was because, "Life is about choices, and you could make a choice tomorrow that would change the direction and the outcome of the reading."

We shuffled the tarot cards; first her, then me. After I was done and cut the deck, she selected ten cards that she turned over in random order. I took a picture of the ten cards, because I knew that I would never remember them. She told me what each one meant as she placed them in front of me. The first card indicated that I was a *visionary*. She started talking and said, "You are in a transition period, and you have to plan now." She then said, "Trust your vision." She continued by saying that according to the cards, "You'll realize your vision in two to three years. 2023 will be your year. You need to trust and let go." She then advised, "Don't worry about the financial concerns, that will come, and you will be taken care of."

To quote Bill Murray from *Caddyshack*, "So I got that going for me, which is nice."

The following are a few of the other things the cards told her about me:

- "You should write a journal to open up your mind and your voice in order to get things out."

She didn't know I had started writing a daily journal four days earlier as another *first*.

- "You'll be taking a trip later in the year, after June or July, which will be valuable."

I didn't tell her that I was booked to travel in October on a river cruise down the Nile with a side trip to Jerusalem.

- "You need to get rid of the people in your life that are negative and focus on the positive."
- "You should open your heart … You're spiritual."

After the reading and during some small talk, we stumbled onto the subject of meditation, which I had started a few days before for the first time. I asked her a few questions concerning meditation and she asked me a few back. I shared how I'd been *transported to places in my past.*

She was curious, "Where?" she asked.

After I answered that it brought me to the porch of my grandparent's pink house in "the country" in my youth, she said that it brought me to a place of *unconditional love.* She proclaimed, "Love is what it is all about, not happiness, which will come and go. A true love of oneself." She went on, "You need to let go of the negative self-doubt and love and trust yourself."

Since I don't believe in this stuff, I probably filtered most of what she said. I found that I was asking myself, *how does she know this about me?*

Stepping back, I realized she spoke in platitudes, and it was up to me to gravitate to those that applied to me and forget or not focus on those that did not. At one point, she implied or was fishing if I was divorced — I wasn't. I left feeling good. I guess it was worth the time and money for this *first* experience.

*P.S. - **Looking back**: My mom has always had "feelings" from the beyond. I didn't believe it then and still don't. I must admit some of the things she said intrigued me.*

??? – Have you ever tried something you don't believe in out of curiosity?

<u>JANUARY 8TH</u>: CPR CERTIFICATION CLASS

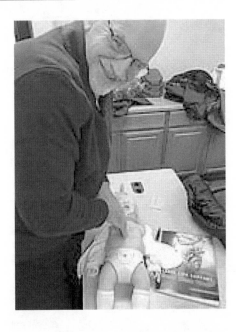

My lips were on the mouth of a dummy laid out in front of me on a table. I had just pounded its chest numerous times. I had joined my wife to take my *first* CPR class. With housing my 85-year-old mother and babysitting our new four-month-old grandson, she wanted to be knowledgeable and prepared. When I heard she was booking the class I asked to join her. I was looking for *firsts* and always had wanted to take a CPR class. We were in a class of a dozen professional healthcare providers for a *three-hour-plus* professional certified CPR class. She had intended to take the one-hour civilian class but booked the longer professional class by mistake. We weren't turning back now. We watched videos and practiced on adult and baby dummies, pumping chests, and blowing breaths of life into these lifeless objects. We practiced for hospital and non-hospital settings. After the training, the instructor handed out a 30-question test to take in 30 minutes for our official CPR certification card. The test was very detailed and surprisingly hard. I passed. I received my course completion card – I'm official! Even though the class encompassed much more than we needed, it was fascinating to see what the professionals must plan for and do. It gave me a great appreciation for what they do and valuable knowledge I can use. Three hours of my life to possibly save another's. Time well spent!

P.S. – Looking back: That was something I had always wanted to do, but without being on the lookout for a first to do, I'm not sure I would have made the time for it.

??? – Do you know CPR? Will you take the time to learn if not?

JANUARY 9TH: LIVE PORTRAIT MODEL DRAWING

As a self-taught, less than adequate watercolor artist who hadn't picked up a brush in over a few decades I decided to challenge myself at the local art studio. I wanted to restart painting again after all these years. I had done a few portraits of my kids back in the day from photographs. I signed up for a live model portrait drawing session having never done it before. I arrived 15 minutes late. The model, a good-looking, African American gentleman with long braided hair and a beard was sitting in the middle of the room on a pedestal surrounded by a half-dozen women, their art easels already set up. The women were diverse from 25 to 75 years of age. There was not much room left, but I found an open spot at a table in the back near the door. Our task was to sketch, draw, or paint a portrait of the live model in front of us, in real time. I had never done it from a live model, in real time, with others. I was NOT comfortable!

I started sketching. I was praying the instructor would be available for some coaching. I was wrong. I shortly realized that I was out of my league, *WAY OUT*, embarrassingly so. I thought the class was more instructional. It wasn't. I had misunderstood and had made a mistake. All the people in the room *were real* artists and knew how to draw. I felt like an impostor. I was in the back of the room. With everyone else in front of me, I could see their drawings. They were good; really good — mine was not in comparison. I quickly became intimidated. I tried to focus and be present in drawing the subtle triangles, ovals, circles, curves, or rectangles in the subject to transfer to the paper. My success was hit and miss. I hung in there for the first hour until break time. They gave the model a breather. I looked at the deformed sketch in front of me and gazed up to see the other pieces of art in progress. I could not bring myself to stay. At some point, everyone would have to share their work for feedback. I knew that I couldn't present mine. It was unfair to me to be sitting in that room of accomplished artists after 20 years, with no training, to go in cold, without help or practice.

This was when I quietly slipped out of to spare my embarrassment. I experienced a *first*, which taught me that I need some seasoning or a visit to YouTube to type in "how to draw a live model" before I put myself in that room again.

*P.S. – **Looking back:** Sometimes you learn from failure. I give myself credit for putting myself in such an uncomfortable situation. I'm glad I had the experience. I now know I need more drawing practice and training before* *doing this again. And I am not including a picture of my drawing; I do have some pride!*

The instructor contacted me the next day via email to make sure I was okay because of my quick exit. When I explained why I was there and why I left, she encouraged me and suggested an online course for learning how to draw: www.thegreatcoursesplus.com. This suggestion would come into play multiple times during the year for various learning opportunities and a few firsts. I also just signed up for a live instructional drawing class.

JANUARY 10TH: VISIT A MOSQUE – ATTEND AN ISLAMIC SERVICE

With my planned travels to the Middle East later in the year, I placed visiting various religious services on my targeted list of *firsts*. I would be visiting a place where many of the world's religions originated and I wanted to gain perspective, knowledge, and understanding of as many as possible. I was fortunate to have Ted, a Muslim practitioner of Islam, on my staff. The mosque that he attended was close to work, and luckily, he was enthusiastic about introducing me to his religion.

We headed out around noon for the 1:15 p.m. service. On the ride over, I quizzed him on what I was about to experience. We discussed the radicalized part of the Muslim religion. I wanted to get past this. We agreed that all religions have a fanatical minority segment that takes the beliefs and teachings selectively and literally to the extreme. My guide that day was a converted former Christian who attempted to explain the "absolutes" of his new religion. He insisted that he could prove the existence of Allah. As a spiritual, but agnostic, reformed non-practicing Catholic raised with that doctrine, I politely stopped him. I wanted him to save his breath. I explained that I believed in something, I just didn't know what it was. I questioned him if anyone knew for sure. I'm skeptical of any religion claiming their God is better than another and having all the answers – be it Islam, Christianity, Hinduism, Judaism, Mormon, Scientology, or any other religion. I believe all claim to have *the* answer and they *all* know and are absolute in their teachings with the exclusion of the others. In my humble opinion, this is what starts hate and eventually wars. This is counter to the core of religion, which is to treat others just as you would like to be treated. I believe at the end of the day it's about love, treating people right — all people. I try to live my religion every day by doing my best to be a good person. Maybe it's too simplistic? What do I know? Maybe as much as the next person? Who knows? I'm not preaching, just providing an insight into my mindset as I walked into this *first*.

We entered the mosque past the armed guard stationed out front. This is a recent sad addition to religious and educational venues with all that's going on in the world. My guide instructed me to remove my shoes and place them in the slotted storage area on the right. We turned to the left, where we had to wash if we were to pray. I wanted the full experience and went to cleanse to receive prayer. The washroom was not a typical one; it had a marble trough with three spigots for cleansing feet. Starting with the right hand, we had to wash our hands completely with soap and water. We then cleaned each arm three times. I Googled "washing three times at a mosque." There is a reason and meaning behind this ritual. The first time is to cleanse physically. The second is to cleanse mentally. And the third is to cleanse spiritually. Makes sense symbolically.

The face and nostrils followed separately, also three times. After we finished our faces, we took off our socks and cleansed our feet with water in the trough. We toweled off and put our socks back on, finally ready to go into the mosque. The interior of the place of worship was modest in decoration — plain walls and no chairs except for two small rows in the back for those who had trouble getting down on the floor. I did ask my host why there were no chairs, and he explained, "To get closer to the ground for prayer." The floor was covered with a deep, plush maroon carpet with stripes (or rows) every four feet, which served as a pew to keep the attendees organized in lines and were spaced to allow for prayer as you touched the ground.

My guide commanded, "Follow me, we are going to pray." As we stood next to each other, I replicated every movement. He raised his arms, went down on his knees, and then bent forward with his head to the carpet, praying. I learned that the prayers he chanted are memorized. All religions seem to have a similar sort of memorized prayer ritual. Islam was no different. After we finished, we sat on the floor propped against the wall and he handed me a Koran with an English translation. I sat and read while we waited an hour for the service to start. In reading, I learned that there were the positives of treating people right. The text also contained hard and fast dialog that non-believers will get their just due and Hell in the afterlife. Some of the wording seemed harsh and degrading (for example, "puny minds of non-believers"), with no wiggle room for understanding and compassion for the non-believers. I'm not picking on Islam; all religions seem to have this dogmatism to one degree or another. Most religions seem to look down in one way or another on non-believers. All are open to interpretation, which can lead to fanaticism. The faith that I was born into and drifted from had the Spanish Inquisition. No one is perfect.

As it got closer to the start of the service, the mosque started to fill until it was packed with all males and there was no room left. The Imam (prayer leader) came out and initially sat on the pulpit (*minbar*). He was a relatively young, good-looking, dark-skinned gentleman dressed from head to toe in white garb. He stood to deliver the Friday sermon (*khutba*) after the beginning chant in Arabic. I mimicked the moves of the congregation the best I could, so as not to seem out of place. No one stared at me, so I guess I did a good enough job.

The whole service lasted about an hour and was mostly in Arabic. The sermon part was in Arabic with English interpretations, kind of like verbal subtitles. The sermon focused on a story of a father and son, with the father teaching his son the keys to life, which included prayer, patience, and helping others. The English translator had an Arabic accent, so it was at times difficult for me to follow. I was able to interpret the point of the story, which was to help people find prayer, and if they resisted, have patience.

After the last prayer, everyone got up and headed for the shoes stored outside of the prayer area.

I noticed that there were no women and asked about this on our way out. My host explained that they have their own separate place of worship in the mosque next door, as they were not allowed to mingle with the male congregation. This kept thoughts and prayer pure without temptation. My *first* experience in a mosque was complete. I cherished the experience of knowledge.

P.S. – Looking back: *This was a valued first and a great experience. It provided me some understanding of this religion I had not had previously.*

??? – Have you ever ventured outside of your religion to experience another religion to gain understanding?

JANUARY 14TH: HEART ABLATION

(Unedited journal entry)

… This is NOT a *first* that one puts on their to-do list, but a heart ablation procedure was a *first* for me. I had been diagnosed with AFib (an out of rhythm fast heartbeat) the year before. The doctor unsuccessfully tried to shock it back into rhythm months ago. Because of the long-term toll AFib can have on the heart, the doctor recommended stepping up the treatment to an ablation. A cardiac ablation is a procedure that scars tissue in your heart to block abnormal electrical signals. A long flexible tube (catheter) is threaded through blood vessels to your heart. They enter through the groin. Sensors on the tips of the catheters use heat or cold energy to destroy (ablate) the heart tissue. Yikes! So, there I was at the hospital in Camden, New Jersey. I showed up at 10 a.m. as instructed for a four-hour procedure. I would have to stay overnight, another *first* in my adult life – there is always a silver lining!

I went through registration and then off to one of the pre-op rooms where I got into my birthday suit and stylish hospital gown. The anesthesiologist stopped in for a brief visit and asked me a bunch of questions. We ended up talking golf and comparing notes on our golf groups. A few nurses came by only to ask multiple duplicate questions I'd answered previously. They took my blood pressure, did an EKG, and hooked me up to an IV. I was ready to go. The nurses were great and funny. So was my wife. When the nurses asked who she was her reply was, "Yes, I'm his wife … his girlfriend couldn't make it." Love her! We waited for about a half-hour, and then one of the nurses wheeled me through a maze of tight corridors to the operating room.

The doctor greeted me with a laundry list of potential risks, including death, along with a detailed account of what he was about to do to me. He inquired how I was doing. I assured him that I felt relaxed and fine, but more importantly I wanted to know, "How was he doing?" He responded with thumbs up, and I was pushed through the door to the awaiting operating room that contained a half-dozen pretty nurses who began to prep me. One nurse shaved various parts of my body for the application of dozens of connections both front and back. I tried to take it all in. There were a dozen computer screens and many spider-armed pieces of equipment. It was noon, and I was about to be put to sleep by my golfing anesthesiologist.

That was the last thing I remembered until my eyes opened around 4:15 p.m. I was in the recovery room with my heart back in rhythm – *YEAH!* Driving the speed limit to work seemed much harder and more stressful. The doctor said I could go home, which squashed my planned *first* for an overnight stay in a hospital! I'd have to think up a new *first* for tomorrow.

I was also back in business as I waited in the recovery room. I had coerced the nurse into handing me my cell phone from my stored valuables nearby, so I could clear out and respond to my seventy-three emails along with a half-dozen texts. My wife had absconded with my phone over six hours earlier. All I needed to be released was to make sure my plumbing was working. The route the doctor took to get to my heart was through my urinary tract. They wanted to make sure they didn't break anything. Thank God they didn't, and I was discharged at 7 p.m.

P.S. – Looking back: A year later my heart is still in rhythm! The feeling of not having to worry about this is freeing. It is a weight off my mind and heart. Every surgery carries a level of risk. When they tell you the outcome of death is a very slim possibility of the procedure there is obviously a concern. But it was well worth the risk for a "normal" life.

JANUARY 15TH: TIE A BOW TIE

What does one do when they are home recovering from a heart ablation looking for a *first* to do? They type into YouTube "how to" and scroll through what comes up to get to *tie a bow tie*, of course. It looked easy enough. Little did I know! Being the annoying recovering patient, I asked my wife to assist me in this *first* by going to the store to pick me up a bow tie to tie. I didn't own one and neither did my son. God bless her.

If the *Guinness Book of World Records* kept track of eye-rolling, my wife would have qualified that day. She watched in amazement as I tried and failed, time after time, to tie that darn bow tie. I came to find out it is either not easy or I'm not very smart, I'm terribly uncoordinated, or all the above. I think I accomplished another world record: my claim to fame is that I found more ways to tie a bow tie incorrectly than anyone else that had tried before me. I viewed different videos for various perspectives. A few hours in, after many failures, I decided to practice on a small, round pillow. The pillow helped. It was much harder than I had anticipated, but I stuck with it to tie my *first* bow tie. It was a lovely light blue patterned one, in case you were curious.

??? – Have you ever tried to tie a bow tie? I'm curious if you would find it easier than I did? Is it just me?

JANUARY 16TH: RUSHED TO EMERGENCY ROOM

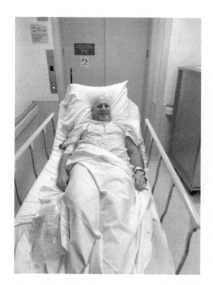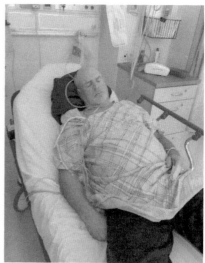

(Unedited journal entry)

… I thought I was out of the woods from the procedure and had texted my partners that they would see me today. I felt pretty good during my bow tying escapades of the day prior. During the night and through the early morning, I started having difficulties. I couldn't and didn't sleep; I figured I'd eventually drift off watching TV. I figured wrong. I kept getting shorter of breath, I felt clammy from a fever, and was having chest pains. It felt like someone was sitting on my chest. I just told myself to *suck it up*. I was two days out from the ablation. The second day of recovery was normally the toughest or the pain pinnacle. I emailed my partners around 4 a.m. saying that I had not slept and was in some pain. My plan was to try to get some rest and come to work late. I kept trying to get to sleep to no avail. The shortness of breath progressed. I could feel the fever. I waited as long as I could, but finally called my wife from my spot on the couch at 8 a.m. to wake her up and request a ride. "I think you should take me to the ER," I pleaded. A *first*!

She was frightened and slightly panicked. I have been blessed with good health and don't go to the doctor or the hospital. She knew something had to be wrong.

We drove into rush hour traffic back to the hospital where I'd been a couple of days earlier. I tried meditation during the 45-minute drive, but it only worked sporadically. I felt like I'd been beaten up. I wasn't sure if I was having a heart attack or if I was just overreacting.

We pulled up to the emergency room door. The wheelchair to take me in seemed to take hours. Someone wheeled me into the ER, and a swarm of hospital workers descended asking me questions. They poked and probed, took blood, and ran numerous tests. My heart rate was elevated, so they gave me something to calm my heart rate and anxiety as they debated the possibilities. They appeared stumped as they ruled out a heart attack.

I stayed in the ER all day. Many other patients littered the hallways. I was lucky to have one of the ER rooms. Either my insurance was better or my case more serious. During the array of tests, medications, and consultations, it was determined that they were admitting me to stay overnight. My *first* for tomorrow was secure!

??? – Have you ever been scared by the fear of the unknown?

JANUARY 17TH: OVERNIGHT STAY IN A HOSPITAL

After the failed attempt of an overnight stay in a hospital a few days back, I achieved this *first* this day — some accomplishment.

The reason for my first stay overnight was in debate. My doctors and nurses were not exactly sure what my situation was. They guessed it might be either pneumonia and/or pericarditis, which is when fluid builds up around the heart. Both were possibilities with an ablation procedure, I was told. One conjecture was that an infection could build up in the fluid in the lungs and around the heart after anesthesia; apparently the lungs can sometimes be slow in waking up. I waited for my discharge home later that afternoon.

*P.S. – **Looking back:** I was not discharged home that day. I ended up being in the hospital for the next four nights until my fever broke and was on oxygen the whole time. I obviously did not plan both those last two days of firsts. But I counted them because they were both firsts for me — Besides my birth and getting my tonsils out at the age of four, I don't remember either one, so they don't count.*

The doctors were never comfortable with their diagnosis, which made me wonder: did I have COVID-19? It was January, and the medical community didn't know much about COVID-19 yet, nor was it discussed. The symptoms were coincidental. I will never know. One thing I do know is that I couldn't breathe, and I was on oxygen. I don't get scared often. I must admit I was a little frightened on that ride to the hospital the morning of the 16th.

JANUARY 18TH: LISTEN TO A PODCAST SERIES

My overnight stay turned into an extended stay due to my continued fever, fatigue and difficulty breathing. I was told I'm here till my fever breaks. I was lying in my hospital bed feeling beat up when I received the following text from my wife: *I just listened to the first part of Ronan Farrow's podcast* Catch and Kill. *I think it would interest you. Have you ever listened to a podcast before?*

I hadn't. She was looking out for me and my *firsts*. I quickly and excitedly replied, "I've never listened to a podcast. That's a good *first* for me."

I'm ashamed to say I never really knew what a podcast was. I had never paid attention to them, and I didn't even know how to do it. I just thought it was someone broadcasting, with a tin can and a wire, out of their basement somewhere in the middle of nowhere, talking about nonsense.

My wife came to my hospital room to kindly show this dinosaur how to find and download podcasts. We searched for *Catch and Kill* and downloaded the five episodes on my phone. Ronan, the son of Mia Farrow and Woody Allen, is the journalist who broke the Harvey Weinstein story in the *New Yorker*. The *Catch and Kill* Podcast was about how that story came to be. I pressed "Episode 1: *The Spy*" and started to listen. I was immediately captivated by the interview with the spy (private investigator) Igor Ostrovsky, who was hired by the Weinstein Group to follow Ronan because he was sniffing around the story. Wow, I'm sometimes too naïve, unaware, or ignorant to consider the lengths that some powerful people will go to for self-preservation. I couldn't stop after episode one – I was hooked. I sat there with my wife for the next three-plus hours and listened to all five episodes.

The last episode led the listener into today, as Harvey Weinstein headed into court after dodging, paying off, bullying, and utilizing his power, with the help of enablers, to abuse women for sexual favors. As it ended, I turned and looked at my spouse quizzically and commented, "I just don't get someone like Harvey Weinstein."

P.S. – Looking back: *I have checked out other podcasts since. I am now hooked. I find myself listening to different series on my drive to and from work. They've also become an educational tool to learn about topics I'm interested in. This would come in handy for my quest to learn about the many* *religious services on my to-do list I'd like to attend. This is just one of the many examples of looking for and experiencing firsts that have broadened me as a person.*

??? – Have you downloaded a podcast to learn more about a topic of interest?

JANUARY 19TH: BINGE-WATCH A SERIES (*THE VIETNAM WAR*)
(Unedited email entry)

… Yesterday was an audio *first* (podcast). Today was a visual *first* as I binge-watched the entire ten-episode Netflix series *The Vietnam War*, a film by Ken Burns and Lynn Novick. The series was over 1,000 minutes (16 hours) of programming at one sitting. I had the time – I'd been advised not to return to work until I was cleared of my pneumonia. I was a hostage on my couch. Someone had mentioned how good this Netflix series was, and I'd made a mental note. I settled in to take advantage of this unique opportunity of time on the mend.

Ten episodes from the beginning – Episode I: *Déjà Vu* (1858–1961) to the last, *The Weight of Memory* (March 1973–present day), educated me. It opened my eyes. It gave me a much greater perspective, appreciation, empathy, and understanding. Intertwined were individual perspectives from all sides. Like many, I never really knew why the United States was there other than we were "fighting communism." I came to learn that it was much more complex and not as simple or as straightforward as that. In any conflict, there are always three sides to the story, with the truth usually somewhere in the middle. I had heard one side. Conflict, in my estimation, is due to misunderstanding and miscommunication. This was no different. History and people keep repeating themselves. That is not to say that selfish people without a conscience, with oversized egos and individual agendas despite the greater good, also play a part.

The Vietnam conflict divided our country – there were protests, lost lives at Kent State, and all the histrionics were intense. I was at times proud and at times ashamed of my heritage as an American citizen. I was proud of the good intentions of individuals and our country, the courage of the men and women sent to war. I was also proud of the people who stood up for what was right. I was ashamed of the lies and cover-ups that put the lives of our youth in peril. I think people who make decisions about going to war should serve in one. They should experience a family member or friend perish. If that happened, I think there would be much more reluctance and more humility to find common ground. It was also somewhat scary to see how thin the veneer between civility and savagery was, as demonstrated by the Mỹ Lai Massacre. How did we get there as humans?

I learned that Vietnam was a French colony (just as the United States had been to Britain) in the 1800s and became a Japanese colony during World War II. After WWII, it reverted to France and divided with the communist-influenced Viet Minh, led by Ho Chi Minh. The United States took the reigns over from France in the late 1950s by misreading Vietnam as a Cold War communist play, like Korea. It was the end of a colonial reign. The United States supported and backed a corrupt leader in South Vietnam. We were backing a bad horse, and we knew it. Instead of recognizing it and admitting their mistake, our government's arrogance led them to lie to their own people. They perpetuated a war that they knew long before it ended that we could not win through five presidents – not good. They were more concerned with re-election or political face-saving than the lives of the soldiers they were sending to their deaths. It was sad.

I came to appreciate Ho Chi Minh. He cared for his people. All he wanted for the Vietnamese people was what we strive for here: Life, Liberty, and the Pursuit of Happiness. When his request fell on the deaf ears of the American government, he turned to alternate opportunities to reach his goal for his people — his mistake. But we had the right of first refusal, so to speak. We could have backed a good horse and chose not to. The dominoes and bad decisions fell from there. The series was a fascinating look back with perspective. The lives lost during the conflict were costly and needless.

At the end of this *first*, it was about forgiveness, healing, and moving on.

P.S. – *Looking back:* *This series affected on me. I learned a lot and it also gave me another first to add to my to-do list for another day this year, visiting the Vietnam Memorial in Washington, DC.*

<u>JANUARY 23RD</u>: WEAR HIGH HEELS

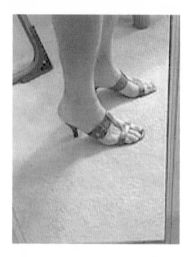

If I had a thought such as "I wonder what that feels like" I explored it as long as it was legal and didn't hurt anyone. Wearing high heels fell into this category of *firsts*. Like most straight men I had never worn high heels before in my life. I'd often marveled and wondered how women walked around all day in them. I was not looking to be Bruce or Caitlin Jenner, nor do I have a fetish to cross-dress as I ventured into my wife's closet looking for a pair of slip-on high heels to try. I promise, this was a *first*. I found a nice pair of brown leather two-inch pumps with buckles and beige stitching. Okay, I know two-inch pumps may not officially be considered high heels, but they were to me. They would have to do for this first experience. Apologies if the title of this entry is misleading. These were the only pair of my wife's size nines I could find that were remotely close to fitting. Luckily the back is open and the front forgiving. I stuffed my fat feet into the strained footwear and paraded around the empty house, gaining knowledge and appreciation of what it was like to walk in them. I was in a pair of shorts and took a picture of my furry bare legs in the mirror. OMG. Let's say I don't think I would elicit many dates with this get up. Thank goodness I was alone in the house. After a short period of time, they started to hurt. I give women and cross-dressers credit; it is not easy. How do they do it for a whole day? Thank goodness I didn't fall.

JANUARY 26TH: INTERVIEW MY MOM FOR POSTERITY

If your mom is like mine, she must get her hair done to *go to* her hair appointment, so she doesn't look bad for her hairstylist. I'm not joking. I love her, all 4-foot 8 inches of her! She'll go through multiple changes of clothes before leaving the house to make sure she is color coordinated and looks just right. This daily fashion show is at the expense of any scheduled appointment or agreed-to time of arrival.

My planned *first* today was to capture this *queen*, my mom, in a videoed interview about her life, for the *first* time, for posterity's sake. I compiled 30-plus interview questions I wanted to ask. Although I must admit, I did Google "top questions to ask your mother." I borrowed a few and married them to the others. I didn't print all of them here to save space, but hopefully you'll get the idea. Following are a few of the questions I posed to my mom:

- What did you love to do as a kid, before high school?

- *"Roller Skate. I used to put the skates onto my shoes and skate in the street. On Saturdays we would go to the rink to skate."*

- What did you love to do in high school? What do remember most about your teenage years?

- *"Going to high school football games with my friends."*

- What do you remember most about your mom and dad — do you have a favorite memory or story?

- *"Their love and care for me."*

- What was most important to each of them?

- *"Family."*

- How did you meet dad? Where, when?

- *"When I was around 13 or 14 years old my girlfriend introduced us. He was part of the neighborhood crowd."*

- What was the best trip you took in your life?

- *"It is a toss-up between Ireland and Hawaii. Hawaii was beautiful, but Ireland was the most fun."*

- What was your favorite family vacation? Why?

- *"The Outer Banks, because all my kids and grandkids were together."*

- What did you believe about yourself that helped you become a good mom and wife and deal with hard times?

- *"My mom and dad taught me to do the right thing. To respect people."*

- What times in your life truly "tested your mettle," and what did you learn about yourself by dealing (or not dealing) with them?

- *"The accident I was in with the man that was to be my fiancé. I was 16 years old. He died in the accident, and I almost lost my leg.*

I still have the physical pain from the crash. I learned that you can't change things and you just have to go with it and move on."

- Which three events most shaped your life?

- *"One, meeting your dad. Two, having my children. Three, having my grandchildren."*

- What do you remember about when each of us (me, my brother, and sister) was born?

- *"Joy!"*

- What three words represented your approach to parenting and why?

- *"One, set limits. Two, set the right example. Three, grow your children to be good people."*

- What message do you have that you want us to always keep in mind?

- *"Family is everything."*

- Tell us about Tony Cash? *(Laughter)*

- *"He was a hallucination."* (For the readers, mom has had a few urinary tract infections, accompanied by some very vivid hallucinations. During one of these episodes, she woke me up in the middle of the night and asked me to tell Tony Cash to stop singing so loud in her bathroom because she was afraid he would woo my son's girlfriend away from him. There was no singing and no Tony Cash. I Googled "Tony Cash." I thought he might be Johnny Cash's brother, but he doesn't exist. Mom realized this after she was hooked up to an IV at the hospital. We kid about it now. I could write another book about the hallucinations – too funny.)

- What three words best describe the person you have tried to be in life, and how you want to be remembered.

- ■ *"Love, happiness, and grateful."*
- • What are your thoughts on medical marijuana?
- ■ *"Necessary. A breakthrough for those of us in pain. It helps people."*
- • What have you learned about other people in life?
- ■ *"Sometimes they will disappoint you, but most are good."*
- • What do you think the world needs more of right now?
- ■ *"Understanding. We have to get along."*
- • What do you believe people want the most in life?
- ■ *"Love and happiness."*
- • What are you most proud of in life?
- ■ *"My family."*
- • What message would you like to share with your family?
- ■ *"Life is short, live it."*
- • Are there any questions I didn't ask that I should ask? Anything I missed that you would like to tell us?
- ■ (Her response brought laughs from everyone listening and was the perfect end to the interview.) With a perfectly straight face she said, *"Yeah, you didn't ask me if I'm pregnant or not? I'm not."* *Boom*, my mom just dropped the mic on me — interview and *first* over.

P.S. – *Looking back:* *This was the day that Kobe Bryant passed.*

In listening to her answers, it struck me that I could have answered many of the questions the same way. The apple doesn't fall far from the tree.

JANUARY 28TH: DETAIL INTERIOR OF CAR

I typed "How to" into YouTube as potluck to see what came up. I was in search of a *first* with nothing planned. I played a game with myself like

I used to do with my kids when we went out on an "adventure." We would get into the car with no knowledge of what we were going to do. We would do whatever first thing of interest we came across. My so-called car drive to my adventure of the day was my YouTube search. Detailing the interior of a car came up. I had no idea how to really do it like a professional. I like things clean and organized, so I was motivated. I watched the 11-plus-minute video a few times, then started to gather up various cleaning supplies and a vacuum cleaner as instructed. I pulled my car into the garage and went step-by-step per the video. A few hours later I was done! I'll spare you the particulars. You can YouTube it. Car immaculate – another *first*!

??? – Do you ever head out without a destination in mind just for the adventure and experience of whatever you may find?

JANUARY 31ST: LUNCH WITH DAUGHTER AT HER WORK

I was discussing my year of *firsts* with my kids a few weeks back during a Sunday family dinner. It must have had an impact. The next day, my daughter texted me: *For your year of* firsts, *you can always have lunch with me at my work. We haven't done that. I could do it Friday.* She was excited. So was I; it was a great idea! We made a date for lunch.

My daughter is a proud health and physical education teacher at the local middle school. Our lunch turned into a mini take-dad-to-work day as she showed me off. Father and daughter relationships are special, and it was extra special just sitting and catching up over a few slices of pizza from the local Italian restaurant. We left a few minutes for selfies to document this *first*. A kiss, a hug, and I left feeling very proud of her. My heart smiled. One month of *firsts* down – eleven more to go!

· · ·

The *firsts* continued into the balance of February, and into the beginning of March. I didn't miss a day. They were a healthy mix of typical bucket list items, learning opportunities, a quest for understanding, experiences, and fun as you will see in subsequent chapters. Some were funny, like baking pot brownies on February 21. I learned by typing things into YouTube.

At this point in the year, it was all fun and games. Who knew what lay ahead? These *firsts* changed dramatically in March with the future of my life's work in the balance. It would change my journey again and would impact the rest of my year, and the lives of many others.

CHAPTER THREE:
A QUEST FOR UNDERSTANDING

To quote Albert Einstein, "I have no special talents. I am only passionately curious." I ain't no Einstein, but I was curious about many things that the *firsts* satisfied. The pursuit of these *firsts* presented many opportunities to quench my curiosity on numerous subjects. Some of my *firsts* were influenced by the events of that year. I sought to understand the many religions since I had a scheduled trip to Jerusalem later in the year. I found myself thinking, *I wonder what that is like?* I would then plan to experience it. I gained appreciation and empathy. I grew as a result. I gained knowledge.

FEBRUARY 2ND: ATTEND A JEHOVAH WITNESS SERVICE

I had just spoken with my Jehovah Witness-practicing cousin, who prompted me to Google "Jehovah Witness near me." I was easily able to "Find a Meeting" from their home page www.JW.org, at a Kingdom Hall just 22 minutes away.

Unsure of myself, I texted my cousin to let him know what I was about to do and asked for any words of advice. He laid it out for me. The first part is a talk on a subject and the next part is a study article. He then shared, "Today would be a great one for you. It is about getting things done!"

He also added, "People will be dressed up; maybe put on a tie." I took his advice, ran upstairs to change, sans tie, and off I went.

As I pulled in, the parking lot was full. All the people heading for the door were well dressed. Everyone seemed happy, welcoming, nice, and engaging. I was a minority without a tie and without color in my skin — neither appeared to be an issue or a concern. I was one of just a few

Caucasians in the church. I was five minutes early and found a seat in the crowded room on the outside middle right. The service started promptly on time with a song, and two large TV screens displayed the words. Once the song finished, a gentleman — a visitor from another congregation I believe — was called to the stage.

The first half-hour was, as my cousin had said, a talk on a subject, which that day asked the question: "Are you happy?" I thought I was, until the leader informed us that we really weren't. Oh well, what do I know? The discussion turned into how "you can be truly happy by following *a true* religion, Jehovah." The sermon meandered into the creation of man, Adam, and Eve in the Garden of Eden. Jehovah (God?) had given us (man) everything and we screwed it up by not following his orders, which led us to where we are today; a mess.

The leader seemed to mock the many "false" religions (other than Jehovah), and how they are responsible for all the conflicts and the wars. In this context, he also seemed to mock science by asking the congregation in what seemed a sarcastic tone, "Who believes they come from apes?" There were laughs throughout. "Of course we don't, because we were created by God."

I sat silently in quiet disbelief. The orator shared that he had just changed jobs and asked, "Who likes their job?" I was about to raise my hand when I noticed that everyone was shaking their heads *no* along with the person who asked who followed with, "We work because we have to, not because we like it or get any fulfillment out of it." I was in the minority on this one.

At one point, a well-dressed Caucasian metrosexual that was sitting directly in front of me got up, went into the aisle, and proceeded to sit next to me. He asked, "Would you like a Bible?"

I was stunned but didn't show it. I politely replied, "I'm fine, thank you."

He then returned to his seat in front of me. I had been sitting there totally engaged, listening to the lecture. How did this person, who had not turned around once, know that I did not have a Bible? Why did it matter? I looked around for cameras and didn't see any. I wondered if someone else in the congregation texted him from the back. I couldn't figure it out. I became much more aware of my surroundings. Everyone had an Apple iPad Mini, a Kindle, or an actual printed old-school Bible they were using to follow along intently as the lecturer randomly referred to various scripture readings to make his point. He read the scripture very slowly and deliberately. Once done, he'd then interpret the reading to make it fit the point he was making. There were constant nods in agreement from the crowd, with occasional moans of approval. It seemed like indoctrination to me, like my experience at the mosque, or at Mass. Different, but the same — us against them.

The "us" were the smart and saved with all the absolute answers. The "them" were the ignorant and condemned; they were clueless non-believers that needed education and salvation. I was born and raised Catholic. Although I am non-practicing, the Catholic church does the same thing — it's no different. As an older adult, I just don't get it. It seems to be a familiar pattern of dogma. All religions have their redeeming qualities of the universal "golden rule" (good stuff) to lure you in, then they go astray in drawing their declaration of war against "them." I'm not sure this is fair, but that is what was going through my mind as I listened. The lecturer ended with a song. He then called upon a dignitary from the congregation to take over the second part of the service.

The next part was the study article, and as my cousin had said, it was about "getting things done." I sat up to listen. Before a minute had gone by, my metrosexual friend got up and sat down next to me *AGAIN*! This time, he asked if I wanted a copy of *The Watchtower* so I could follow along. Again, stunned, I managed, "Sure, thanks."

He then got up and walked to the back and out the door. He returned a few minutes later with a 32-page pamphlet (The Watchtower) containing the study articles for December 30, 2019, to February 2, 2020. I opened it to page 26 and started following along with the article, "Complete What You Started to Do." This seemed harmless enough, with the possibility of picking up some useful pointers.

For the next 90 minutes, I sat and listened to a curious repetitive sequence of the leader deferring to a designated reader on his left. The designated reader would read a few lines at a time from the pamphlet, and then he'd sit down and defer to the leader. The leader then would look to the congregation for what I thought was feedback, questions for further discussion, or both, none of which happened. Instead, the called-upon congregation members then basically repeated word for word what the designated reader had just read. If the designated reader read four sentences, four separate congregation members were selected to repeat almost verbatim what was just read — line for line. I kept waiting for something special or enlightening to take place; it didn't. I wasn't sure if I was missing something. The leader would call on "brother" or "sister" so-and-so from the crowd who had raised their hands to participate in this ritual. He'd give each a "well done" and move on to calling on the next person for the next ninety minutes. The leader reminded us that everything and every answer came from Jehovah.

The outline to help us "Complete What You Started to Do" contained two parts. The first was *Before making a decision* and was then followed by *After making a decision*. Each part had five steps that included a mix of prayer, consultation with God (Jehovah), golden rule-isms, and common sense. The leader punctuated each section by calling out Bible verses for the congregation to read to tie into the point.

The interior of this house of worship was sparsely decorated. Other than the pews we sat in it didn't resemble a church, with the two big screen TVs and a stage at front with a few folding chairs for the leaders. The interior was dated. At the conclusion, we sang one more song. The lyrics were very simple and preachy. It told of good and bad. It stressed going out and knocking "door-to-door" to spread the teachings of Jehovah. As the song wound down, I was the first one out of the door. It was just shy of two hours from when I entered.

P.S. – *Looking back: I started this day with a plan to experience iFLY Indoor Skydiving. When I called in the morning though, they had sold out of spots. With it being a Sunday, I looked for a religious service to attend and spoke to my cousin. I adjusted my firsts in similar ways throughout the year when my plans did not work out.*

??? – **Would you challenge yourself on the next open weekend to Google the nearest religious service that you have never experienced and attend?**

FEBRUARY 4TH: IFLY INDOOR SKYDIVING

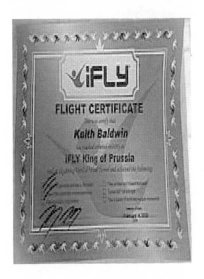

By chance, I found myself between appointments and around iFLY. I took a shot at a spontaneous *first* and dropped in to discover an opening in their schedule. I signed in at the front desk with a young woman and struck up a conversation. One of the questions she asked was if this was my *first*

time. I explained it was a part of my *year of firsts*. She was intrigued and demanded some examples. She became "inspired" as I read her my long list of *firsts* from my phone. I kept a list of possible firsts in the notes section of my phone to refer to in times of need. The conversation ventured into my daily journal documenting these firsts with a hope of it becoming a book. Her eyes lit up and she asked if I would mention her in the book. I wrote "Julia" down on the back of the photo voucher to remember her name and keep my promise.

Once registered, my instructor Jack sat down to introduce himself. I learned that he has been an instructor at iFLY for the last two years in addition to providing real skydiving lessons out of an airport in South Jersey. Coincidentally, I golf at the course next to that airport and have watched skydivers land on the course while I played. Jack was one of those wayward souls who had fallen from the sky during our Sunday rounds of golf — small world. After observing a few people ahead of me "flying" in the wind tunnel, I had an idea of what I was in for.

I was handed a helmet and a left-handed glove to cover my wedding ring that I can't get off my finger. I emptied my pockets of everything that could dislodge and become a flying object into one of the lockers. I was then ushered to a training room to watch a 15-minute instructional video. Jack reentered the room and went over the hand signals he would use to communicate with me. The ability to talk does not exist with the winds at great speeds. He demonstrated the necessary posture for a good flight: hands spread over my head, head up, and legs straight out, slightly bent and apart. It was like taking a good belly flop into a pool. I sauntered out and entered the tunnel prepared. I had paid for two one-minute flights. The first was introductory, and the second a "high-flying" flight.

The operator behind the glass cranked up the air in the tunnel and set my timer to one minute. Jack stepped in and I entered the portal to the tunnel in the posture instructed and just fell forward. I was flying! The rush of air had me floating. Jack, who was standing on the netting six feet below, periodically guided me with a push here and a pull there to keep me in line. Did I say I was *flying*?! WOW, very cool! The minute seemed to stretch to 15, with Jack bending my legs slightly to bring me in for the landing into the portal to the outside. We high-fived each other as I walked out to take a seat.

A few minutes later I was up again for my second high-flying flight. This time Jack grabbed the fabric at my elbow and then the knee of my flight suit. Poof! Off we went spiraling up in tandem, *fast!* Up into the 25-foot tunnel we went, spiraling around the tube — thrilling. For the next 40 seconds we went up and down, round and round for a thrill ride that replicated free falling out of a plane. I thought about the scene in the movie *Point Break* when Patrick Swayze and Keanu Reeves jump out of the plane and tangle in the air. Jack may have looked like Keanu, but I was no Swayze. It was exhilarating! Then we had to land; my time was up. Jack magically guided us down.

Apparently, Julia was excited about my quest of *firsts* in 2020 and had told all the instructors in the place. I know this because after my flight Jack commented, "So you're the one. Julia told us all about what you are doing."

As I disrobed from the jumpsuit, I was handed my official flight certificate. I had my proof — I'd done it!

*P.S. - **Looking back:** Julia, I kept my word. I mentioned you in the book! The pandemic would cancel my plans to do the real thing out of a plane, which was one of the* firsts *I wanted to attempt. At least for this year of* firsts *I had this simulation to count.*

??? – Have you ever wanted to parachute out of a plane, but were too afraid? Have you considered iFLY as a safe substitute?

FEBRUARY 9TH: ATTEND A MORMON SERVICE

Another Sunday, another religious service to experience! I awoke and Googled "religious services near me." I found the Church of Jesus Christ of Latter Day Saints (Mormons). It was in my town. I plugged the address into Waze, not knowing exactly where it was. That week, I had been listening to a *World Religions* podcast by J.R. Forasteros to prepare myself for experiencing different religions. The podcast covered Hinduism, Buddhism, Judaism, Islam, Atheism, and had just finished with Mormonism. I had never attended a Mormon service before. The extent of my knowledge on the Mormon faith was limited to seeing the play *The Book of Mormon* on Broadway the year before. I knew that Joseph Smith presumably found some gold tablets in a garden in upper New York a few hundred years ago for the "First Vision" that presented an altered course from Christianity. The podcast on this religion helped to fill in the blanks.

I put on a shirt, tie, and jacket and took off for the morning service. I found the Meetinghouse (as referred to by the Mormons) directly across the street from the high school where my kids had gone. I had driven by it numerous times but had never noticed it. I walked through the vestibule, hoping to sneak past the bishop who appeared to be guarding the entrance. I didn't make it past the oversized Brother, who was conducting the service that day. He extended a hand and introduced himself.

I settled into the last row of the sparsely appointed place of worship. There was a lectern in front on a raised platform with three rows of seats behind, as well as an organ where an organist played quietly. In front were five rows of pews, followed by approximately ten rows of padded chairs. I was on one of these padded chairs in the cheap seats in the back. The service started precisely at 10 a.m. with the church a third filled with approximately 60 people. There was a noticeable lack of diversity. The folded photocopied paper was the "Sacrament Meeting Program," the playbook for the next hour.

Brother Rich read a few select announcements from a list in the program of 16 upcoming events and meetings. He shared, "If you are looking for a person to change your life, look in the mirror." I nodded my head yes in agreement. In between the hymns, a few names of people that had been "released" were announced, accompanied by gratitude and thanks. Then another list of people who had been "called" was announced. Each reading of names was followed by a request for *yay* or *nay* votes from the congregation. All the names received unanimous yeahs, except from me. I abstained. I wasn't sure exactly what these people had been *released from* or *called to*. I quickly pieced it together when the released and called were summoned to the pulpit to give their "Testimony."

The first was an older gray-haired woman who had been "released." She wept through her entire testimony of her past year as president of one of the church subcommittees. I couldn't hear or understand which one. She was not a public speaker. She was someone from the small congregation selected as a volunteer and delegated part of the work that the church needed. She kept saying that she was not "worthy" when "called" to serve by the bishop, who is the leader of the congregation. She wept, explaining she was humbled, grateful, and learned a lot through the process. She said God had gotten her through the times of doubt.

The next was a young mother, with baby in hand, who had been "called." She was summoned to the lectern to provide her "testimony" on being "called" (selectively volunteered) to serve on another church sub-committee. She apparently was part of a military family that moved quite a bit. She thanked the congregation for making her feel welcome and a part of the church. It struck me that these religious gatherings served a human need of feeling a part of something.

The last "testimony" was from a couple. They had been part of the church for the past few years and were leaving. They had also been "called" in the past and were now being "released." All were emotional and thanked God for choosing and leading them.

In the middle of the hymns and the testimonies was the serving of the Sacrament. A few (very) young boys in neat white dress shirts at the front right altar said a few words that I could not hear. Then they emerged, with two other young clones holding silver-handled serving trays. They walked pew by pew, row by row, passing the trays through the congregation. As a congregate took the silver tray, they plucked a piece of bread from the tray, placed it in their mouth, and passed it on. Once the tray was passed throughout the whole church, the four youngsters returned to the front and grabbed four new trays and started the process all over again. This time the trays held plastic thimble-sized cups of water. Everyone selected one, drank, and passed it on. I was thinking, "the church is only a third full. If it was filled, we would never get out of here." It took a *long* time for everyone to pass the two rounds of silver trays and partake. Before it was over, the pastor mentioned that someone in the congregation had a *first* for the day (other than me?). Had they found me out? Nope, it was the organist, who for the *first* time played in front of the congregation. There was one final quick prayer by one of the called upon and the service ended.

As I drove off, I saw one of the young Sacrament distributors spreading the leftovers from the silver trays on the church's front lawn. I guess the birds celebrate Sunday service also.

This day was also the *first* time I ever went to a father and son game of the Philadelphia 76ers. I had given my son the tickets for his birthday with this intent. While at the game, we caught one of the free t-shirts that are blasted out of a hand-held cannon into the crowd during intermission for the *first* time ever. It was a good day of a few *firsts*.

P.S. - *Looking back:* *I didn't know it at the time, but that was the last religious service I would attend in person for the rest of the year. I thought I had the rest of the year to fit them in. The pandemic would prevent this from happening. It is something I will do as soon as things open again, God willing. I find the similarities and the subtle differences fascinating. My observations with my experiences and through my eyes are not intended to offend.*

??? – How many different religious services have you attended? Have you criticized without experiencing or understanding?

FEBRUARY 11TH: WORK WITH MY WIFE AT HER JOB

(Journal entry with a few edits)

… Going to work with my wife was one of the items on my to-do list. She liked the idea and planned for it, saying, "Let's do it later in the year — during the holiday season, when I'm really busy."

Fate and the damaged retail marketplace did not allow the wait for that coming holiday season. The week before, she had received a call informing her that after more than 20 years with her infant wear company, they were discontinuing her entire retail rep division nationally. She was the representative for numerous stores in the area carrying the brand. Macy's and Kohl's were her main stores. She had a flexible schedule that allowed her to go into these stores and merchandise the clothing departments to maximize the sales of the clothing line. Sales were always strong at her stores. She never cut corners; she always worked hard and put in an honest day's work. She cared, and she had established good relationships in all her stores. I was proud of her.

That day ended up being her last with her company. It was time for "bring your husband to work day." If I was going to experience this first, it had to be that day. She was already inside working in the department when I happened upon her. I stood and watched for a moment without her being aware. She was hard at work sorting and merchandising the racks of new products that had come in. She saw me out of the corner of her eye and put me to work. The department was a mess. There were clothes that were not on the floor, which were left in the back. The ones on the floor were all mixed and misplaced. I started sorting the muddled rack into similar styles and then sorted in order from infant to nine months. I had to ask if a few styles were for a boy or girl. Some were a little hard to tell, at least for me. She answered, "*If it has pink in the design — girl!*" Or "*See the ribbon in the design — girl!*" Once the sorting was done, I integrated the new recruits into the existing clothes on display. My retail background from 45 years ago resurfaced. I worked and emptied the whole three-story rack. As I finished, my wife looked at her watch and said with despair, "Three minutes left." It was a sad anticlimactic ending after more than 20 years. Her company, the stores, and the relationships she built will miss her.

*P.S. - **Looking back:** It was fun going to work with my wife. It gave me an appreciation of what she had done all those years. I think she appreciated that I took the time to understand.*

??? – Have you ever gone to work with your spouse or significant other to see, understand, and appreciate what they do? Have you ever been given a pink slip after many years of work due to a shift in the economy?

FEBRUARY 12TH: MEDICAL MARIJUANA CAREGIVER CARD

My *first* official medical marijuana caregiver card arrived in the mail today! I had helped my mom obtain her medical marijuana card a few months back for her pain management. Medical marijuana would assist in her withdrawal from the fentanyl patch, which the doctor had strongly suggested. After she secured her card, I took her a few times to the dispensary. Without the card though, I was on the outside looking in, literally.

I could see my mom looking back at me helplessly through the glass of the lobby of the dispensary. I stood powerless watching her cry for help with her sad puppy-dog-like eyes. I was not allowed in without a caregiver card, which I did not possess. She would sometimes emerge with an additional redundant product that an employee had insisted she might need. She only had to pick up and pay for what the doctor prescribed. I thought I had scripted it perfectly. While at the pickup counter, an employee would ask her questions she apparently was ill equipped to answer, "Do you want any additional items?" She was out of her element. One day she purchased an extra $120 of merchandise – *cash*! Did I mention all transactions are in cash and expensive?

This pulled at my heartstrings and motivated me to apply for a caregiver card. I walked out one day determined to get my card. I went online and signed up, and paid the $100 registration fee, then waited a month for this *first*.

??? – To what lengths would you go to help your parents?

FEBRUARY 14TH: DISPENSARY WITH CAREGIVER CARD

My mom awoke in the middle of the night crying. She was in extreme pain and was looking for relief. The only solace I could provide was to tell her that I was going to pick up more medical marijuana lozenges in addition to some more pain-fighting strains of marijuana I was researching. This was my first opportunity to use my newly acquired caregiver card.

While waiting for my card to arrive, mom had run out of her medical marijuana lozenges.

The next morning, I woke up and Googled "what medical marijuana is best for pain medication?" I saw a top 10 list. I compared this against the dispensary's available stock. I settled on Kush #7, which is sold in bud form. Since I knew mom would *never* smoke it, because to quote her, "I'm not going to become a hippie!" I would find recipes to bake it in (for another future *first?*).

At the dispensary, the young girl behind the counter confirmed what the internet had revealed — Kush#7 was the best for pain. She gathered my order from various drawers filled with inventory behind her; lozenges from one drawer, oil from another, Kush #7 from another. She handed me the marijuana buds in a zip lock bag with a professionally printed label that described the contents. It took me back in time to my illegal teenage years, minus the professional label. Yes, I was a young derelict growing up. It was a lifetime ago. It was hard to believe that I was purchasing pot *legally*, for my mom no less. She was at home eagerly awaiting my return with her stuff; almost 50 years ago, she'd grounded me for having it in my possession. It was a surreal *first*. I guess I was now her supplier!

P.S. – Looking back: *The day we first entered the discussion with my mom about the possibility of using medical marijuana for her never-ending pain was unique. I wish you could have been a fly on the wall as the pain medication doctor and I talked her into considering this. It was hysterical. To quote her "I'm not going to be a hippie." I assured her there were other ways to injest, like edibles, where she was not going to be asked to smoke pot. I also assured her she didn't have to purchase tie-dye clothing and we were not going to a Grateful Dead concert. Slowly and methodically, with the help of the physicians, she came around to the idea. It has helped her. Now she asks me if she can have her "goodies." As a flippant teenager, I would have prognosticated that this day could and would NEVER happen. Not in my wildest dreams could I have pictured this. Never say never! Little did I know that this* *would be a precursor to the Twilight Zone experience that the year would soon become.*

??? – Have you ever had an older relative resistant to the use of medical marijuana due to preconceived ideas of the product?

FEBRUARY 15TH: RACE CAR AT LAS VEGAS MOTOR SPEEDWAY

I rolled up to the Palms Hotel & Casino in Las Vegas around noon for my annual trek to my industry's trade show. I dropped off my bags at the bell desk and summoned an Uber to take me to the Vegas Motor Speedway. Prior to arriving, I had researched things to do in Las Vegas that I had never done. At the top of my list was driving a race car. I saw that they accepted walk-ins with hourly lessons until 4 p.m.

A $16 Uber ride of twenty minutes brought me in front of the Las Vegas Motor Speedway to Exotics Racing for this *first* — driving a race car. I walked in and signed up for five laps in a Porsche 718 Cayman GTS for just under $200. I had never been in nor driven a Porsche. I started with a training video, led by a live instructor, in a room with 30 other waiting drivers. The racing "lines" to take in and out of the turns were stressed with the key word being "smooth." The racing line is the fastest line or arc through a corner on a race circuit. The trajectory of the racing line depends on the severity of the corner, how long the following straight is and what kind of car is being driven. The goal is to always carry as much speed in the braking zone, through the corner and onto the next straight. This also meant not making quick or jerky motions with the steering wheel, brakes, or gas. Being smooooth was stressed! As the instructor concluded our session, he must have been reading our collective minds when he said, "Don't worry about remembering all the details we just gave you," (we didn't) "there will be an instructor next to you in the car who will be telling this to you in real time. This is just for an overview preview." We all breathed a sigh of relief. Off we went onto the track in groups of three in SUVs for a two-lap test drive with a chauffeur. There were a few precise instructions of exactly when and where to brake and accelerate around the course, marked by various colored cones. The first lap was slow so we could see the track we were to drive. The second lap gave us a feel of the G-force created around the turns at increased speeds...hmm. The first lap was how I normally drive: fast. The second one was really fast, and I felt the G-forces they had hinted at. I did feel a slight sense of carsickness and hoped it wasn't going to be an issue on my five laps.

A tall, young college kid named Ian called out my name — he was my guy. They outfitted us with racing helmets, and I walked outside to find my white Porsche among Ferraris, Lamborghinis, Aston Martins, and other vehicles worth small fortunes. My internal voice asked if my overstuffed, aging body would flex and bend to fit into the restricted space so low to the ground. It was a challenge, but I finally fit and strapped in. Ian briefly went over the instructions again as I slowly pulled up to the stop sign at the entrance to the track. Once the coast was clear of the other cars whizzing by, we were off with his instructions to "Hit it!" I was into turn one with my young instructor calmly providing guidance.

"Accelerate." "Brake hard." "Left, left." "Go hard to the cone." "Go, go, go." It was a blur of concentration, and with each lap I pushed to improve.

It was not an easy oval of a few banked curves and long straight-aways. The course was challenging, with six sharp turns that were difficult to navigate. I pushed as hard as the caution sign in my brain would allow. I needed much more experience than five laps if I wanted to truly let go. The fifth and final lap came just in time, as my carsickness returned. I had exceeded 125 miles per hour, passed two cars, and one had passed me. I was not the worst nor the best with much room for improvement. I found myself being overly cautious going into the turns thinking, "*Don't crash!*"

*P.S. – **Looking back:** I walked away wondering how the professionals do this for a living. They travel at much greater speeds and for 500 laps! One hundred times the laps I had just completed. OMG…500 miles of starting and stopping, into and out of sharp turns at high speeds, focusing constantly for hours, all with many more cars than the five cars that I had to contend with. God bless them. That was my* first *and my* LAST *time as a race car driver. I'm too old to make it a career. A memorable experience that I recommend as a* first.

??? – Have you ever challenged yourself to race a car on a racetrack? Are you curious about the experience?

FEBRUARY 19TH: *CHER LIVE* IN VEGAS

I was late — an hour late after a protracted business dinner. I was alone and had found a last-minute single seat at the Park MGM sold-out show as a walk up. I walked in on the Sonny and Cher number, *I Got You Babe*. Cher was singing the duet with the deceased Sonny via the two large video screens flanking the stage. Sonny on the screen. Cher live and on stage going back and forth. She lamented that this was the *first* time she could bring herself to sing this to virtual Sonny. You could feel the compelling sweet connection and the deep emotion. If it was an act, it was a great one. I don't think she ever got over their relationship.

Cher worked her way through her hits, with an ABBA set in the middle. She ended with her personal hit, *Believe*. She looked amazing, with constant wardrobe and hair changes. From black, to brunette, to blonde, to redhead, and back again. Her voice for a 73-year-old was flawless. I assumed she was singing *live*. I had never seen Cher before, a *first*. I caught the last 90 minutes of her show. I'm glad I did — great show.

P.S. – *Looking back:* *I would recommend her show to anyone.*

??? – Have you ever seen Cher? Have you ever purchased a last-minute single seat to a show?

FEBRUARY 21ST: BAKE POT BROWNIES FOR MOM

I started to doze off, having returned home late after traveling all day from my meetings in Las Vegas. I had been up since 4 a.m. west coast time and losing three hours with the time change didn't help. But I couldn't go to sleep and break my streak of *firsts*. I shook myself awake. I felt slightly panicked with the pressure of not doing a *first* yet.

I had the quarter ounce of Kush #7 medical marijuana I intended to use for pot brownies for mom. I picked the marijuana up for her with my new caregiver card from the dispensary. I Googled "pot brownie recipes." It seemed like a lot of work and time. Then I had the brilliant idea of getting one of those quick brownie mixes and adding the Kush #7. I searched the cupboard and came up empty. Mom liked regular brownies. I headed to the grocery store at 8:30 p.m. and picked up Betty Crocker Supreme Fudge Brownie Mix. I wonder if Betty Crocker is rolling over in her grave? I'm sure this was not her intent when she concocted her brownie formula years ago. I retrieved the concealed bag of Kush #7 and split the quarter ounce in half. The internet recipe said to use an eighth of an ounce, so that was what I was going with. I hurriedly cut the buds with a knife into spice-sized flecks. I stirred the supplied mix with the required egg, milk, and vegetable oil and placed the batter into the nine-inch square greased cooking pan. I then sprinkled the cut-up cannabis on top. The oven was set at three hundred and fifty degrees, and I put in the pan. Ms. Crocker, please forgive me. I'm sure I wasn't the first to do this, nor will I be the last.

My wife, who was upstairs watching TV in bed, came cascading down the steps frantically complaining of the smell coming from the oven. The house smelled like pot – it was strong. She was not happy; I knew I was in trouble. I think she was revoking my husband of the year award. "Open the windows! This is ridiculous! Are you nuts?"

Oops – what did I know? This was the *first* time I had done this. I begged forgiveness and pleaded ignorance. I didn't know the smell would be so intense and pervasive. I lifted the brownies out of the oven and cut them into squares for mom to try the next day. Mission accomplished for a hurried and not very well thought out *first*. I fell quickly to sleep, spent from the travel and a week in Vegas.

P.S. – Looking back: *My mom and I would partake in the result of this calamity in the coming days. Although not overpowering it did provide a slight buzz of sorts.*

A few months after this episode, my wife was attending the Philadelphia Flower Show with a friend. She happened upon a medical marijuana education booth and asked what strain was best for pain. She shared the story of that night and my attempt at brownies. The person at the booth was dumbfounded and then bent over in stitches laughing hysterically. My "brilliant idea" was a terrible, but possibly funny idea! You must make butter out of it first. Apparently, the correct way to do what I had tried to do is to bake the buds first to extract the oil. This oil and not the uncooked buds should have been put into the mixture. This is what apparently made my house in need of fumigation. The person in the booth could not stop laughing at my missteps. She even called over several colleagues to have my wife retell the story again. Before long, there were a half – dozen people gathered around laughing uncontrollably at my stupidity. To quote Forest Gump, "Stupid is as stupid does."

??? – Have you ever tried pot edibles? Do you know that you must extract the oil before baking pot brownies?

FEBRUARY 22ND: HOME-BREWED BEER

I had secured a promised *first* from my beer-brewing lifelong friend Brian months ago. I made him commit to include me in on the concoction of his next batch of beer, which we had put on the calendar for today. He brews approximately six times a year for a total of sixteen times to date. I was looking forward to this six-hour labor of love.

Brian was in the basement already prepping when I arrived. His wife Colleen had vacated the house due to the smell created by brewing the hops. As I descended into the basement, I observed several pieces of brewing equipment: A brewer, something called the sparge heater, a fermenter, and a chiller, as well as other unfamiliar paraphernalia. I constantly asked throughout the day, "What is that? What is it used for?" I was a pest, but my host was gracious and patient as he consistently answered my intrusive questions.

The machinery was diverse and expensive. Brewing is not a cheap hobby. It is a time-consuming chemistry experiment with a possible payoff a few weeks later; hopefully something enjoyable to drink and savor, or not. Brian's partner in brewing Tom had joined us. The first batch my brew master friends Brian and Tom ever made was, in their words, "undrinkable." It was too sweet. Their best brew was a "mistake." You never really know until consumption time. The machinery they have purchased along the way has assisted with the consistency and a higher percentage of success.

There was a three-page brewing checklist on the counter. It looked more like a chemistry experiment than a recipe. The list contained the following:

- Prior day preparation: consisting of the yeast starter
- Brew day preparation: consisting of mash day prep, sparging, boiling, fermenting, dry hopping, and kegging

The last page of the checklist read "Downtime Activities." It was all well scripted, fascinating. The recipe took up four pages for the brew we were mixing that day: All Grain American IPA — "Snowflake of Love." There were 20-plus steps of various ingredients listed consisting of different varieties of malt, oats, hops, and yeast that had to be added at specific times and temperatures. In between the various procedures, we laid out the bags of hops and other ingredients like we were preparing to cook dinner. We measured out the ingredients and placed them in order of introduction to the brew. You can't add the wrong stuff at the wrong time. A few days before, the yeast had been prepared in a large beaker. The beaker of yeast was swirling with the use of a magnet. I'm still not sure why.

We started by pouring the previously measured minerals and grain into the brewer and added water to bring to the temp to 152 (*not* 151 or 153!). Once at 152 degrees, it then needed to boil at 212 degrees, adding grain along the way, to create the "mash." We sanitized everything throughout the entire process with a special sanitizing agent; my friend stressed that sanitation is very important. We also "measured the gravity" of this concoction by drawing out liquid with what looked like a mini-turkey baster into a "vessel" (cup). Then we placed the drops from the vessel onto some sort of "gravity" detection machine hooked up to my friend's computer. I knew it was meaningful because my brew masters discussed the gravity being slightly off the recipe's instructions. But this could change and be okay with a later gravity reading. It was way over my head, but I nodded as if I knew what my brew master friends were talking about. There were numerous brewing terms thrown around that day like gravity measuring, sparge, Fermcap, pitching yeast, wort, and many more. Who knew that brew masters had their own language?

We then drained and threw the mash out in the backyard, leaving the grain-flavored boiled water. In pouring the water, which they let me do, I had to go slow and disperse it evenly so it filtered through all the grain. There were so many steps, I'm sure some of the details written here are backward, missed, or outright wrong, but hopefully it paints a broad-stroke picture, like a watercolor painting.

Each step had to be timed: Mash water prep (30 minutes), sparge (60 minutes), boil (60 minutes), and so on, with multiple steps in between. I added two separate vessels of hops into two separate strainers that we placed into the boiling mixture. I also added Fermcap to the mixture before the hops to keep the mixture from boiling over. They shared that this was by far more than they had ever done before. This was going to be a "hoppy IPA."

Once the hops had soaked in the drained liquid mixture, I was called upon to "pitch the yeast" from the beaker in the other room into the heated stew. Once the yeast went in, we had to aerate the "wort" (brew mixture?). For a minute, we fed the wort oxygen with some apparatus to stimulate the yeast (I think?). Once aerated, the wort had to cool to 60 degrees while being transferred to the ferment machine through a multiple-hosed cylindrical contraption running cold water, which was hooked up to the house water.

Once we transferred the flavored liquid to the fermenter and set it at 65 degrees we were done – at least for that day. We took another gravity test. There was a cooled water flow hooked up to the fermenter to regulate the temperature. I was educated that fermentation temperature is the key. We did 65 degrees for five days, then raising three degrees for a diacetyl test, whatever that is? (I Googled "what is a diacetyl test" and got this: "[Diacetyl test] is a simple method to check if your yeast has finished reabsorbing the diacetyl." Diacetyl is a chemical used as an artificial food flavoring.)

We spent the next half-hour doing cleanup. I was told that there was still some "dry hopping" to be done in the coming days. This involves adding some additional hops in three and six days. My brew masters had a few *"firsts"* of their own that day. This was their hoppiest beer to date. It required extra steps that they had never performed before. I know this was a lot of unneeded or unwanted detail, but I wanted to communicate the complexity of the process. I headed home having completed my *first* brewing of beer.

When I got home, my friend texted me; *"1.002 Final Gravity will give us 5.9 ABV."*

Ahh, the gravity test measures the alcohol level of the brew. I came to learn that the difference between the first and the last gravity test determines the alcohol content.

*P.S. – **Looking back:** It was such a great experience. I learned so much. I had so many questions. It was also a great excuse to spend time with a lifelong friend that I do not get to see often enough. A win-win!*

I returned weeks later to partake in our efforts. It was good. We had succeeded. It was the first time I ever drank a beer I helped brew!

??? – Did you ever think that making beer would be so complex?

FEBRUARY 29TH: WEAR GOLF KNICKERS

As a self-proclaimed recovering shy person, I am usually a basic conservative dresser. Therefore, my *first* time wearing Plus Fours, or golf knickers, was a stretch for me. I had my wife order them online prior to my annual golf trip for this planned *first*. I broke them out at the Conservatory Golf Course at Hammock Beach Resort in Florida. I had never played there before; another *first* for the day. I looked better than I golfed in my dark gray knickers with matching gray and white argyle socks. My friends were impressed.

*P.S. – **Looking back:** This was THE extra Leap Year Day that became my book title and made my year of firsts unique. I spent it with dear friends playing golf. Golf is just a facilitator for the cherished friendships, and time spent sharing laughs with good-natured competitive jabs — it doesn't get much better.*

??? – Are you shy and afraid to put yourself out there? Will you look for an opportunity to stretch yourself by taking a chance for the first time?

<u>MARCH 6TH</u>: DAD'S ASHES IN MY GOLF BAG

I will never forget the day my dad told me, near the very end of his life, "I'll never golf again." It was his nod to the inevitable and his way of putting me on notice. Until that time, the hope of a recovery was always in the balance. Even in his decline, he would ride in the cart, hit a few drives, and chip and putt. In short order, he was reduced to just putting. Toward the end, he'd putt with his tank of oxygen in tow. It had become a fixture at his side. Finally, the weekend came when he couldn't even get out of the cart to putt. His energy to do so was gone. That was the day he declared that he was done playing golf. The sadness and finality in his eyes is something I will never forget. That was his final stubborn resignation to the disease that had consumed him — cancer. We both knew the outcome that was shortly ahead.

It has been almost 12 years since my dad passed. He was an avid golfer who loved the time he spent with his crew on his annual golf excursions and every weekend at the local municipal course. His group had the first two tee times every Saturday and Sunday morning at dawn at the muni. It was his religion, so to speak. I inherited his passion for the game, and I'm a disciple in my own golf congregation. I'm both grateful and fortunate for both.

It was this memory that motivated me that night to choose this *first*. I find myself wiping tears from my eyes. After all these years, the memory of holding his hand as he took his last breath is still fresh.

The urn with his remains stared me in the face from the mantle in our living room. It was at that moment that I decided my next *first* would be to play my future rounds of golf with a small portion of my dad's ashes in my golf bag. It was something I think he would appreciate.

I located a small container that could securely hold some of the embers and doled a few tablespoons into the empty vessel. I know this sounds strange or maybe even creepy or morbid, but to me it felt right. I took the small bottle of remains and marked *"Dad"* with a black marker. I placed the container into the side pocket of my golf bag — a *first*. I now keep a little of dad in my golf bag as I enjoy what he enjoyed, golfing with my friends. There is not a doubt in my mind that he'll enjoy being out on the links once again. My game could also use the guidance of a single-digit handicapper.

P.S. – Looking back: *This came in handy when I visited my grandparents' grave for the* first *time later in the year. I have also occasionally sprinkled a few ashes here and there on a few courses I knew he enjoyed.*

??? – Are there uncommon things (like the ashes in my golf bag) that help you remember the special people you have lost in your life?

.   .   .

CHAPTER FOUR:
—YOU'VE JUST CROSSED OVER INTO... THE TWILIGHT ZONE— UNWANTED FIRSTS

"You unlock this door with the key of imagination.
Beyond it is another dimension: a dimension of sound, a
dimension of sight, a dimension of mind. You're moving into a
land of both shadow and substance, of things and ideas.
You've just crossed over into... the Twilight Zone."

This was the opening to the early 1960s science fiction television series of the same name. I often refer to the year 2020 after the pandemic hit as the Twilight Zone. The *Twilight Zone* episodes, as described by Wikipedia:

> "... were in various genres, including fantasy, science fiction, absurdism, dystopian fiction, suspense, horror, supernatural drama, black comedy, and psychological thriller, often concluding with a macabre or unexpected twist, and usually with a moral."

Sounds like THE perfect description for the year to me. It started early in the year with a few unusual *firsts*, and then continued after March 20th, with what seemed like science fiction. Following are a few of my episodes during a year like no other. I'll share the following journal entries of other unwanted *firsts* from March that led up to my weeping.

MARCH 9TH: BUSINESS INTERRUPTION CLAIM

(Journal entry with a few minor deletions to shorten)

… I HATE this *first*! I inquired about business interruption insurance today for the *first* time in my 40-plus-year career because it was looking like there may be a shutdown in the future that would interrupt our business. The ominous plot was building fast from day to day. Today, the news was an 8 percent drop in the stock market in one day. All social functions in Italy just closed! The travel industry is taking a pounding, led by the cruise industry and the airlines. No one wants to be stuck on a boat quarantined for weeks on end. Here in Philly, the Convention and Visitors Bureau announced the cancellation of two major conventions coming to town in the next few weeks. Local schools are having dialogue about closing for the semester and having the students work from home. A local prep school customer closed until further notice. *CRAZY!* We'll see what the response to my email request to my insurance agent brings. I'm saying a prayer, which is *NOT* a *first*!

*P.S. – **Looking back:** We never filed a claim — not because it would not have been warranted but because of an exclusion clause in all these policies that prevented the opportunity to collect on it. Some businesses were trying despite this. A few lawsuits were in the courts to be determined sometime in the future.*

MARCH 11TH: MEDICAL MARIJUANA LOZENGES

There was a building pandemic hysteria. I couldn't do anything to affect it. I worked on some contingency strategies over the last few days to plan as best possible. But how do you plan for something that has never happened before? This was the backdrop to my *first* for today, experiencing medical marijuana lozenges.

I am the chief caregiver for my 85-year-old mother, now on medical marijuana. Her pain doctor asked me to document her dosage and its effects so he can adjust the medication. When I ask her, I don't exactly get good feedback to help me help her. That is, unless you consider the response "*I don't know*" helpful. We started this journey earlier in the year with an assigned counselor at the dispensary who recommended she start with a quarter of a lozenge to evaluate the effects. Her doctors were trying to wean her off fentanyl. We have since moved mom to one whole lozenge dose when she requests relief for her leg and back pain. Ever since the first weekend when mom took *five* lozenges and zonked out for an entire day, we realized that we needed to be more involved with the distribution of her medical marijuana. She thought of them like candy: "*Oh my.*" From that weekend forward, we became engaged as her pseudo "distributor."

So, with the purest of intentions, looking out for her best interests, I went to mom's "stash." I felt it was important to experience and understand the effects that she was feeling. I bit off slightly more than a quarter of a watermelon-flavored lozenge and waited. After a half-hour, I felt a little something. An hour later, I felt just a little bit more. I thought I should be experiencing the full effects by now. I felt slightly mellow, but nothing debilitating. Pushing the envelope, I bit slightly more of the lozenge, now consuming over a half, and waited again. I never made it to document the effect of this last bite because I nodded off to sleep. I had digested my *first* medical marijuana lozenge for the day.

P.S. – Looking back: This was the night the NBA season was suspended until further notice due to the Coronavirus. I was watching a Sixers game. All the news and non-news channels were consumed with reports on the Coronavirus. I remember reaching out to my business partners after the news of the NBA cancellation to comment that, "This is not good," and, "We will need to batten down the hatches." That became an understatement.

Regarding the medical marijuana, it's been effective in helping mom manage her pain while reducing her dosage of other narcotic-based painkillers. What had been a dangerous "gateway" drug to her when I was growing up is now improving her quality of life. I should have known then that the year would be like no other.

??? – Do you remember what you were doing and where you were when you realized the world as we knew it was about to change due to the pandemic?

<u>MARCH 12TH</u>: A PANDEMIC (LIFE CHANGES)

(Unedited journal entry)

… This *first* for me is also a *first* for America and eventually the world. The headline on CNN's website today read: *America's Way of Life Changes Indefinitely.* It has. The following three items were *Breaking News* at 6:10 a.m.

- Disney is closing its flagship theme park in California
- NCAA is canceling March Madness. Never in its history has it been canceled. A *FIRST!*
- Cruise lines Princess and Viking halt all cruises as virus spreads

This way of life-change caused by the Coronavirus became an internationally declared pandemic. We have entered a very strange, bizarre time. Professional leagues (NBA, NHL MLS, MLB) are suspended. Schools are closing. Events are being canceled. The stock market has taken a dive. The world as we know it seems to have been placed on hold. It feels like we have all been written into an unwanted bad B-movie script. It just doesn't seem real. It is a *first* for me and many.

We had an emergency management strategy meeting at work to plan and deal with these circumstances. My mantra was: *We are NOT going to panic, and we will work the problem while leaning on our core values to make decisions.* We survived 2008–2009, while many others in my industry did not. The problem this time is the timing. This is hitting during our industry's busiest quarter of the year. This is a gale force storm, and it is going to be difficult to navigate, but we are not in this fight alone. The nation and every small business are under siege. It is frightening; it is time to get ready for the fight. For the record, I don't like this *first*!

P.S. - Looking back: *Who would have ever thought? We did exactly as I wrote that day … "NOT panic and work the problem, while leaning on our core values." This has become a big part of the motivational speech I'm working on to share what I learned from 2020. It seemed like fiction.*

??? – How would you react in a time of crisis?

<u>MARCH 13TH</u>: *THE BEST MAN* (A PLAY)

Friday the 13th — what a day. I started the day addressing my staff about the personal and business concerns presented by the Coronavirus. I ended it by experiencing the public effect of it as I recorded my *first* time seeing the play *The Best Man*, described by the Walnut Street Theatre website as:

> "... *Power, ambition, and secrecy are in the air...it must be election season. Set at the national convention in Philadelphia, Gore Vidal's* The Best Man *takes you into the back rooms and hotel suites where two candidates are vying for their party's nomination. It's your inside look at the dirt-digging, double-dealing,*

triple-crossing deception of presidential electioneering ... and what could be more fun at the start of a Presidential campaign season! However, leave your party affiliation at the door; The Best Man *plays no favorites as theatrical fireworks are lobbed from both sides."*

As the week and the day played out, I wondered if I'd have to find a last-minute *first* to log. The day before, Broadway went dark for the foreseeable future. In Philly, our cultural centers, the Kimmel Center, and the Academy of Music, also hit the pause button. Disneyland and Disney World stopped operations that day. It was Friday the 13th, which seemed appropriate for the eerie, surreal happenings occurring. So it was reasonable to assume the Walnut Street Theater would cancel also. I also needed to mention the following online report from local ABC affiliate Channel 6 that came out just after noon:

Friday, March 13, 2020 12:30AM

PHILADELPHIA (WPVI) – *Philadelphia officials have banned public gatherings of over 1,000 people for the next 30 days over Coronavirus concerns. They are also recommending there be no gatherings of more than 250 people for the next 30 days.*

The Walnut Street Theater holds just over one thousand. I Googled "is the Walnut Street Theater still open?" The results were non-committal. I went to their website; nothing stated that the show had been canceled. So I called and I called. I sent an e-mail through their website, but the automatic reply said I'd receive a response between 24 to 48 hours. With the curtain call scheduled in six hours, I called again. The phone rang about a dozen times before someone picked up — a live voice! They informed me that the show was still on. I wondered what effect the Coronavirus would have on the attendance. Normally, most of the theater's audience consists of senior citizens, the population at highest risk with this pandemic.

The traffic as we traveled into Center City, Philadelphia, had noticeably thinned for a Friday night. Our second hint that this would be a peculiar *first* was the parking lot closest to the theater was empty. We arrived only five minutes before the play was to start. That lot was usually full, which often meant we would have to go farther down the street to access additional parking. As we walked in minutes before, where people normally filled the halls with lines at concession stands, there were just a few couples meandering around. Maybe everyone was already in their seats? We walked through the mezzanine doors to find a few dozen people seated. A female attendant came through to tell us we could move anywhere in the theater we'd like. Seats were obviously available. We looked at each other in shock. It was a ghost town. It was eerie. It was strange. It felt like The Twilight Zone. As the performance unfolded you could hear every single response from the audience. There was one large guy with a very loud and distinctive laugh that drew everyone's attention. At times, the actors responded directly to the crowd as if we were part of the play. It was a unique experience. The Walnut Street Theatre, founded in 1808, is America's oldest theatre. I must believe this was a *first* for the theatre also.

P.S. - *Looking back:* *This would be the last public gathering of the year for me and for many. It was also a topical play with the upcoming contested presidential election. The theater would be closed for over a year.*

??? – When this all started to happen did you ever envision this continuing for over a year?

MARCH 14TH: AXE THROWING

I had planned for months to attend the Atlantic Ten Basketball Tournament at the Barclay Center in Brooklyn with my son for my *first* for today. I had never been. We had tickets, but the pandemic had taken care of this *first*, canceling every sporting event for the foreseeable future. We replaced it with axe throwing – a *first* that would reveal a hidden talent.

Our instructor Josh went through his training talk about how to throw the axe. Josh was a long-haired millennial that threw bullseyes effortlessly. He obviously used his downtime practicing what he was preaching. My mind went to my horseshoe ringer throwing mentality from my youth. It was all about focus and the flip. Growing up in "the country" at my grandparents' house with horseshoe pits, my cousins and I became quite accomplished at horseshoe throwing. For summers on end, we'd have epic horseshoe tournaments. It got to be a ringer fest; we were that good. If you were going to keep playing, you had to throw ringers. To do so you needed to rotate the horseshoe, so the open end came to open at just the time it hit and slid onto the awaiting pole. The axe was much the same way. You needed the sharp blade to rotate at just the right time to strike the awaiting wooden target.

The target had circles starting from the outside moving inward marked 1, 2, 3, and 4, with a red bullseye in the center of the circle worth six points. There were also two much smaller little blue circles on the top left and right. We learned these were "kill shots" for 10 bonus points. If the axe did not stick, it was worth zero points. Zero points happened frequently; it was not easy. The "kill shots" could only be done at the end, during the tenth frame, and you had to call it. If called and hit, it counted as 10 points. A perfect score was 64 four points – nine bullseyes for 54 points and a "kill shot" worth 10. There was a large board with about a dozen small photos on it under the designation of "MVT" (Most Valuable Thrower). For your photo to qualify to join this "Axe Hall of Fame," you had to score 55 points or more.

I started hitting my rhythm, with my focus and confidence growing with each bullseye hit. I'd take a deep breath to relax before each release and just let it go. I was entering "the zone." As I started racking up bullseyes and wins against my son and the others, Josh hung in the background watching. He started watching more intently as I came close to reaching the 55-point total needed to gain MVT fame. He saw this and challenged me; I felt honored.

Josh led off with six consecutive bullseyes. I was on his heels with 5 out of 6. He was impressed, and I was focused. The competition was palpable. He threw with such confidence, sure that he wouldn't miss, until he gave me an opening in the seventh frame by missing the bullseye. I couldn't capitalize and entered the tenth frame trailing. Josh threw first and hit a bullseye to achieve the MVT board-worthy total of 56. I was at 46 after the ninth frame. My son and my friends were cheering me on. I had one last chance to tie my mentor and achieve fame. I had to call and hit the "kill shot." I wanted it *bad*. I took a deep breath to focus on the target calmly and confidently. I released the axe with ease and confidence to nail that small blue two-inch diameter "kill shot" at the top right of the board in the center! I gave a Tiger-style fist pump of achievement. I had done it! I tied Josh and qualified for "fame" on my last pressure-packed throw. I had never thrown an axe before in my life and I had NEVER qualified for a "Wall of Fame" — a double *first*. I had my picture taken and it was placed on the board for posterity. This distinction and a few bucks will get me a cup of coffee.

P.S. – *Looking back:* *I retired on top. I have not been back.*

??? – Have you ever stumbled across something that you are naturally good at?

MARCH 16TH: WORRIED FOR THE FUTURE OF MY BUSINESS

(Journal entry, with a few minor edits)

… I can honestly and sadly say that for the *first* time in my life, I'm worried about the future of my business, Spike's Trophies' Ltd. The mayor of Philadelphia had a press conference this afternoon to close all non-essential businesses for the next two weeks. We're non-essential we thought, but as a manufacturer we were unsure. The happenings leading up to this have been unpredictable and unprecedented. It seems that in one week the world has stopped. Orders and events have been canceled left and right. Today along with the city shutting down, our customer the Penn Relays canceled their April event for this year. It is the first time in their 125-year history that they have done so. This was just one of many. Schools — which are 20 percent of our business — have closed for the foreseeable future with my guess until the next school year. No graduations or year-end awards, tournaments are being canceled. The phones have stopped ringing and the traffic in our showrooms has reduced to a trickle. This is supposed to be our "busy season." Things have changed — quickly. I knew we were in for a rocky ride last Friday. Now, three days later, I'm afraid for the continuation of the business. At our meeting this morning I instructed my controller that I was taking a pay cut. We met again this afternoon, after the mayor's announcement to game-plan again. We agreed to meet tomorrow morning after we slept on our decisions from this afternoon. Every resolution we make becomes outdated — quickly. The target keeps moving.

This afternoon we decided to close on Saturdays. We spoke to our bank and discussed options. They were supportive and asked us for three months' worth of cash flows in order to discuss a strategy. We stopped all part-time hours. We discussed laying off employees, an unwanted first for us. My solution in the past has always been to think, plan, and work my ass off. I'm not sure if that will get us through this time. I pledged to my partners that if we were going down, *"We are going down swinging."*

I texted my wife: *Any interest in happy hour? I need a drink.* This is not like me.

She texted back: *No one is allowed in restaurants. Only take out.*

I was so engrossed in work I had forgotten that restaurants and any public gathering places were on lockdown. Next thing you know they'll shut down the bridge and you won't be able to jump from it (kidding...sort of). I fight thinking negative thoughts. After 40-plus years of hard work in climbing the ladder and building a business something I have no control over, a once-in-a-lifetime event could destroy it. Let's hope and pray that this is not the outcome. I guess we'll see how this plays out.

I got up at 3:30 a.m. last Friday morning and wrote the following script for my weekly 10 a.m. Monday staff meeting today. I read the following copy word for word to my employees:

We have entered into a very strange, bizarre time. There is a new reality we have to deal with today. I am personally doing a year of firsts, and unfortunately America joined me for a first yesterday, as America started to shut down temporarily. Can I ask for a show of hands of who woke up Monday of this week and thought, "Professional leagues would be suspended (NBA, NHL, PGA, MLS); that NCAA March Madness would be canceled (a first!); that schools would close; that Broadway would "go dark"; that annual events would be canceled; that we'd have a travel ban; that the stock market would take a dive? The world as we know it seems to have been placed on hold.

This is something that is a first for everyone in this room and in this country. There is no playbook or history to draw from in making decisions. I don't know how long this will continue; no one knows. We will do our absolute best; you have my/our word. It doesn't seem real. It is and we have to deal with it. The only thing similar is the financial crisis of 2008-2009. The difference now though is the speed that things have changed. In 2008-2009, it took over 200 days for the stock market to lose 20 percent of its value. It took 20 days as of yesterday for the same 20 percent loss in value in the stock market. In 2008-2009 we survived, but many others did not. I expect and will plan for the same here, God willing.

We will deal with these circumstances by responding with: no panic and by working the problem, while leaning on our core values. We will do it with clear, calm, focused minds. Worry and drama are wastes of time and energy. We need to be present and not distracted. Thought and solutions are the answer, not complaining about the hand we have been dealt, which we cannot control. We have to control what we can control.

During these unusual times, until we all figure out where this is leading, we will look to do and help with the following, which we can control:

1. *Look at your personal and our business spending. Look for any cost-cutting possibilities to save money. Stop any unneeded spending. Conserve cash at all costs. There is difference between a "want" and an absolute "need." Filter out the want.*

2. *Installing hand sanitizer stations in the showrooms, maybe create some bump elbow signs?*

3. *Get forehead scanners to check temps.*

4. *Aggressively send people home who come in sick, including myself. I have to change. I used to wear as a badge of courage coming to work when under the weather, putting on my game-face to play hurt. In today's environment, it is a stamp of stupidity.*

5. *Stop all overtime until further notice.*

6. *Keep showrooms open, unless shut down by the city.*

7. *Start to put pressure on all monies owed, concentrating on accounts past 30 days. In times like these, cash is king.*

8. *Escalate any requests for canceled orders to discuss potential alternate options. Ship the awards direct to the recipients if the event has been canceled.*

9. *We will continue to monitor the situation and may look to implement initiatives, like a reduced workweek schedule, if needed.*

We need to all put on our big boy and big girl pants and deal with the reality of some upcoming difficult times. If we all pull together, we will be stronger for it.

The possible good news is that Wuhan, China, where this started over three months ago, appears to be on the other side of this. My hope is that whatever measures we have to put in place will be temporary in nature to weather this hopefully short-term storm. Unfortunately for us, in our industry, the timing could not be worse as we head into our busy season, the time we make our money for the year. We are looking to make lemonade out of this batch of lemons that has been presented to us and to the nation.

I /we care about each and everyone in this room. Let's circle the wagons and have each other's back by doing our/your jobs correctly and efficiently! Questions?

There weren't many questions. I think everyone understood the gravity of the situation at hand. To say this is an unforeseen and unwanted *first* is an understatement.

P.S. – *Looking back:* *I would never have guessed that I'd be sitting here writing this book a year later and we are still dealing with the ripple effects of the pandemic. I'm guessing that we'll be dealing with this the rest of this year and beyond. Oh, and I can't believe we have survived so far.*

??? – How would you have reacted if it was your business and the livelihood of others on the line? What would you have done differently?

MARCH 17TH: NO SALARY – WORKED FOR FREE

I have no entry for today. I wrote *"NO SALARY"* on my desk calendar to mark my unwanted *first* for the day. I stopped paying myself that day. That day and the following one must have been a blur. I never found the time to write a daily journal entry. I looked back into my emails from the day to try and piece together that day and only found this email to my controller:

From: Keith

Sent: Tuesday, March 17, 2020 7:18 PM

To: John

Subject: Salary suspension

I just spoke to my wife. I'm prepared to suspend my salary for the next month to help out. We'll be OK.

Keith

I followed this up with another email the next morning at 7:37 a.m. to my bookkeeper and my controller, who had questioned my decision, with the same message:

As of today, please suspend my salary until further notice. Please no questions. Just do. Please. This is my decision.

Respectfully,

Keith

P.S. – *Looking back:* *I'm not sure I believed what I wrote in the email above that "we'll be OK." Maybe I was trying to convince myself? You do what you must do to save the ship. I never really worked for the money anyway. This just confirmed it. I thought that I'd stop my pay for a month to help. That month turned into many more. I became richer through the experience beyond my imagination. Riches come in many ways. I would come to appreciate this more and more as the journey through the year continued. I told my wife later in the year that I did the best work of my entire life for* free.

??? – Have you ever worked for free for the good of a cause? Were you enriched by the experience?

<u>MARCH 18TH</u>: COVID-19 EXPOSURE SHUT DOWN MY BUSINESS

Again, I have no entry for this day. I wrote *Coronavirus infection* on my desk calendar to mark another unwanted *first* for the day.

The day went off the rails in the early morning when employee after employee started to filter into my office with concerns. One employee who was out for two days returned to work. When asked if he was okay due to the increased concern of what was happening in the world, he responded,

"I was home helping my mom who tested positive, but I'm okay because we didn't hug." This set off a chain reaction and I closed the building. I sent everyone home until further notice. I found myself placed on hold with the Centers for Disease Control and Prevention (CDC) hotline for the next hour and a half to get this possibly exposed employee tested. A negative test was required for us to go back to work. I came to learn that I could not expedite a test or the process. We had to sit back and wait for the CDC to contact trace and test the individuals exposed. My employee would hopefully be at the top of this list. I emailed the staff that this could take a few days. They had to sit tight at home until the coast was clear. We would pay them through the end of the week. We were hopeful that we would be able to open the following Monday. That was the *first* time I closed our business due to a possible COVID-19 exposure of an employee.

*P.S. – **Looking back:** This was obviously early in the pandemic when any exposure by an employee shut your business down until all people involved were contact traced and tested negative. It changed dramatically later in the year as we experienced another first during the so-called second wave that hit us.*

??? – Did you have to deal with an exposure to COVID-19 by a friend, a family member, or a business colleague? Did it cause disruption in your life? How did you handle it?

MARCH 19TH: DEALT WITH A THREAT TO A LIFE

(Journal entry, with a few minor edits)

… It was a special edition of The Twilight Zone today. I'm not sure I believe it, and I lived it. I'm just getting back to my desk at 6:30 p.m. I came in at 6 a.m. and at 7:30 a.m., my day transformed as my business partner launched into my office in a panic. He had one of our employees, whose possible exposure had shut us down the day before, on his cell phone. The employee was threatening his own life. He was declaring that he did not want to go on any longer. He was crying hysterically.

My partner had called him to ask if he had heard anything from the CDC about the testing. In short order, we came to find out that his excuse for being out a few days was not true. We asked to speak to his mother to confirm if she had tested positive. We were told we couldn't. He wanted us to take his word that she had not tested positive. It got complicated fast.

I frantically pleaded, "*Stay there, I'm on my way.*" I did not go the speed limit this morning. I screeched into his driveway 10 minutes later as he sat sobbing on his front steps. I grabbed him in a big bear hug. I slowly put the pieces together as I tried my best to calm him down. My employee was understandably upset with the recent trauma in his life. His brother had been murdered during a robbery over a year ago. His father had suddenly passed away a month ago due an unforeseen illness. As I stood with my arms around him, I found out that his uncle's demise was just days away due to lung cancer. This was his mother's brother. His mother was apparently not positive. She had been at the hospital at her brother's bedside the past week.

This troubled soul would leave the house in the morning with his mother thinking he was going to work. He would wait in the neighborhood until she left for the hospital, and then would return home. He needed space. He needed to try to clear his mind. He was lost. The COVID-19 excuse seemed convenient for not coming to work.

He realized overnight that we could not return our employees to work without "official" confirmation from the CDC, which would never come. In his mind, he felt trapped with no way out other than joining his brother and father. I still wasn't sure if he was telling the truth about his mother not having COVID-19. I needed verification. I needed to talk to the mother. She was at the local cancer center with her dying brother a half-hour away. We were on our way. During that very emotional drive, I bared my soul. I shared my doubts of when I was young like him in similar dark places and had considered a similar ending. I acknowledged his losses. I empathized with his situation. I did *my best* sales job on the value of life. I suggested some tools for him to use to find his way out — a step at a time, a day at a time. I suggested doing a *first* every day.

We pulled into the hospital's parking garage. I knew the place well. I ran my company out of this hospital for three months a decade ago. I performed the same end of life duties with my father as his mother was performing with her brother, his uncle. Coincidentally, it was the same cancer; stage IV small cell lung cancer. I'd seen this movie and knew the end all too well.

Entering a hospital at the height of the initial COVID-19 crisis was like entering a war zone. The only problem was that I was virtually defenseless. I had just noticed that I ran out so quickly I'd left my wallet with my IDs on my desk. I was with a hysterically crying young man without any identification. I was going to walk in and try to explain somehow that I needed to find the boy's mom to verify that she did not have COVID-19. There were sentries protecting the front door. I talked my way through somehow. I walked up to a second set of guards positioned at the front desk and started my far-fetched story. One guard peeled away after I mentioned my COVID-19 verification quest. The next thing I knew, the returning guard escorted me out the front door into the parking lot. He had the head nurse of the hospital in tow, and she was not happy.

The head nurse started aggressively interrogating me, "Do we have a person who has tested positive in our hospital?"

To add to this mess, up walks my employee's aunt who asks, "What are you doing here? We were worried about you. Your neighbor just called your mother to say that you were just taken away (abducted) by an old man. She just called me."

Apparently, I was that "old man." They had called the police! I can't make this stuff up. I was now a fugitive with a kidnapped subject. At that moment, by chance, the mother walked through the lobby and the aunt called to her. I was now standing in the parking garage of the Fox Chase cancer center with my crying employee, his quizzical mother, his puzzled aunt, a guard, and one upset head nurse. I was the only one that had the pieces to the puzzle, I think. And I had no identification to verify who this fugitive was. *Are you following me?*

I first tried to calm the nurse down, as the mother asked her child what was going on. Everyone was in a heightened state of either panic or confusion, or both. I noticed the stitched last name of the nurse on the left chest of her medical vest. I asked if she any relation to someone I knew with the same last name. She wasn't receptive until I told her who I was and where I was from. I pointed to the only ID I had on me, my business logo on my left chest. The tone of the conversation turned on a dime. She was indeed my friend's sister *and* she was a customer! She started telling me that she bought all of her nursing plaques from us. We were now best friends. I could now get on with connecting the dots for everyone, which I did. I confirmed that the mother had never tested positive or ever had COVID-19. I confirmed that despite the innocent deceit of her son, she still loved him unconditionally. Everyone was happy. I had my negative COVID-19 confirmation and headed back to the office to inform every one of the good news. I left the others at the hospital to fill in their blanks. It was now the afternoon.

Once back, my work was just starting. I now had HIPPA issues to deal with in communicating with the staff. After legal clearance, we put a conference call together to let the staff know that we were in the clear. We communicated that we were giving them tomorrow off, with pay. We were going to resume business as normal, whatever that meant in these unusual times. We told the staff to enjoy the weekend with their families and get ready to fight on Monday.

As we hung up the phone with the employees around 4:30 p.m. the governor made his announcement, mandating an enforced shutdown of non-essential businesses. That would be us. We started to immediately get texts from our employees asking if they were to still report to work on Monday as we had just told them moments ago. No one could write this script. The management team and I went back to the drawing board. After a few hours of tortured discussion, we concluded that we would put together another conference call tomorrow afternoon to inform the staff that we were laying all of them off and we would be closing. The world had gone mad!

P.S. – Looking back: I came to learn, with this being my first lesson, that this pandemic did not only expose the vulnerabilities of the physical state of the body, but also the vulnerabilities of the mental state of the mind. In short order, my staff member had to deal with multiple family tragedies. The current COVID-19 crisis added to these traumas to cause him to threaten to take his own life. We never truly know what is going on in someone's life. Handle people with care!

MARCH 20TH: LAID OFF AN EMPLOYEE – ALL 45 OF THEM

It's 5 a.m. on Friday March 20th. I'm heaving, standing in my shower. I'm crying uncontrollably. I am about to perform an unwanted *first* today in my quest of my *Leap Year of Firsts*. For the *first* time in my life, I am going to lay off an employee. It isn't going to be just one it is the entire company — all 45 of them. Many of these people have worked with me for many years — some for 40 years, others 25 plus, with the majority over five years. They are family. They have families. I care for them. I love them. I was them; I am them. I know the impact this will have on their lives, and it is not my fault. It is not their fault. It is the hand that the pandemic has dealt the world. I get it. I understand. That doesn't make it hurt any less.

Earlier in the day, I had a tough conversation with my company's banker. I let her know the predicament of our impending closure. I was transparent. I was practicing what I preach in times like these, honest communication. She was understanding and compassionate in offering additional loans to keep us afloat. I turned her offers down. Our future is uncertain. In good conscience, we can't take on any additional debt. I don't have faith we'd be able to pay them back. I can't do that to my friends.

This moment and the sequence of events that produced this *first* today are best described in the subsequent *Forbes Magazine* article on our predicament:

> "... *Virtually overnight, his customers canceled long-planned events. 'We didn't need the Mayor of Philadelphia or the governor of Pennsylvania to tell us that we were a 'non-essential' business,' says Baldwin. Under a city order, all of Spike's regular venues and showrooms had been shuttered for a week before the governor's stay-home pronouncement left Baldwin no choice: fighting off tears, he was forced to lay off his entire workforce that Friday afternoon at 2:30 p.m."*

My partners and I had gone over every possible scenario. We kept coming back to this unwanted *first*. At 2:30 p.m., I couldn't even muster the energy to control the tears to communicate this news. I was inconsolable. My feelings and responsibility for them was stabbing me in the heart. I was a mess. I had to delegate the telling of the inevitable news to one of my partners. To make it worse we couldn't even tell them in person. We had to set up a conference call. They were all at home due to a Coronavirus scare in our facility earlier in the week. I'm sure they had a clue as to what was coming. The afternoon prior, the governor had made a declaration that we were non-essential.

We received texts from the employees throughout the morning asking: *What are we going to do?*

Our answers were consistent: *We'll talk about it at 2:30 p.m.*

After my partner communicated the unavoidable bad news, more questions came — questions about their future, our future. Our answers lacked any certainty - either: "*We don't know ...*" or "*We'll do the best we can.*" Despite our feeble replies, something remarkable happened. Several of them asked if they could still come to work next week even if we couldn't pay them. Somehow, they managed a smile through the pain. *Remarkable. Blessed.*

I had started the year of 2020 committed to doing something EVERY DAY for the *first* time in my life. I was documenting these *firsts* in my *first* ever daily journal when the effects of the storm created by the worldwide pandemic hit. Never having risked my life climbing Mt. Everest I can only imagine what it would be like clinging to life on the side of that mountain during a surprise life-threatening storm. The tallest mountain in my life that I had to climb was the buying and growing of my awards business since my teenage years. I was 62 years old and a blinding storm in the form of the Coronavirus had hit. I didn't know if my company would survive. I didn't know if there would be jobs to return to. It felt like impending death. I was crying.

P.S. – Looking back: Being in Forbes Magazine was a big deal and an honor.

??? – Have you had an event in your life where the emotion of a day stays with you and is always close to the surface when recounting it?

MARCH 20TH: HIRED BACK @ 4:30 – PART 2: "MANNA FROM HEAVEN"

The second *first* today is best described by the balance of the *Forbes Magazine* article, "Call Centers Can Help Americans Weather COVID-19 Calamity," written by Richard Levick.

'Manna from heaven,' as Baldwin calls it, arrived just 57 minutes later in the form of a call from Beth Packel, Spike's representative from Philadelphia's Firstrust Bank, who was aware of the company's dilemma. Packel volunteered that one of her long-term customers, AnswerNet, a call center outsourcer operating throughout North America, had just been awarded a large contract to make outbound calls for the State of New York to book appointments for COVID-19 testing.

AnswerNet was suddenly in full agent acquisition mode. It needed 300 workers on the New York State program now.

Packel immediately put Baldwin in touch with Gary Pudles, the president of AnswerNet, who offered agent positions to Spike's entire workforce, at their existing rate of pay!

Baldwin couldn't say "yes" fast enough. Within two hours of dismissing his staff, Baldwin had miraculously hired them all back, filling 45 crucial seats for AnswerNet. In minutes, Baldwin says, the Spike's team went from "non-essential" to "essential".

They were off and running. They worked with AnswerNet through the weekend, from early in the morning until late in the evening, getting everyone prepped and trained to help arrange testing appointments for thousands of New York State residents worried that they had contracted Coronavirus ...".

P.S. – Looking back: This story became the start of our "fifteen minutes of fame." The dramatic pivot brought much attention. The emotion of that day will always live within me. No one will ever truly know. A day I will never forget. This was a "pebble in a pond" moment for me that created many ripples.

First time in my life I ever laid off every employee. First time I offered them their jobs back working as a call center. This was all within two hours of the same day. It seemed fictional although it was very real.

??? – Would you have said yes to the challenge of becoming a call center?

<u>MARCH 21ST</u>: BECAME A CALL CENTER

"AnswerNet" was the singular word I wrote on my desk calendar to capture my *first* that day. That word — scribbled in haste during the mass chaos of converting a trophy company into a call center — would serve as my journal entry for the day. I had no time to write anything else – I was totally immersed and overwhelmed. I don't remember what time I left work that day. I know it was well after midnight.

I will pick up from the Forbes article where I left off in the telling of the day prior to tell the tale of my *first* from that day:

> *"… Creating remote call teams, Pudles notes, requires multiple things to happen simultaneously — and quickly. AnswerNet's team walked Spike's people through their team onboarding process, ensuring that the center systems were compatible with their individual home equipment (personal computer, high-speed Internet, USB headsets, etc.). Each agent needed to be trained via video and screen sharing — and every agent needed to be scheduled and managed based on New York state requirements.*

> *The biggest challenge that occurred while onboarding to Spike's team was an equipment shortage. As states began to announce their first shelter-in-place directives, there was, not surprisingly, a shortage of USB headsets as so many contact centers and other Business Process Outsourcers (BPOs) moved their agent's home. Fortunately, Baldwin was able to locate several dozen headsets in an Arizona warehouse and had them overnighted to Philadelphia. Five days after Baldwin got the go-ahead from Pudles, they went live, working in shifts around the clock.*

> *The calls have at times been inspiring (the AnswerNet team has helped ignite hope for hundreds of beleaguered New Yorkers),*

but at other times been emotionally challenging, since many callers are scared and seeking comfort.

In one instance, their outreach was too late; the person had tragically passed away the day before. The news shook up the team. Still, Baldwin and Pudles couldn't be prouder of the way their people have responded to a calamity that grows worse by the day.

'Every day, I've been emotionally moved by the calls,' says Spike's veteran Max Evans. 'It certainly hits at the heart when you hear the concern and fear in some of their voices. Many are coughing and sick. The gratitude they show us with their, 'Thanks for making calls,' and so much more. Humbling to say the least!'

'I'm so proud of our people, and so grateful for the opportunity from Firstrust and AnswerNet,' says Baldwin. Through April 4, AnswerNet has set up more than 25,000 testing appointments ...

... To suggest that this catastrophe has a "silver lining" is thoughtless as hundreds of Americans succumb by the day. But if we continue to look out for one another – to seize the chances that are out there to help people take care of their medical and financial needs – we can make this crisis a little less awful.

Ask Keith Baldwin and his team at Spike's."

–Richard Levick, Esq. @richardlevick, is Chairman and CEO of LEVICK

For several of our employees who make calls we had to purchase laptops for them. There were restrictions on purchasing quantities due to shortages – but each laptop represented a job. We made the investment and figured a way around the quotas. We had to set up most of our callers in their homes overnight. For those without high-speed internet connections at home we created safe spaces within our building. It was a whirlwind that

I cannot adequately capture here. It would take another book to do so. Your imagination will have to suffice.

P.S. - *Looking back:* *That I even had time and presence of mind to write "AnswerNet" on my desk calendar that day, with everything happening so fast, is amazing. No one will EVER truly know the effort that went into this. Hopefully, I provided a glimpse.*

We worked through Saturday and Sunday night to be able to go live calling at the start of the week — it was remarkable. We "worked the problem," which became a recurring theme for the rest of the year. I am so proud of our people and forever grateful for their ability find a way to say "YES!"

To give you a sense of the calls, I'll share just one of the many emails I received from our staff of callers:

"OMG I started crying talking to this one girl… She sounded really sick and achy. Her birthday is in a few days and her fever just broke. I told her that my friend has it (COVID-19) and his fever pretty much broke after two days and he is feeling like he got hit by a truck, but he is feeling better every couple of hours. She started crying just hearing that she has a chance of feeling better too. I got to be the first one to wish her a happy birthday two days early and she started crying happy tears just to hear something positive. I'm glad we can help people and give them some hope … Wow."

There were many similar types of calls to frightened people. The calls were draining to my staff — but also rewarding. Although I didn't personally make the calls I was behind the scenes playing air traffic controller in coordinating all the moving parts that made these calls possible. This included constantly communicating what seemed like hourly updates from the various parties involved, including the state. I also had to continually work on keeping our spirits and hopes up during the many stresses of the moment.

??? – Can you imagine?

. . .

CHAPTER FIVE:
WHY?

As March progressed, I was working 24/7 for free! I was passionate and inspired despite the seemingly insurmountable obstacles. I was driven. I was doing things of which I would have never thought I was capable. Why — what was fueling me? The WHY is the purpose, cause, or belief that drives every one of us – everyone has a WHY. Do you know yours? Here is what eventually led me to my WHY.

MARCH 22ND: GAVE UP #1 SON STATUS VIA FACEBOOK

I posted the above photo taken in my office on Facebook to document my *first* today with the following caption: *"As of today, I'm 'officially' turning over the title of #1 Son to my brother. He has earned it. He is awesome. He is funnier, more intelligent, and better looking than I will ever be (although shorter; sorry couldn't help myself). Congrats on the new title!*

Wear the crown proudly.

P.S. I confirmed this with mom yesterday. She is aware and has agreed (sadly) of the passing of this torch. With much love!"

In the midst of my personal madness, my younger brother was about to be let go from his job of twenty-six years in the coming month. He was distraught and in an extremely dark place. I had never witnessed this from him in the sixty years I had known him. His quick wit and his sharp zany sense of humor had departed. He could feel his life's work evaporating. He was despondent. He was throwing a grand illogical pity party of negative possibilities for his life. I had just emerged out of my pity party the past week and was looking to assist my brother in ending his.

I spent hours on the phone trying to console him today. I had similar calls during the prior week that compelled me to grab the custom printed pillow cover of my brother and my mother. This was his Christmas present to her so she could go to bed every night with him close by. REALLY? The picture on that pillowcase was a counterfeit. My brother had doctored the photo to show him as the #1 Son and had posted it on Facebook. He superimposed his photo over mine. The real photo was of me and my mom taken at Valentine's Day on our date at her favorite local restaurant. *Hilarious!* I told you he had a screw loose. But that screw had been tightened in this crisis.

To provide context, since my father's passing, to keep my mother's spirits up, I had claimed the fictional #1 Son status. Being the older brother and a year apart, it seemed fitting. We would go back and forth on Facebook with our silly tug of war for the comedy benefit of friends and family. So when I was thinking of a *first* for the day it struck me. "*First*" time I'd give up my #1 Son status. It would give me an opportunity to hopefully put a smile on his face. It was worth giving up the crown, temporarily!

P.S. – Looking back: *My brother is back to his zany self. For a while he was temporarily employed as one of our callers until he landed a job a year later. He has now become #2 again, after I recaptured the #1 slot. Just ask my mom. I love him and am blessed to have him in my life.*

??? – Have you had a sibling in distress that you had to help?

MARCH 24TH: COVID-19 "SURVIVAL GUIDE"

I sent a proposed "Survival Guide" to my awards industry group for the *first* time today. I did so in the following email:

"… I saw several cities and states close yesterday. In my humble opinion, this domino will fall for most everyone. It inspired me to write this last night to share today. Since I feel that I'm a week (a day feels like a year) or so ahead of this, I would like to share my experience of what I've done as a "Survival Kit" from my perspective. My city shut down over a week ago and my state mandated last Friday that we "officially" close as I shared previous. My sharing was not intended to be a scare tactic to create fear or worry or for sympathy. Hopefully it was not taken that way. I wanted to be real. I am NOT fearful, I'm inspired. I wanted to communicate and possibly inspire others that despite some very challenging circumstances we can make it through if we keep our heads and plan properly. I've been suspended from doing business coming up on a few weeks, with no knowledge of when we will reopen. The short version is SAVE CASH at all costs. Again, in my opinion we need to put together a plan to be able to get to three to six months out, without ANY revenue. Hopefully this is over-planning. I think we need to move quickly, the speed of this is fast. To do this you need to shed or suspend every expense possible. Look for every opportunity to obtain cash. We can do this! You need to have a place for your employees to return to. My "why" is to save jobs — safely. Every decision, including laying them off, should be made with this thought process in mind. Extraordinary times call for extraordinary measures!

CASH INBOUND:

1. ***Accounts Receivable***: *Cash is oxygen. Every dollar is a breath of air to your business to live another day. Collect more aggressively than ever. For everything you produce get money up front.*

2. ***Sales***: *If you have them — be as proactive as possible.*

3. ***Line of Credit:*** *Use as needed. It's tough running a business without revenues. I don't recommend it. This is your reserve.*

CASH OUTBOUND:

1. ***Payroll:*** *Lay off staff. Keep the bare necessities and get as close to zero as possible. This will not be easy but needed. Be honest and compassionate; staff understands. They are probably wondering why you didn't do it a week ago. In doing this, you will quickly see who your friends are. I found that I have many. I'm still paying my monthly healthcare expense for the foreseeable future, so my laid-off employees didn't have to apply and pay for COBRA (expensive). If you can do this it will bring comfort to your staff.*

2. ***Bank:*** *Communicate and over-communicate. Be honest in your communication, and keep them in the loop constantly. This assumes you have a good relationship; fortunately we did. I found them more than understanding in the current environment. Negotiate, suspend principal, low interest loans, suspend payments, etc.*

3. ***Accounts Payable:*** *Stop all payments, or at least to everyone you can. Communicate — don't run and hide. Call everyone back and have a conversation to let them know you will pay when you can. Again, they get it. We are all in this together. And, if not, you will quickly see who is with you and who is not when we get on the other side of this. Fortunately, I have not had one negative conversation.*

4. ***Leases/mortgage payments:*** *Negotiate so you do not have to pay for the foreseeable future (three months?). Ask for a few months free rent. Don't be shy, they are expecting it.*

THINGS TO TRY/DO:

1. ***Business Interruption Insurance****: File for it. You will be denied. I just was. I have my denial letter in hand if (when) FEMA gets involved. It will be the first thing they ask you for.*

2. ***Vendors****: Communicate with your vendors. If they call, call them back. Be honest — they understand. I've personally been in touch with all of our vendor partners. I sent them a group email as your president pledging our support. They ALL were supportive and get it. Their responses put fuel in my tank.*

3. ***Grants****: Be on the lookout and apply for all available.*

4. ***Loans (if needed)****: SBA Disaster Loan.*

5. ***Relationships****: Keep in touch with your network constantly. You never know where your opportunities will come from. This becomes a great resource of knowledge. Communicate and utilize your many community relationships. You will find that they are looking for guidance. This communication includes your staff. They are scared. We need to provide hope and leadership.*

6. ***Our website****: I want us to be aggressive here to take advantage of this opportunity.*

7. ***Communication: GREAT, CONSTANT, and POSITIVE! Communication is imperative!*** *I set up an employee email and text chain in order to communicate with them. Gather personal cell phone numbers and home e-mail addresses. Don't be surprised if this is a challenge. Work through it and get them. Your people will want to know what is going on. Give them weekly or daily updates if you can.*

WILD CARD

1. Government support: This is the great unknown. There are so many rumors as to what help and/or stimulus packages will be coming our way — TBD.

We are the leaders in our industry, now more than ever. Let's display that leadership to our staff, our communities, our industry, and ourselves. I have faith in all of you!

Smile, people! Stay focused – our people NEED our leadership! I hope and pray that this gives you a small peace of mind in these turbulent times. Now more than ever, is the time to lean on each other for support and survival. Thank you for allowing me this long-winded email. (Like you had a choice.) If I have any of this wrong, please forgive me with a little understanding and some compassion.

With Much Love,

Keith

P.S. – Looking back: *What possessed me to write and send this? Who was I to send this to people more successful and much smarter than me? What did I really know at the time? I was told later that this and additional updates helped a number of my industry family through this crisis. It provided hope. I had good intentions.*

This is also when I started to realize that COVID-19 was affecting different parts of the country differently.

??? – Have you ever put yourself out there, out of your comfort zone, for others?

MARCH 25TH: CALL FROM AN EMPLOYEE'S FATHER

My cell phone rang late tonight, displaying a number I did not know. The person on the other end identified himself as the father of one of our employees. One of the employees whose job we spared as we became a call center a few days ago. He called to personally thank me for taking care of his daughter and keeping her employed. Wow, that's a *first!* It meant the world to me. I'm a father with a daughter and it brought tears to my eyes. I cried! It was an emotional time. It put hi-test, or premium fuel, in my tank!

The father, who is in the flower business, went on to share the devastation to his own industry. His suppliers (friends) were "burning or destroying fields of flowers in Holland and South America, because they have nowhere to ship them." Their customers (the father and his friends in the flower industry) did not have any sales. We are both in the event industry, so I can empathize with his pain. My friends (industry members and vendors) are in similar situations. We agreed to have a beer (or two or three) when this is all over. I now have a new friend and I cannot wait to meet him!

*P.S. – **Looking back:** These were the kinds of things, positive things, that happened throughout the crisis that continued to put "fuel in my tank" to provide the energy and inspiration to keep doing what I was doing. To this day, I'm still blown away by the call.*

I did finally meet my newfound friend almost a year later to the day. He came to visit me in my office. We shared a celebratory hug to commemorate our survival.

??? – Have you ever received an uplifting call out of the blue? Have you taken time out of your busy day-to-day schedule to reach out and unexpectedly lift someone's spirits? Have you thrown a "pebble" into someone's pond to create a ripple in their life?

<u>MARCH 26TH</u>: A CHECK FOR NO REASON OTHER THAN TO HELP ME

As I sat at my desk running the challenging gauntlet of my day, I opened a handwritten letter addressed to me through snail mail. As I read it, I broke out into uncontrollable sobbing. The emotion became a tidal wave as I read:

"Use this for someone who needs it a hell of a lot more than I do. Keep safe and keep being a good guy. Don't worry, I will get some of it back at golf!"

Enclosed in the letter was a check made out to me for $1,000.

No one had ever sent me a thousand-dollar check — or any amount of money for that matter — just to help me, for no other reason. An inconceivable *first*!

The whole experience had been so surreal, both negative and more importantly positive and inspirational. The letter was from one of the guys in my golf group. I had called earlier in the month saying that I would not be participating in the upcoming spring golf trip. It would be the *first* time I would not be attending in twenty years. I couldn't go away with a clear conscience with what was going on. I was also "conserving cash" as I have been preaching to all my business friends. The golf group had become aware of the reason for my cancellation. This was well before the trip would officially be cancelled altogether due to the pandemic.

I did not cash the check. The sentiment and meaning behind that selfless gesture of extreme kindness was worth a million times more than the face value of the check.

I texted my friend the following: *I just received your letter. I'm in tears and speechless. One of THE nicest things someone has ever done for me! This is my "first" for today. Never in my life has anyone EVER sent me a check for no reason. WOW. You just provided "High Octane fuel in my tank." Inspired … I can't cash it. I Love you Brother.*

It seemed that I was humbled and inspired every day by some gift of kindness. It was overwhelming at times. What a life. I am truly blessed for the many friends I have!

P.S. – Looking back: *The letter and check hang on a plaque outside my office under Plexiglas with other memorabilia from the past year. The copy I had engraved on the plaque reads:*

*From a Friend to a Friend / An Act of Kindness in Challenging Times /
Inspired & Humbled / Forever Grateful / Coronavirus Crisis / 2020*

*I look at the plaque to inspire me to "pay it forward" everyday! That was a
"pebble" moment for me that created ripples. One such ripple happened the
following day as I ventured to help another company. I was gathering many
inspiring real-life stories to share. What a ride. Crazy things were happening.*

**??? – Has someone ever given you a gift you couldn't accept? A gift where the
thought was much more meaningful that the actual gift?**

MARCH 27TH: WORKED ON ANOTHER BUSINESS

The local, small business community is an ecosystem unto itself —
we're all interconnected. I received communication from one of the owners in my community sphere that Michele was close to shutting down her
catering business's operations. She was in tears. She was about to affect a
few hundred lives of people who had worked with her for years. She had
enough work in the queue to keep a skeleton crew of a dozen core workers
for a week. I was in the same shoes a week prior with my business. The
events she catered were evaporating. I knew the agony well. I was motivated and inspired by her pain. That and she had made me "husband of the
year" (for a day) four days ago. I had purchased my *first* pre-made dinners
from her business, which I brought home to my wife to win my award. I
owed her!

My friend is much smarter than me. She just needed someone to
ask some dumb uneducated questions to be a catalyst. I filled the role. I
assisted in a small way to get her unstuck with my ignorance. I hit send
on an email challenging her to find a way to keep her staff employed by
assisting front-line workers at local hospitals utilizing these pre-made family dinners. *First* time I ever proposed a microwaved business strategy for
another company to save a friend's business and the jobs of their employees. It released her brilliance. We brainstormed and worked throughout the

day to come up with a one-page plan. We would fund a program through the various local hospitals and/or outside sponsors. It would consist of a week's worth of pre-made food to feed the families of the front-line troops of nurses, doctors, and hospital staff.

We listed the benefits of this global approach for the local hospitals we would pitch. The program would lessen the stress of the workers' families by taking care of dinner for the week. No food shopping (not venturing out to the store = safety). No time spent cooking during this extremely stressful time. Great food as validated by my wife on March 24th. For the hospital, it would be free delivery in refrigerated trucks – free food for their overworked heroes (aka front line workers). The staff would be grateful, just as my wife was when I brought those meals home. This would be their "why" and our plan.

*P.S. – **Looking back:** It worked. The story got picked up by the local press; a corporate sponsor was touched and sent a check for $50,000. My friend was off and running. We had saved jobs and she had saved her company. Win-win-win. She supplied thousands upon thousands of meals to a number of area hospitals for their staff in a time of crisis. It worked out and she survived! Again, no one will ever know what my friend in the catering business really went through, and that includes me.*

Now the crazy thing was getting the workers back. At the time, many were scared to leave their homes. She had the opposite problem to deal with now. She had the work, and now needed her people back to help with this work. This would become a problem for numerous businesses as the pandemic continued. The catering business and their employees survived with this influx of new work created, and I was off to see who else needed help.

A retired naval officer friend of mine provided some sage advice from his military training concerning saving lives when someone is drowning. He cautioned that you can only save one person from drowning at a time. If you try to save multiple people at the same time, you will drown. Bring the person you are saving safely to shore before you jump back in the water to save

110

someone else. This became useful advice that I would follow in helping other businesses during that time.

<u>MARCH 28TH</u>: 115 MPH ON I-95N TO "WHY"

I woke up with the insatiable need to transfer my thoughts onto the easel in my office. The notepad by my bed would not do for some reason today. I know — crazy. I was in my car and off to work within minutes. It was before 6 a.m. on Saturday. I was on a vacant Interstate 95 North headed to work, fast. I consciously felt an adrenaline rush. I felt focused and wired and had to get to work. Admittedly, I am a fast driver, but that day it was different. I looked down at speedometer and saw that I was going 115 miles per hour! The speed limit was 55. I know this because earlier in the year I drove the same route to work at the actual speed limit. I honestly thought I was doing 70.

I vaulted up the steps to my office, grabbed my marker, and wrote:

My/Our "WHY" = Save Jobs (safely). Save a Job, Save a Life

That was what I woke up with – why was I working 24/7 – for free? Why was I so energized and inspired? Why was I so emotional? Why did I care so much it hurt? Why could I find clarity in the chaos? It hit me. In some strange Twilight Zone way, it made sense. *First* time I drove that fast outside of a motor speedway. *First* time I wrote my "WHY".

Since the start of this insanity, it seemed that despite whatever challenges were in front of me I was waking up inspired. I woke up and grabbed my notepad to write an idea or a possible solution for the challenge I went to bed with the night before. I should have been curled up in a ball depressed, but I wasn't! I can't figure it out. People kept asking me if I was okay out of concern. Some thought I might be on drugs, but I wasn't.

I moved the easel from the conference room into my office. It was where I worked the daily problems. The easel pads were big post-it notes; I had the walls of my office and conference room plastered with these. I was like some mad scientist. It was an out of body experience at times. *Why?*

P.S. – Looking back: *This "why" inspired a number of other firsts during the balance of the year. It made me do things I would have never thought of doing. It gave me the courage to take chances, to put myself out there, often for others.*

??? – What about you? What fuels you? Do you have a "WHY" that inspires you?

APRIL 1ST: DID NOT ACHIEVE A WRITTEN GOAL

I don't write many goals, so when I do, I commit. I may not achieve them all, but I have never given up on any of them, until today — a *first*. This was the culmination of almost a year's worth of work on this written goal. I was inspired by the happenings of the past few weeks to attempt to accomplish my goal of terminating a *Hatfield vs. McCoy* feud that had been going on for the past few years. This feud had broken many hearts, including mine. As an apparent elder statesman, I was brought into this war, at the request of one of the combatants, to hopefully broker peace. It was not of my own doing, but I was willing to take on the challenge for the betterment of both parties who I cared deeply about.

The feud started from — what I could tell — a miscommunication that created hurt feelings. Nothing more, nothing less. Nobody committed a crime. No one was killed. It came down to a he said, she said case of a gnarled mass of stubborn pride and fragile egos. One side had lent some financial support during some troubled times with resentment of fiscal responsibility. The other side felt judged and looked down upon. The money was inconsequential and more of principle. Not something to break up a friend or a family over in my opinion as the outside mediator. These feelings hardened over time with continued misunderstandings and fueled with harsh and often very cruel words from both parties. It kept escalating over time till I'm not sure they really knew why they hated each other.

Compassion, empathy, listening, and understanding had walked out the door and it shut behind them.

It was just prior to midnight on April 1st, and I was still at work. I was beat and needed to go home so I'd have the strength for tomorrow. That morning I'd woken up inspired to conclude this fight. Perhaps the conflict was marinating in my subconscious or maybe it dominated my previous night's dreams? This was to be my shock and awe campaign. I thought about all involved. That was the *first* time I ever emailed everyone involved on my quest to bring them together. It was my last stand, and I was going on the offensive. They were stuck in the past over petty inconsequential debated issues, which in the larger picture of life were meaningless — at least to this outsider's eyes. They could not or were unwilling to choose to forgive in order to move forward. They would all tell me, "*I'll forgive, BUT ...*" Then they would attempt to explain once again how justified they were in holding the grudge. Forgiveness does not come with a "but." I became a broken record. I had tried every heartfelt trick in my bag to find the light switch to illuminate forgiveness for them. They needed to emerge from the darkness of their rooms of hatred and contempt for each other. I had met with each one individually. I went out to dinners where I would sit and listen to all sides. I spent hours on the phone trying to communicate with empathy and love. They were both right and they were both wrong. Both sides had blood on their hands. I now have an appreciation for Middle East negotiations. I sent books with personalized handwritten messages of forgiveness inside of each front cover. The book *Life Is Magic* is by Jon Dorenbos, who I saw live. He gave the most inspirational speech on forgiveness ever. He forgave his father for killing his mother. Now that is forgiveness. He did it for himself to be a better parent to his new child. He had figured out that holding onto that lifelong grudge was eating him up from the inside. He had to forgive to survive so he could lead a better life, for himself and his family. It was a powerful message on forgiveness that I was attempting to transfuse. I composed and sent custom greeting cards with pictures of better times with the lyrics to the Don Henley song *The*

Heart of the Matter on the card. I featured the chorus which spoke to getting down to "the heart of the matter," which is "Forgiveness, forgiveness." I included the CD with the same song in the card. I had a mutual friend create a video to share his experience of suddenly losing his entire family. He shared that life is too short and how critical it is to appreciate your friends and family while they are still here. He wanted to communicate forgiveness and love before it was too late.

It was the *first* time I learned to sign language: *I love you* and *forgiveness*, which I used on them in an email sent. Each outreach was ultimately unsuccessful. I played good cop with my ears and heart open. I also played the role of bad cop to try and shake them out of their rut. One night in my role as a bad cop I scared my mom and wife. They both came running into our living room to make sure all was all right. They heard me scream at the top of my lungs through my cell phone to the deaf ears on the other end of the line. This is not my personality, but I was trying anything to shake their trance. I was trying to get through for naught. I negotiated a peace treaty, only to have it fall apart. I did a host of other things. I offered to pay the one side back any out-of-pocket money they felt they were owed. I even prayed they would find forgiveness in their hearts; nothing worked. I came to realize that you can only control yourself. In life, forgiveness is an individual choice. I came to the conclusion that no matter how many times they claimed to forgive, their actions said otherwise. I had failed and was giving up on achieving my written goal for the *first* time of my life. My last offensive stand had not worked. My heart frowned.

P.S. – Looking back: *I wish I had a different* first *for that day. It breaks my heart to include this. I have not had any contact with the "other" side since. From what I understand, the division and lack of forgiveness continues to this day, with sadness in their collective hearts. They unfortunately don't know what they are missing (my opinion of course). Life is too short. I gave it everything I had. I'm proud of the attempt I made. I could not get the parties to realize that the pain inside is devouring them and robbing them of joy. It is* *restricting their capacity to love. They are not stuck because they can't forgive; they are stuck because they won't forgive. I have come to learn that you can't help someone who doesn't want to help themselves. I'm open at ANY time to be there for them. I love them, both "sides." Although I failed, I exposed and exhausted my heart, soul, and mind with my efforts. Who knows, maybe they will read this, and they will pick up the phone or visit to personally forgive, without a "but?"*

I've intentionally left this passage vague to protect the feelings of those involved.

??? – Do you know of a similar situation? Do you have a fractured friend, family, or business relationship that causes you heartache? Do you hold a grudge and are unwilling to forgive? Does this lack of forgiveness hurt you or the other person more? Is it worth it?

CHAPTER SIX:
15 MINUTES OF FAME

This expression was inspired by Andy Warhol: "In the future, everyone will be world-famous for 15 minutes," which appeared in the program for a 1968 exhibition of his work at the Moderna Museet in Stockholm, Sweden. Never having experienced my 15 minutes of fame, the following were all *firsts* for me.

APRIL 2ND: POSTED SELFIES OF EMPLOYEES – MY HEROES

I posted the following copy with numerous selfies of my staff in their headsets for the *first* time today with this caption:

Thank you to our Spike's heroes, who are making calls for the State of New York through a partnership with our call center friend to book appointments for Coronavirus tests for its citizens. Working remotely and safely we miss them! They have made us an "essential" business that we are proud of. The work has been at times inspiring. We're helping to make a difference in providing hope. Other times it can be draining. The people we are calling are afraid and need much comfort. I am so proud of our people. No one will ever know how much!

P.S. – Looking back: *I will always be so proud of and forever grateful to these heroes. No one will ever know the fear and the anxiety in addition to the gratitude that these callers faced on a daily basis on the other end of the line. They were calling into the boroughs of New York City as the body bags were piling up outside of city hospitals. They hoped and prayed they were calling in time to help. Sometimes they were met with the devastating news that they had not. At times, the person they were calling to set up the COVID-19 test for had succumbed to this horrid disease.*

The callers needed to be constantly reminded that in helping just one person set an appointment, they had made a difference. These daily "hugs" of support were needed to keep them calling. At times, it was not easy — just ask the callers, my heroes.

??? – Who are the unsung everyday heroes in your life?

APRIL 6TH: ARTICLE IN *FORBES MAGAZINE*

A *Forbes Magazine* article that featured my company and me went live today. You will find this article in the firsts of March 20th and 21st. So as not to be redundant, I only mention the honor of our inclusion in *Forbes Magazine* here. It will also save space. It was my *first* time ever appearing in a *Forbes* article.

*P.S. – **Looking back:** This was the start to our 15 minutes of fame. People were looking for a positive story during the shit storm that was happening. Apparently, our pivot to a call center to save jobs became one. We weren't looking for the spotlight. It found us.*

??? – Have you ever experienced 15 minutes of fame?

APRIL 7TH: INTERVIEWED FOR A PODCAST

The second act of my 15 minutes of fame was my *first* podcast interview on the Lion's Den today. The 20-minute podcast was for a local business broadcast hosted by a digital media CEO who focused on special guests from across the country to offer the latest insights, advice, and expert opinions. The video and audio series were put together to motivate and inspire others during those trying times.

My purpose of the broadcast was to tell our story of the opportunity that impacted our company as we joined the front lines as a call center. My host wanted to dive into why relationships matter now more than ever. I was honored and emotional as I told the story of how relationships assisted me in keeping our employees employed. As the host, who also knows me, stated, "You wear your heart on your sleeve." Unfortunately, I do at times.

*P.S. – **Looking back:** Things like this just added to my day. Instead of going home at midnight, it would mean leaving at 1 a.m. If I thought I could help one person by providing hope, I said yes. I would manufacture the time, despite not having any.*

??? – What things make you so passionate that you will sacrifice your own free time to do them?

APRIL 8TH: PASSOVER SEDER (VIA ZOOM)

My friend Lisa had invited me to attend her family's Passover Seder in person months ago. She wanted to help me with my *firsts*. I reached out assuming this *first* would not happen due to COVID-19. My friend instantly offered to host me virtually with a Zoom invite. I connected and virtually "sat" at their family table, where I was introduced to her children. I was about to experience my *first* Passover Seder.

For my gentile friends, the Passover Seder is the ritual feast that marks the beginning of the Jewish holiday of Passover. I learned from reading up on it that it occurs on the eve of the fifteenth day of Nisan in the Hebrew calendar. A Hebrew day begins at sunset, which is when we started the Zoom call. Passover lasts for seven days in Israel and eight days outside of Israel. The Seder is a ritual performed by multiple generations of a family involving a retelling of the story of the liberation of the Israelites from slavery in ancient Egypt. I observed this as the different generations on the Zoom call took responsibility for different parts of the story. Traditionally, families and friends gather in the evening to read the text of the Haggadah. The Haggadah contains the narrative of the Israelites' Exodus from Egypt, special blessings and rituals, commentaries from the Talmud, and special Passover songs. Seder customs include telling and discussing the story, drinking four cups of wine, eating matzah, partaking of symbolic foods from the Passover Seder plate, and reclining in celebration of freedom.

On the Seder plate there are five or six different Passover foods, each symbolizing a unique element of the Exodus story. At various points in the Seder (which means 'order' in Hebrew), participants partake in these different foods to reenact the events of the Exodus tangibly and gastronomically. Following are the foods and the symbols they represented.

Matzah symbolizes the hardship of slavery and the Jewish people's hasty transition to freedom. When the Israelites learned that the pharaoh had agreed to let them leave Egypt, they did not have time to bake bread for their journey. A plate of at least three covered matzahs is set next to the Seder plate. The matzah is partaken from ritually three separate times during the Seder. *Karpas,* a green leafy vegetable, usually parsley, is used to symbolize the initial flourishing of the Israelites in Egypt. This is dipped into bitter salt water, which represents the tears shed by the Israelites. *Maror*, or bitter herbs, is another one of the Passover foods on the Seder plate and it symbolizes the bitterness of slavery. *Charoset is a* paste-like mixture of fruits, nuts and sweet wine or honey, charoset (also spelled haroset) is symbolic of the mortar used by the Israelite slaves when they laid bricks for Pharaoh's monuments. *Shank Bone*, or z'roa in Hebrew, represents the sacrifice offered by the Israelites on the eve of their exodus from Egypt. A roasted lamb bone is traditionally used to represent the z'roa, however any piece of roasted meat may be used. *Egg*, which is a universal symbol of springtime, new beginnings, and rebirth — all themes that are echoed in the story of the Exodus.

This larger piece of matzah is called the afikomen, a word that comes from the Greek word for "dessert." It is so called not because it is sweet, but because it is the last item of food eaten at the Passover Seder meal. Traditionally, after the afikomen is broken, it is hidden for the children to find. The afikomen represents this sacrifice, and it concludes the Passover meal with the eating of a small piece of the afikomen. When Jesus celebrated His last Passover with His disciples, He gave them matzah as the symbol of His body.

I was blessed and fortunate to be included in the family Seder. I had come prepared with my own matzo and wine, which I ate and drank from my desk at work. I am forever grateful for the education and hospitality.

*P.S. – **Looking back:** I still smile at the thought of the generosity of the invite and of sharing this cherished religious family experience.*

??? – Have you ever joined in on a religious ceremony that was not of your religion?

APRIL 9TH: PPP LOAN APPLICATION ACCEPTED

On April 3rd, we submitted our PPP application for the *first* time. PPP was the *Paycheck Protection Program* part of the CARES Act. The *Coronavirus Aid, Relief, and Economic Security* Act (CARES Act) was signed into law on March 27, 2020, in response to the economic fallout of the COVID-19 pandemic in the United States. I wanted to win a *"first place trophy"* for being the *first* to submit the application to our bank. I needed to create urgency. To me, this was a game of financial musical chairs for survival. I didn't want us to be left standing without a loan when the money ran out. This was life and death for businesses at the time. The effort to learn and gather the information to file the loan was a full-time job unto itself. It played a part in my working 24/7. The challenge became greater because we were trying to hit the moving target of the constantly changing rules and regulations concerning this loan. Everyone seemed to be making it up as we went along. We were playing a game where the rules changed constantly, and it was a tough game to win. This just added to the insanity.

That day was the *first* time that the business received approval for such a loan. This is a short passage representing hours of hard work and nerve-racking sleepless nights. How long could we tread water before drowning was always on my mind as I awaited this life preserver. Our business was not on firm footing by any means, but at least we were alive.

P.S. – *Looking back:* *This was one time I was satisfied with a "participation" trophy. We were not the* first, *but I was told we were one of the first groups of companies to get its applications in with the bank. Gathering and submitting the financial information needed was rushed, chaotic, nerve-racking, and mind-numbing. The PPP loan became one of the lifelines that kept us viable.*

??? – Have you ever felt the pressure of a business failure that would affect many lives?

APRIL 10TH: SENT "PEBBLE" POEM PRODUCT OF GRATITUDE

I awoke with a deep sense of gratitude for all that had happened despite the recent onslaught. I was grateful for the call at 3:27 p.m. on March 20th that provided the vehicle to keep my employees employed and us as a business essential and afloat. I had expressed my feelings verbally, but I felt that it wasn't good enough. I wanted Beth, my bank representative who provided the opportunity to become a call center, to have something from me that years from now she could look back at with a smile. I wanted to take this emotion of gratitude, capture it, and create a permanent memory. This person could have chosen to call anyone about the call center opportunity, but she called me. She also walked me through the PPP SBA loan process, so we became one of the first loans the bank approved a day earlier. Amazing! I thought her worthy of this honor of my *first*. She is one of my heroes in this Twilight Zone episode of the previous month. Her deeds impacted me and others. Her actions allowed me the freedom to "pay it forward" to others, to make more "ripples" by helping. She is the perfect first person to receive one of these MyExpressio items from me — truly emotions to memories. MyExpressio is a product idea and business plan generated from my time in the Goldman Sachs 10,000 Small Business program to provide a simple and lasting way for people to show pride, joy, love, sadness, happiness, admiration, appreciation, or affection by communicating their words positively and permanently to express their true passionate feelings quickly with heartfelt sentiments. I would like to make the world a better place.

I engraved the following "pebble" poem into my selected award item. It was a four inch by six-inch carved acrylics stand up piece with a red highlight reflected from the bottom. I wrote a personal handwritten note to specifically communicate how much she had done for me and others.

Just as ripples spread out
When a single pebble is dropped into water,
The actions of individuals
Can have far-reaching effects.
—Dalai Lama

. . .

You will never know the effects of your actions
And the impact they had on many lives!
I do, and I'm forever grateful!!
With Much Love, Keith
2020

P.S. – *Looking back:* I sent out a few other "pebble" mementos with hand-written cards to others who impacted me along this journey. Forever grateful!

??? – Have you taken the time during the chaos of daily life to let someone know how much you appreciate them? To tell someone how much you love them and share your emotions?

<u>APRIL 11TH</u>: STAFF FEATURED IN THE *WALL STREET JOURNAL*

As a continuation of our 15 minutes, Aaron Zitner, a writer from the *Wall Street Journal*, reached out to me for an interview. I placed the spotlight on my staff that was making the actual calls for the State of New York setting up COVID-19 test appointments. It was the *first* time I was able to have a few of my heroes (staff) not only get their names in this *Wall Street Journal* article, but their photos also. This lifted the spirits of the entire call center staff — a proud *first*.

We also had to make and place a large sign in front of our building that day that read: "*When you see cars here, we are assisting New York State with healthcare issues. We are essential!*"

We had to communicate this because the Philadelphia Department of Licenses and Inspections (L&I) paid us a visit. They had received a complaint from an anonymous person who observed a few cars in the parking lot of this supposed non-essential awards business. L&I had come to shut us down as a non-essential business. They were going to fine us for being open. I never had someone from the city knock on our door to shut us down as a non-essential business before — another *first*. Once we produced the legal paperwork from the State of New York documenting we were now an "essential business" as a call center, they could not have been nicer. To avoid any misunderstandings in the future, we placed the sign on our front lawn. Sign of the times…crazy times!

P.S. – *Looking back:* *The lamination of this article hangs on the wall outside my office. Still proud of my heroes!*

The visit from L&I was confirmation that we would have been shut down and out of business as a non-essential awards business.

??? – Have you ever had your picture in the Wall Street Journal?

APRIL 16TH: CRIED ON TV (6ABC)

I recorded my *first* TV interview for *Action News* (6ABC) a few days prior. The spot played today on TV. I received many calls, texts, and emails congratulating me. A couple people noted that, "It is okay that you got emotional." I then realized that they didn't cut out the part of me crying in telling our call center story, as I had requested. I hadn't seen the spot; I'd been working and didn't have time to watch. I was also embarrassed. The station sent me the link to the broadcast to view.

In addition, our PPP SBA forgivable loan money hit our bank account that day at 11 a.m. for the *first* time. Even though we saved jobs with our call center gig, it didn't save the company. We still had rent to pay, a mortgage, healthcare, and utility costs to cover. We still owed money to a number of our vendors who were waiting for a check. We had outstanding loans at the bank. I could go on; it's tough running a business without any sales or profits. I wouldn't recommend it. The *first* that day would provide some needed breathing room for the business finances.

*P.S. – **Looking back:** I never saw the broadcast. I never opened the link to view it. I did the interview, I lived it. I knew what I said and how I embarrassed myself. I didn't need to rub salt into my wounds. It was not the first time I would embarrass myself that year. I learned throughout that year to accept my many imperfections and move on. This day was one of those days. I accepted my imperfection of not being able to control my emotions while on-air. I moved on.*

??? – Have you ever embarrassed yourself in front of many people? How did you handle it?

APRIL 18TH: COMPANY FACEBOOK PAGE UNPUBLISHED

We were blindsided — the punches have kept coming. For the *first* time in my life, Facebook took down our business page. With our showrooms shut down, Facebook had been our access to the outside world to help create some sales. We were fortunate to acquire masks to distribute while everyone else was having trouble getting them. Our customers and the public were clamoring for facemasks in order to go out safely. The assumption was that when we announced that we had PPEs available to our followers, Facebook shut us down. Facebook was apparently clamping down on PPE suppliers abusing the platform for less than honorable intent. I got it, but our company was not one of the bad guys. We just happened to get caught in this widely thrown net. I felt like a boxer who took another good shot to the jaw. I wobbled but didn't go down.

In addition to this *first*, I experienced survivor's guilt today for the *first* time.

Survivor's guilt: (noun): *A condition of persistent mental and emotional stress experienced by someone who has survived an incident in which others died.*

My heart hurt hearing about all the PPP rejections my friends and business colleagues were experiencing. I was inundated with tears from many friends the past few days that got shut out of receiving their life saving loan. This gave me an understanding of the definition above. I had received PPP funding while many others had not. The music stopped and they didn't have a chair, but I did. I was thrilled and grateful — please don't get me wrong! The PPP loan and call center engagement obviously made the challenges comparatively less than those of many others. The following will give you some insight into my feelings. I'm not the only one with tears to shed. This was what I received the night before from my bank:

Very rough day here. Thirty percent of our customers that applied did not get their money before it ran out. Lots of tears for both customers and lenders. We don't know of anyone that came close to 70 percent funded ... We have a lot of non-customers that applied. We couldn't get to them.

We were one of the fortunate ones. From what I understand, our bank did a lot better than most. I'm not sure if that is any consolation. The bigger banks seemed to be the worst — tough days. You may wonder where all the emotions came from; here are a few pieces of evidence.

P.S. – _Looking back:_ _We remained in Facebook's "time-out" for the next few months — unbelievable! The exasperation led to the first time I appealed to Mark Zuckerberg personally on his Facebook page on April 25th, without a response. I finally received an audience with a Facebook representative on June 12th. I think an audience with the Pope would have been easier! The odyssey to get this done took many hours of wasted work during a time when I didn't have the time to waste. When people asked why I was working 24/7 that was just one of the many reasons._

The PPP loan was finally retooled and opened up again providing access to many of the unfortunate companies that were shut out that day. I lost my guilt when this occurred, and my heart smiled.

??? – Have you ever experienced survivor's guilt?

APRIL 20TH: WORKED THROUGH THE NIGHT WITH NO SLEEP

It was 11 p.m. on a Monday night and I was still at work; like I said, I'd been working 24/7. I received a call from my call center contact informing me they just were awarded the contract from the State of California unemployment office and needed to fill seats immediately. She defined "immediately" as 9 a.m. the following morning — a ten-hour deadline! She asked, "Can you get one hundred callers?"

I can't remember if I verbalized it or thought it: "I'm good, but I'm not that good." I was on it and went to work, through the night, without sleep, for the _first_ time. Hey, I needed a _first!_

I had primed that pump by communicating, "Please let me know if you need any more callers. I'll fill whatever number of jobs you need." My "why" was driving me. My mysterious confidence came from the many people I knew who were hurting and losing jobs. This included friends in my industry around the country. It was late and I was hungry, so I decided to go home to catch an after-midnight dinner. I had not eaten. After dinner, I put together as many FAQs as possible on the call center program highlights through the night. I took a quick shower and headed back to work to email the list to my friends around the country to see who needed a job.

P.S. – Looking back: *I still can't believe I did this. I was possessed in some way.*

??? – Have you ever been driven by passion and worked all night with no sleep?

<u>APRIL 21ST</u>: SAVED 123 JOBS — ANSWERING CALIFORNIA UNEMPLOYMENT CALLS

I have no entry from yesterday and today. I am writing this from memory. Despite my bad memory, that day is etched in my memory banks. After working all night, I emailed what I had composed. My guess is that somewhere around 7 a.m. I sent it locally and nationally to my network in the survival mode side of the pandemic. In order to secure the spots, I had to submit a spreadsheet with the names, email addresses, and telephone numbers of the proposed employees. At 9 a.m., I *had one* caller. I felt bleary-eyed and disheartened. I called to negotiate for more time and committed to delivering one hundred jobs if they could give me until noon, my new deadline. I started juggling all the incoming questions from my FAQs group email.

I set up a Zoom conference call with all interested parties from around the country. I fielded their many questions. I explained how this opportunity had saved the jobs of my employees and others. I was grateful to share this with my friends to assist them in saving jobs for their employees. I cautioned that it was not for the faint of heart. This gig was NOT easy!

I was frantically cutting and pasting the information coming at me from multiple interested parties into the spreadsheet that I had to forward to secure these jobs — from San Francisco and Oxnard, California, as well as Dallas, Texas. It was crazy. At noon, I had about 80 and I continued to gather and enter. I called and negotiated another hour. At 1:27 p.m., I submitted a list of 123 callers to take unemployment calls for the State of California! The state needed help *now*, inundated with calls from desperate people. The rest of the day was a fire drill coordinating all the details.

P.S. – Looking back: It seems like fiction to me, like I'm making this up.

APRIL 22ND: LOST 123 JOBS – ANSWERING CALIFORNIA UNEMPLOYMENT CALLS

I was on a Zoom call at 8 a.m. with one of my CEO groups when I received a text from my contact at the call center that read: *Call me immediately.* I had not had much sleep the previous few days so my emotions were raw. I placed myself on mute on the Zoom call and called her to see what was up. She asked if all the people I had submitted for call center jobs had official background checks within the past year. I knew that most, if not all, had not. Who does? She proceeded to tell me that the state had rejected ALL of our submitted callers because they all needed background checks to qualify. I wish I had been informed. The target kept moving. I quickly ended the Zoom call. I jumped up and shut my office door, turned off my computer, and had a good cry. I didn't want my fellow CEOs or my staff to see me in this state. For the *first* time in my life, I had just lost the 123 jobs I worked so hard the past day to secure.

P.S. – Looking back: We ended up figuring out a solution a few days later. We spent over $100 per employee for expedited background checks in order to get the employees hired to save jobs. I wouldn't take no for an answer and kept asking how we could get quick background checks to get them hired. I kept working the problem. It was worth the investment in many ways. What a roller coaster ride.

<u>APRIL 24TH</u>: FEATURED AS A HERO ON ZOOM MEETING

There I was, a picture of me on-screen of the concluding Zoom of my business relationship group meeting with the caption: *Our Hero*. I was stunned. Extreme embarrassment soon followed. There were screens of people in attendance. A hundred or so. I am one of the lesser, smaller members. Maybe this is a result of my fifteen minutes of fame. Maybe some of the things I was doing to help others in times of need were found out? I didn't know.

This Zoom in normal times would instead have been an elaborate breakfast meeting at a prestigious venue with a live presentation by a high-level speaker; usually about two hundred plus C-level executives attend. Because of the pandemic, the Friday morning ritual changed to a virtual environment. The featured speaker that morning was Captain Scott Kelly, who shared topical tips on isolation after having just spending a year in space. Scott Kelly is a former military fighter pilot and test pilot, an engineer, a retired astronaut, and a retired U.S. Navy captain. He is also the author of the book *Endurance, My Year in Space, A Lifetime of Discovery*. A veteran of four space flights, Kelly commanded the International Space Station (ISS) on three expeditions and was aboard the year-long mission on the ISS. In October 2015, he set the record for the total accumulated number of days spent in space, the single longest space mission by an American astronaut. Given the Coronavirus-imposed isolation at the time, the talk was timely. Scott Kelly took us inside a sphere utterly hostile to human life. He described navigating the extreme challenges of long-term spaceflight—the devastating effects on the body, the isolation from everyone he loves and the comforts of Earth, and the pressures of constant close cohabitation. All things we were experiencing from our COVID induced isolation.

Some of the valuable timely tips shared were to follow a schedule, but pace yourself. He counseled to go outside to experience nature and find a hobby if possible. He suggested keeping a journal and staying in contact with loved ones via Zoom, Facetime, or by picking up the phone for a conversation. Scientists have found that isolation is damaging not only to our mental health, but to our physical health as well, especially our immune systems. Technology makes it easier than ever to keep in touch, so it's worth making time to connect with someone every day. I saw several members joining me in nodding my head in agreement.

At the end of this opportune presentation my picture flashed on the screen to my surprise and self-consciousness. I'm claiming this as a *first*. Something like this had never happened to me — humbled.

*P.S. – **Looking back:** My motor had been running so fast for the past month that I hadn't taken the time to reflect on what I was doing. This gave me a much-needed respite, albeit brief, for some self-evaluation. I felt exhausted and stressed out from the overwhelming time commitment of the pandemic-induced frenzy. This recognition gave me the impetus to push even harder. I guess the business of recognition that I am in works.*

??? – Have you ever been embarrassed and fueled by surprise recognition?

APRIL 27TH: NATIONAL RETAIL FEDERATION'S (NRF) SMALL BUSINESS SPOTLIGHT

I received a call today that I was going to be the focus of the National Retail Federation's (NRF) Small Business Spotlight — yes, for the *first* time. I was one of 20 retailers selected nationally. The Small Business Spotlight stories were sponsored and presented by QVC and the Home Shopping Network. The NRF in Washington, D.C. wanted to promote small businesses to help them get back on their feet. This resulted from my *Forbes Magazine* story on our call center pivot in addition to my work with other local companies in my attempt to save jobs. NRF contacted various Chamber of Commerce organizations around the country asking for nominees from their membership, and the Philadelphia Chamber nominated me. The caterer I worked with to re-employ her laid-off employees also happened to be the Chamber's personal caterer. Who knew? Word had traveled — I guess my 15 minutes was not over yet.

P.S. – *Looking back:* *What an honor, as well as the beginning of other incredible* firsts.

??? – Have you gone out of your way to nominate someone for recognition?

APRIL 28TH: COLD-CALLED FOR AN INTERVIEW BY KYW-RADIO

Someone from KYW News Radio knocked on our locked front door, although we were still closed as a non-essential awards business. He was there unannounced and wanted to interview me. KYW is the top-rated radio program in Philly. I honestly thought it was a prank by my staff; sometimes they did things like this to me. I figured they might be practicing one of our core values: FUN! To convince myself that they were not joking, I made my way downstairs to meet this intruder.

Paul Kurtz is a Philadelphia native who has been working as a reporter and anchor for KYW News Radio since 1984. He attended the local Roxborough High School and Temple University, where he majored in journalism. He stood in the showroom with his elbow (COVID-style) extended in greeting. He has won numerous awards including the prestigious Edward R. Murrow National Award for reporting. He introduced himself and explained that he had heard of our recent press and wanted to see the operation for himself. I gave him a tour. He stopped and briefly spoke with one of our callers making the calls into New York city to set up COVID test appointments. We talked and he interviewed me for the next hour or so. The questions were wide ranging, from the turning of the business into a call center to the state of our current non-existent usual awards business. We were discussing and trying to solve the problems that currently existed in the world. The one thing that stuck with me was an assignment he reported on the week before. He had covered one of the food lines that had popped up as the result of the growing unemployment

A LEAP YEAR OF FIRSTS

rate. The line was long and populated by unfamiliar types of people. Paul looked at me emotionally and said, "There were people in that line just like you and me — people who held jobs, good jobs, throughout their lives and had never been unemployed before. They were in line because they could no longer afford to feed their families."

*P.S. – **Looking back:** That interview resulted in a feature on Antoinette Lee's show on KYW News Radio on May 8th. My company and I were the focus of their "Philly Rising" segment where they featured local businesses helping their communities. The website lead for the story on stated: "Philly Rising: By word of mouth, Northeast Philly store owner finds jobs for his non-essential employees." The segment was only a minute and a half long, but it was a first for me and my company!*

Paul Kurtz's food line story, the increasing unemployment, and a number of other experiences that year would lead me to one of my firsts on December 5th. It all had a cumulative effect and an impact on me. It emboldened me in my efforts to save jobs. It made me empathetic and curious of the effects of not having one. It drove me.

??? – Have you ever had to stand in a food line to feed your family? Have you been close to doing so?

APRIL 30TH: CALLED A BOOK PUBLISHER

When I started my first daily journal on January 2nd, I halfheartedly thought I'd turn it into a book for me and my family. Because of the things that were happening and the experiences I was living, I started to think bigger and picked up the phone to call a real book publisher for the *first* time. I called my friend at Book Baby for a referral with his company. Book Baby is a local self-publishing house that is a member of my manufacturing CEO group — it's all about relationships! I took a tour of their facility a couple of years ago and was somewhat familiar with the process. Despite how busy I was, I wanted this to be my *first* for today.

P.S. – Looking back: I guess this is when it hit me. *This book became real on that day.*

??? – Have you ever had an idea for a book? Have you ever wanted to write one? Have you taken the first step and put your ideas on paper? Will you make today the first day to do this?

. . .

CHAPTER SEVEN:
"IN THE MIDST OF CHAOS, THERE IS ALSO OPPORTUNITY" — SUN TZU

I received the following email in April, while in the middle of our fight for survival, from one of my friends in the small business community. I thought it appropriate to share:

> Keith — I think you need to have this Sun Tzu quote: "In the midst of chaos, there is also opportunity," engraved and mounted on your office wall. While the world around us is caving in, you continue to weed through the chaos and find opportunity for yourself and all of us. Thanks for keeping all of your brothers and sisters in the game.

I wasn't conscious of it at the time, but as the year of chaos played out, opportunities did present themselves as revealed by some of the following *firsts*. I also shared this quote with others as I attempted to pay it forward in my aim to provide hope.

MAY 1ST: WEAR TUTU AT BOARD OF DIRECTORS ZOOM MEETING

As I arose from behind my desk, my ravishing pink tutu came into full view. The executive director of my national industry group Award Associates of America was concluding our *first* Zoom board of directors' call. I am the current president of the organization. We had convened to cover the many stressful issues of the times. I purposely planned my *first* time wearing a pink tutu to a business meeting in an effort to cut the tension.

Actor John Krasinski's *Some Good News* quarantine YouTube series inspired this *first*. It was offbeat and accomplished its intended goal of cutting stress while placing a smile on my face. Mr. Krasinski signed off straight-faced and got up to walk away. He was wearing a colorful tutu. A light bulb moment for a *first*! I immediately texted my wife and asked her to order me a pink tutu. I thought it was a perfectly normal request. She didn't but she did it anyway — she's the best!

I achieved my *first* and broke the ice of a tense call. I brought some smiles to faces with a few chuckles from my friends. What else can they expect from their president in a time of crisis?

??? – Have you ever tried to break the ice by making a fool of yourself?

MAY 4TH: NO MACHINES RUNNING MID-DAY, MID-BUSY SEASON

"Eerie" [**eer**-ie] *adjective*, meaning: strange and frightening. That word struck me as I walked through my production department mid-day, mid-May, mid-busy season and NO ONE was there. May is usually the busiest month in the year for an awards manufacturing company. My industry refers to it as "the busy season." Normally, any other year at this time dozens of people would be running around with their hair on fire trying to get time-sensitive award orders out the door. There were no orders, there were no employees. Most were home making calls for the call center. It was eerie, and very strange and frightening. I had been doing this for over 40 years and could honestly say that was the *first* time that had ever happened — a much unwanted first. Another Twilight Zone moment. As I walked through the building, I felt like someone had dropped me into the middle of an episode. I looked around to see if I could find any hidden cameras —. unfortunately there were none. That was reality.

P.S. – Looking back: A year later, it is somewhat better but not what it used to be. My guess is it will not be for some time. We are all hoping and praying for next year to be back to a normal busy season.

??? – What was your other worldly "Twilight Zone" experience during that uncertain time?

<u>MAY 5TH</u>: MARGARITAS AT LUNCH AT WORK

Crazy times calls for crazy measures. Day drinking in the middle of the work week in our supposed busy season seemed like a perfect plan. For Cinco de Mayo, we set up a margarita bar in the warehouse for what was left of our staff working in the building. We had a blender and served different flavors, frozen and non-frozen, with or without salt, poured into red Solo cups. We even had a friend show up dressed as a taco. It doesn't get any better than that in tough times!

Seriously, we were relying on one of our core values during a very stressful time: *FUN*! It took the edge off and it was a good day. It was also a good thing we didn't have any awards to build that afternoon.

*P.S. – **Looking back:** This was unthinkable.*

??? – Have you ever thrown a mid-day Cinco de Mayo margarita fest at work before?

MAY 11TH: *TWILIGHT ZONE* EDITION OF THE SPIKE'S COMPANY NEWSLETTER

I had been writing a weekly newsletter for employees to keep them informed and on the same page for years. There is no special name for it, just the Spike's Newsletter. During the crisis, I stopped due to the lack of time to produce it. That and I seemed to be directly communicating with most of them daily. This day was the *first* time I restarted the newsletter after hitting pause to become a call center. It was the *first* of the *Twilight Zone Editions* of the Spike's Newsletter. I won't bore you with the entire five-page newsletter; I'll just share the beginning of it as follows. (*Unedited newsletter entry*):

> ... *I had no idea the last time I stood in front of you all on Monday, March 16th, which I documented in the attached news-letter, that almost two months later I would be writing this next newsletter. Who knew the world would hit the "pause" button and would change so fast, so suddenly? Some of you are not old enough to know* The Twilight Zone *reference; ask your parents. It was a TV series about the bizarre and unusual from the early sixties. Every day since we met seems to be a new episode in this Twilight Zone, often with unbelievable plot twists throughout each episode, each day, each hour. We now have new terms like ... Social Distancing ... Pandemic ... Self-Quarantine ... and COVID-19 – crazy.*

> *Reading the "Coronavirus recap" in this last newsletter, I don't think I would change much. I still believe what I wrote then. Obviously, A LOT has happened the last few months that we have been a part of. In preparation for hopefully being able to start to bring some of you back, when we are allowed to, I would like to recap what's been happening and what we hope will be happening. Some things you are aware of, some you are not. Following in no particular order are a few things that have*

happened and that are happening. As you will see, we have not been sitting back having a pity party for ourselves on a lost traditional busy season. There will be casualties in this war. We are NOT going to allow us to be a casualty of this. We will NOT go out of business – NOT going to happen – PROMISE! We may be bloodied or bruised in this, but we will NOT be knocked out! Figured you may have some free time for some reading, so here you go. We are turning this "pause" and challenge into an opportunity …

P.S. – *Looking back:* *I was bold in my predictions. I'm not certain if I was so sure deep down. I may have been trying to convince myself. I was trying to fabricate and provide hope — I think.*

I ended the Twilight Zone-*themed editions of our newsletter at the end of the year. I resumed our ordinary newsletter in January 2021. I wanted to start to transition the company back to a semblance of normal.*

??? – What were some of your Twilight Zone experiences in this very unique year?

MAY 13TH: STARTED A HAND SANITIZER BUSINESS

Today, we produced our *first* sample of the new product we created — personalized hand sanitizer.

We printed a custom label and hand-filled the two-and-four-ounce spray bottles. Our automated filling machine that we ordered was due any day. This new essential product would replace, for the foreseeable future, our standard now non-essential trophy figure on a marble base for our new "abby-normal" busy season. Hopefully you get the Young Frankenstein reference. If not, please search YouTube for *Young Frankenstein abby-normal* and enjoy. In plain language it was not a "normal" busy season by any stretch of the imagination.

The marble base became the plastic spray bottle. The trophy figure became the screwed-on spray top. The turning of the trophy wrench became the filling of the bottle. Finally, the engraved trophy plate became the printing and application of the personalized bottle label. The time invested, the cost, and retail of the respective trophy and hand sanitizer were virtually the same, "abby-normally."

The key to this product became the sourcing and importing of the two-and-four-ounce spray bottles. There was a shortage, and they didn't exist. We magically made them appear through hard work, relationships, knowledge, and some luck. We sourced the liquid domestically — and listing the ingredients correctly took much research. All this took time, and a lot of it.

*P.S. – **Looking back:** This capped a week of multiple firsts including supplying various Personal Protective Equipment (PPE) items. May 6th was the first time we received an order for 4,992 canisters of disinfectant wipes. The next day an order for hand-held thermometers — these were the expensive electronic legit ones sold in pharmacies. Never in my wildest dreams did I think that our trophy company would be selling these items.*

That was in the Wild West days of PPE supply when no one could get disinfectant wipes, hand-held thermometers, and hand sanitizer. Everyone needed and wanted these products. People from the many business relationships that we had built over time were reaching out to us to solve these supply issues. That was only the beginning. Bigger things followed later in the year. We found a way to say "YES," one of our company's core values.

??? – Have you ever gone totally out of your comfort zone to take a chance?

MAY 14TH: SIGNED TWO NDAS IN A DAY

As people tried to pivot during the COVID-19 crisis, it seemed like everyone was attempting to get creative on how to adjust. *Pivot* became the overused word of the day. A new need for improved personal safety in several different fields, caused by the pandemic, created an influx of new product ideas. The quote from Sun Tzu, the Chinese strategist, "In the midst of chaos, there is also opportunity," was literally playing out in front of my surprised eyes. A few of these ideas and opportunities reached me by way of two Non-Disclosure Agreements (NDAs), which I signed to assist two friends in different industries this day. Companies and startups use these NDA legal documents to ensure that their good ideas won't be stolen by people they are negotiating with. One was in the golf industry while the other was in the dental industry.

NDA #1

The one friend in the golf industry, who owned and ran a half dozen local golf courses, was restricted to one person per golf cart due to the safety protocols put in place. This friend, who was kind enough to write the foreword to my book, happened to be Ron "Jaws" Jaworski. This restriction didn't seem like a big deal, unless you are in the golf industry. The courses didn't have enough golf carts to host golf outings and would need double the number of carts, which would not be cheap to purchase. We wanted to come up with a safe solution to put two people back in the golf carts, which would solve the problem.

Another small-business colleague, Dana, who I thought may be able to assist me came to mind. Dana's company had been recently sold, shut down locally and had moved leaving their local workers stranded and out of work. The company had produced outdoor retractable sunshades for the boating industry. They had the knowledge, sourcing, and staff needed to produce a removable and flexible safe divider to golf carts. This would allow two golfers per cart. My "why" of saving jobs turned on a light bulb. I could possibly have saved a few of the lost jobs of Dana's relocated company.

I reached out to both parties to try to connect the dots. There was nothing in it for me other that creating a few jobs. Dana and her husband, the manufacturer, Ron the golf course owner, and I met to discuss and design the new product. The manufacturer put together the NDA. I signed the NDA along with the golf course owner, who happened to be kind enough to write the foreword for this book. We were off — developing a prototype, logo, pricing, and whatever we needed to launch the product *fast..* We toyed with the names: Flexi-Guards, Jaws of Life, Safety Jaws, Safety Shade, Jaws Shade, Sneeze Shade, and Sure Safety Guard. We settled on PARtition, with the tagline "Protecting the Player, Preserving the Game." We would offer to print sponsors' names on the PARtition to help the golf course fund the expense. We had a concept that worked and designed the PARtition in a way that was easy to install and remove and wouldn't compromise the integrity of the carts. Our goal was to have a product to demonstrate before the end of the month.

NDA #2

The second NDA was for Rob Kaz, a friend who is an orthodontist, as well as an excellent tinkerer. His job entailed putting braces on his patients, which meant exposure to the droplets that carry the COVID-19 virus. He had an idea to solve his personal challenge of working safely on his patients. He reached out to me for manufacturing assistance. He had built a prototype from various parts in his office, his home, and ordered items from Amazon. He had done his own research and development. Before involving me in the production, I had to sign my second NDA of the day — amazing. What did I know? I signed the NDA. After work, I visited his office to see what we were dealing with in order to help.

The Dental Aerosol Safety Hood (D.A.S.H.) was a customized acrylic hood with a strategically placed vacuum system. This contraption allowed the orthodontist or dentist to work safely. The idea was to place the acrylic hood over the patient, while sucking the air particles produced by the patient out of the protective hood. The open bottom allowed the doctor to work on their patient freely and safely. My friend hooked up a fog machine to demonstrate the movement of the air particles under the hood — ingenious.

*P.S. – **Looking back:** As soon as we had the PARtition product developed and ready to produce, the one person per golf cart restrictions were dropped. The need for this new product dissipated. Poof, it was gone in a second. We always knew it was speculative. It was a fun learning experience nonetheless. I'd do it again.*

The other product, D.A.S.H., is still around. I facilitated the introduction of the orthodontist to a manufacturing friend to make it happen. Although not the biggest seller due to limited exposure and marketing, it was and still is the best product in the field for the purpose of safety.

I also signed an NDA for a clinical trial for a Point of Diagnosis (P.O.D.) project in April, a protocol that was developed to return people back to work safely. I was to be the subcontractor on the job. My role was to supply the Personal Protection Equipment (PPE) needed for the project. I hosted the trial in our facility. I also participated with a scientist and a medial staffing partner in the test. We performed time studies on processing employees quickly, safely, and efficiently. We had custom software with verifying questions for the employees, hand-held thermometers, social distancing floor graphics, all the PPE needed to keep everyone safe along with trained medical staff to implement this process to clear employees to enter the workplace safely. Isn't that what a trophy company is supposed to do, really? The Point of Diagnosis (P.O.D.) project fizzled. The federal money planned for this launch fell through. The customer ended up processing their employees in-house. Out of the NDAs I signed one became an actual product. D.A.S.H. was that product. No one got rich, but it did solve a problem. Sometimes the opportunities don't work out.

There are some very talented people in the world who when chaos hit seized the opportunity. My friends who created the PARtition and D.A.S.H. are a couple of them. I became an inventor for a short period — connecting the dots for others to help save jobs.

??? – Have you had an idea for an invention before? Have you attempted to bring it to life?

MAY 30TH: CANCELED NILE RIVER CRUISE AND JERUSALEM TRIP

As mentioned previously I had organized another "trip of a lifetime" for a group of friends and my wife and I over a year ago. We prepaid for the trip down the Nile and to Jerusalem. We had to decide six months before to pull out to qualify for a full refund, and that was the last day to make the decision. The following was the email I sadly sent to our travel agent that day:

> It is with deep regret and sadness that I am writing you to cancel our upcoming Nile River cruise and side trip to Jerusalem … I would like a full monetary refund due to the imposed decision date. I really wanted to go, but this far out there is too much uncertainty in the world to gamble the amount of money spent...

> Respectfully, Keith

P.S. – *Looking back:* *This ended up being the correct decision. We could have never traveled overseas in 2020.*

??? – What exciting plans did you have to cancel due to the Covid lockdown?

MAY 31ST: CLOSED SHOWROOM DUE TO CIVIL UNREST IN CENTER CITY, PHILADELPHIA

The lead story in the *Philadelphia Business Journal* read "Breaking News: Philadelphia Restricts Vehicle Access into Center City in Effort to Prevent More Damage." Due to the restrictions, we were unable to access our Center City showroom located one block from City Hall. This news caused us to close the location until further notice for the *first* time due to civil unrest. The showroom had been there for over 30 years. What had started as peaceful protests ignited into vandalism and destruction a few blocks removed from our showroom on JFK Boulevard in One Penn Center – the historic Suburban Station Building. Along the streets of Chestnut and Walnut in Center City Philly stores were broken into, looted, and set fire to. Less than a block down the street from our showroom on JFK Boulevard police cars were set ablaze in front of a statue of Frank Rizzo, a former mayor, and police commissioner. The statue was spray painted, and unsuccessful attempts were made to tear it down. The Pennsylvania National Guard was called in to retore order. The civil unrest was in response to the unwarranted killing of George Floyd; sad times.

P.S. – **Looking back:** *I understand, support, and empathize with the protesters. I don't get and condemn the looting and lawlessness. Incredibly, our Center City location remained closed into 2021. Never in my wildest dreams would I have thought we'd close our premiere, high-rent, Class A real estate Center City showroom for a year. As of mid-year 2021, Center City is still a ghost town for the most part until the vaccine is fully distributed and people can congregate again.*

JUNE 1ST: CANCELED AWARD ASSOCIATES OF AMERICA'S SUMMER MEETING

Every year, my national industry group hosts a summer meeting. A few hundred of us flock to the selected host city for education, sharing of ideas, a trade show, and relationship building. This year was my second time hosting this summer meeting. I have been a member of the Award Associates group for over twenty years. Today I sent the following email (*unedited journal entry*) to the group as the host for my *first*.

POSTPONED till 2021

Sad, strange day in the City of Brotherly Love. On a day that the city of Philadelphia was on lockdown due to civil unrest, we held a board meeting to discuss the results of the survey we took on the upcoming summer meeting in Philly this September. I came prepared with a virtual option for those not feeling safe or not being able to afford to come. I honestly wanted to host it this year to show resilience and perseverance in not letting the current challenges derail us. But the vote wasn't close. It was roughly 20 percent "yes, we'll come" and 80 percent "no, let's postpone". This was from both the members and the vendors. I get it; there is just too much uncertainty to move forward this year. So the board voted unanimously to postpone Philly till next year. It is the right thing to do.

The good news (????) is that I have experience postponing and re-planning a summer meeting. I have only hosted one other summer meeting. As most of you know, the last one was to start September 11th. YES, that September 11th! Our executive director and I canceled that meeting that morning, right after the second plane hit the towers. We had members in the air that morning on their way to Philly. We hosted the following year. So, this is unfortunately not uncharted waters for this meeting. I'll be calling the hotel tomorrow to let them know. I had already put them on notice. I'll start to work on a new date for 2021 and will let you all know once we get it all figured out.

I apologize; this has got to be my fault in some way. Can't be this lucky, or is it unlucky, with summer meetings. I can tell you one date next year's summer meeting will NOT be ... September 11th! And, as I have mentioned before, after 2021, you will NEVER be invited back — you're welcome. I think I have worn out my welcome.

With much love and some sadness, Keith

The other unwanted *first* that day was a sign of the times. It was the *first* time an employee, who was working from home, called out sick to take her kids to New Jersey to her mother's house because of the riots in her

Philadelphia neighborhood. She didn't feel safe at her home; a seemingly fictional first — sorrowful.

P.S. - *Looking back: That was absolutely the correct decision to cancel the meeting. A second wave of the virus started to hit in the third quarter that shut down a lot of things for the second time. As I sit here writing this a year later, we rescheduled the date to September 18, 2021. The vaccines are starting to be effective, and we are currently a go-to host this year.*

P.S. – What events did you have to cancel or postpone due to the pandemic? A wedding?

<u>JUNE 2ND:</u> QVC AND HSN LIVE

A month prior, a producer from QVC contacted me; he'd been assigned our story for this spotlight. He had collected a video interview, pictures for background, and other "compelling assets" that he put together for the prerecorded part of this feature. The piece he created would run through the end of the year on both QVC and HSN. The goal was to communicate how people could help us.

My first live QVC appearance took place with Terri Conn. Ms. Conn called me 15 minutes prior to the appearance for a pre-interview. She had done her homework, visited the company website, and viewed the prerecorded spot I had done for her producer a few weeks back. The producer of my spot put together an introduction piece that was to proceed my live appearance. He made something out of nothing. Terri asked me what I wanted to discuss. She'd heard a lot about what I was doing and asked me to tell her more. I wanted to mention my bank and my call center partner who had allowed me to keep my people employed. I wanted to mention my national industry partners who were also hurting. I was looking to drive traffic to their locations nationally, if possible. She allowed me to cover all three of my objectives. I told Terri that this was emotional for me. As I was saying this, she started to get emotional herself. I pleaded, "Thanks, that doesn't help me. I'm already afraid of getting emotional over all this on air and embarrassing myself." She was gracious, kind, and assured me it was okay and to be myself. I hung up and waited, somewhat nervously.

Terri and I went on, right on time, at noon. The prerecorded segment took up the first few minutes, and then I was *live*. I discussed the points I wanted to cover and got through it well. Although I can't remember what I said; it was a blur. As Terri thanked me to sign off, I stopped her. There was one more thing, I raised a plaque up to the camera and started to read:

In appreciation to

QVC & HSN for your exceptional and caring support of the small business community nationally during these very challenging times,

THANK YOU for your sponsorship and coverage of the

National Retail Federation's

Small Business Spotlight

Forever Grateful

Spike's

June 2, 2020

I could feel the emotion rise in my voice as I got to "thank you," but managed to hold it together — not Terri though. Touched by my sincere presentation of recognition and gratitude, she could barely make it to the end as she started to cry — the power of recognition. This is what and why we do what we do as an awards company. I was deeply touched.

I did three other live segments with three other hosts, and each one got easier. Here are the other three hosts:

Bobby Ray Carter (HSN at 1:55 p.m.)

Shawn Killinger (QVC at 9 p.m.)

Adam Freeman (HSN at 10:55 p.m.).

I almost forgot to mention that during halftime of the four appearances, my wife showed up with dinner. It was Mexican food *with* margaritas! I finished both and went back to work before the 9 p.m. appearance. I had to grab a coffee to stay awake.

I finished the last live appearance a little after 11 p.m. By the time I wrapped up at my desk at work and traveled home, it was well after midnight. I was toast! What a *first*!

P.S. – Looking back: *We received a few orders for masks and a few smaller orders for hand sanitizer. There was some increased traffic on our website as well as phone calls. Not the tidal wave that would crash our website as feared. We had prepared for the onslaught. Oh well, something was better than nothing. It was a fitting end to my 15 minutes of fame, and a surreal experience.*

The spotlight faded fast. The next night, I ended up sleeping in my office at work for the very first *time. The challenges seemed to never end.*

JUNE 3RD: SLEPT OVERNIGHT AT WORK

(Unedited journal entry)

... Early this afternoon, the lights started to flicker when a storm started coming through. THEN we lost ALL electricity ... a BLACKOUT! We had nuttin'. I'm laughing my ass off right now. I miscalculated; I thought the locusts were next; I didn't count on a blackout. Do I contact Noah for an ark? NO ONE will EVER buy my book as a nonfiction. I'm going to market it as fiction.

I just received this headline from the *Philadelphia Business Journal* minutes ago after hitting send to my journal entry: "National Guard to Be Deployed to Neighborhoods; Mayor Kenney Unclear on City Entering "Yellow Phase" of Reopening." We were supposed to be able to open next week. That was now in jeopardy due to the civil unrest.

My industry group's executive director had threatened to quit because of the group's new website and issues with its developer. There was a brewing mutiny by our California callers due to the onerous oversight from the state. All our calls being made were monitored. The times on the calls, along with every break was tracked. We had quotas for calls per hour that would not let our callers deal with the many complexities and heart wrenching issues being presented by the unemployed callers desperately looking for their benefits. I was told that my home, which also lost power in the storm, would not have power for days. My *first* would be sleeping at work that night. I had an overnight kit in the bathroom as well as a shower for situations like this. I kept an extra set of golf clothes in the trunk of my car, in case a golf opportunity occurred. Being able to play golf at that time seemed like another lifetime. There was a couch just outside my office. There were a few sample logoed blankets in the showroom. I dug up a throw pillow that was hanging around and I was set.

I was feeling defeated. I texted my lifelong friend: *"First time since this all started that I felt beat up. Yesterday's temporary fame from the QVC appearance was just that – temporary. A negative thought – How much can one man take – crept in that day. I fought it and I was going to 'work the problem' and wake up inspired to tackle tomorrow's challenges."*

My friend called and asked me a few questions and listened. It helped to clarify my thoughts and I stabilized enough to be able to go to bed in a better frame of mind, so I woke up with solutions and felt inspired again. I felt grateful to have friends that I could reach out to who didn't tell me what I wanted to hear, but what I needed to hear. I sent my friend the following for his help that night: "*Thx for the part you played in 'packing my parachute.' Back to grinding. I found the following to be very insightful. I wanted to let you know that I really appreciate the time we spent together tonight."*

I shared the following story with my friend:

"This is a wonderful way to look at life! A wonderful story. Yes, we all need our parachutes in life. Charles Plumb was a U.S. Navy jet pilot in Vietnam. After 75 combat missions, his plane was destroyed by a surface-to-air missile. Plumb ejected and parachuted into enemy hands. He was captured and spent six years in a communist Vietnamese prison. He survived the ordeal and now lectures on lessons learned from that experience!

One day, when Plumb and his wife were sitting in a restaurant, a man at another table came up and said, 'You're Plumb! You flew jet fighters in Vietnam from the aircraft carrier Kitty Hawk. You were shot down!'

'How in the world did you know that?' asked Plumb.

'I packed your parachute,' the man replied.

Plumb gasped in surprise and gratitude. The man pumped his hand and said, 'I guess it worked!'

Plumb assured him, 'It sure did. If your chute hadn't worked, I wouldn't be here today.'

Plumb couldn't sleep that night, thinking about that man. Plumb says, 'I kept wondering what he had looked like in a Navy uniform: a white hat, a bib in the back, and bell-bottom trousers. I wondered how many times I might have seen him and not even said, 'Good morning, how are you?' or anything because, you see, I was a fighter pilot and he was just a sailor.'

Plumb thought of the many hours the sailor had spent at a long wooden table in the bowels of the ship, carefully weaving the shrouds and folding the silks of each chute, holding in his hands each time the fate of someone he didn't know.

Now, Plumb asks his audience, 'Who's packing your parachute?' Everyone has someone who provides what they need to make it through the day. He also points out that he needed many kinds of parachutes when his plane was shot down over enemy territory — he needed his physical parachute, his mental parachute, his emotional parachute, and his spiritual parachute. He called on all these supports before reaching safety.

Sometimes, in the daily challenges that life gives us, we miss what is important. We may fail to say hello, please, or thank you, congratulate someone on something wonderful that has happened to them, give a compliment, or just do something nice for no reason.

As you go through this week, this month, this year, recognize people who pack your parachutes. I am sending you this as my way of thanking you for your part in packing my parachute. And I hope you will send it on to those who have helped pack yours!

Sometimes, we wonder why friends keep forwarding jokes to us without writing a word. Maybe this could explain it! When you are very busy, but still want to keep in touch, guess what you do — you forward jokes. This lets you know that you are still remembered, you are still important, you are still loved, you are still cared for, [so] guess what you get? A forwarded joke.

So, my friend, next time when you get a joke, don't think that you've been sent just another forwarded joke, but that you've been thought of today and your friend on the other end of your computer wanted to send you a smile, just helping you pack your parachute.

P.S. – Looking back: *I had a number of concerned friends reach out to me about the stress I was going through and the hours I was putting in. I had assured them I was good and felt inspired. That day was the first crack in the armor. I felt it. The hint of depression showed its ugly head. Thank God I had a friend that day, at that moment, who packed my parachute. A friend who listened and asked me some great questions. I was in a freefall and needed the parachute he provided in order to land safely. A "pebble" moment for me.*

??? – Do you pack parachutes for others in need of one? Do you find yourself throwing pity parties when life kicks you? Are you able to limit them to move forward with the help of an ear and a few good questions from a friend, or with help from someone you don't even know who is packing parachutes?

<u>JUNE 7TH</u>: WEAR A PINK TUTU ON THE GOLF COURSE

The "General," my golf partner for the day, was in the midst of the best round of his life, a 78. Our golf match this day placed The General and I against the undefeated duo of the "Commish" and the "Professor." My golf group has nicknames. Mine is Spike for obvious reasons thanks to my awards company of the same name. As we came to the 13th hole, after another par from The General, we increased our match lead to six. The Professor said to me, "No offense, but The General is beating us all by himself." After finishing the hole, I let the three of them walk ahead of me to the next tee. I had placed the pink tutu my wife bought me a month ago in my golf bag for just this opportunity for a *first*. I put away my pride and put on my pink tutu. I joined my foursome on the 14th tee. I proclaimed that, "If I can't support my partner with good golf, I'm willing to cheerlead for him." I then broke out into a cheer for my partner on the tee, "Go General, go!" I received the laughs I sought in addition to some doubtful stares that seemed to question my sanity.

We closed out the match on the following hole. I had my winnings, all six dollars of it, tucked into my tutu by The Commish. I proudly wore my striking pink tutu until we finished the last hole.

*P.S. - **Looking back:** Love the friendships and the laughs — priceless. For your viewing pleasure, I included a picture from that day on the cover of this book.*

??? – Are you the proud owner of a pink tutu? Would you ever wear it out in public?

JUNE 16TH: A CALL LIKE NO OTHER

That day was another sad *Twilight Zone* reality from "the front." One of our employees, making the unemployment triage calls for the State of California, had an actual suicidal call the night before. That was the *first* time I received a call from my partner notifying me of the situation. That happened on our watch. The California citizen calling had committed suicide while on the call. Distressed by his current situation, he had lost everything: his job, his home, and was living in the car he was calling from. We did all the right things. We had three supervisors on the call with the police on their way when the caller decided he had enough — sad, tragic, tough. Real life shit. NOT the trophy business, I can tell you that. I have left this intentionally vague. I'm thankful our employee had a strong grounded faith that he relied on. He found peace in the fact that he knew he had done everything he could to help this individual. This exposed the ugly and unfortunate underbelly of the pandemic.

*P.S. - **Looking back:** That put an exclamation point in my* why *of helping save jobs. Save a job, possibly save a life. We continued into 2021 answering these calls. It took a toll on our employees, there were other close calls. They are heroes.*

??? – Do you know the resources available to give someone who is suicidal?

The National Suicide Prevention Lifeline is 800-273-8255 and the website https://suicidepreventionlifeline.org/

JUNE 17TH: SING AS FRONT MAN OF BAND

I had my tonsils out when I was five years old. That is the excuse I use for my horrible singing voice. I'm horrible. I cannot carry a tune. My daughter had made me promise to never sing in public because it would cause the family shame. To this point I had kept my promise. So, the prospect of this *first* was horrifying.

One of my partners Gary has a band that rehearses in our warehouse a few nights a week, sharing some wine between sets. Thus, the band's name the Warehouse Winos. They are a classic rock band and have become quite good over the past few years from their humble beginnings. I love live music of any kind and am fortunate I can take it in occasionally for free on these nights of practice. I've become the group's groupie of sorts giving them my singular standing ovation at the completion of their songs. Lucky them?

I came down to catch a few live tunes and decided I would ask if I could front on one of their songs. They enthusiastically agreed. I had thought this out and had requested a specific Doors song because of the monotone lack of range singing by Mr. Morrison. The song was "Waiting for the Sun." Well, they didn't know this one and started to break out into another Doors song they wanted me to try, "L.A. Woman." They encouraged me and I tried to sit on a stool with a microphone in my hand to sing in front of a band for the *first* time in my life. What a train wreck. First, I was scared out of my mind to expose my lack of talent. Second, I had no idea of timing for when to jump in. It was awkward. One of the normal lead singers tried to help and support my vocals. I wasn't giving him much to work with. I tried the best I could. All in the spirit of a *first*! I blurted out a few lines here and there. I'm not sure it counts as fronting a band, but for my purposes it will have to do. The timing, or confidence to just jump in was harder than I had envisioned. Jim Morrison is rolling over in his grave.

P.S. – Looking back: What was I thinking? But in an odd way it was freeing. Who really cares? They have been trying to encourage me to learn one song and join them on stage when they are out playing one night. Who knows?

??? – Have you ever tried something for the first time that petrified you? Something you knew you had no talent for, but tried it anyway?

JUNE 25TH: TAILGATE SHOW FOR COMPETITORS

First time we ever hosted a promotional product tailgate mini-trade show for competitors in our parking lot to help the local multi-line factory representatives! We had six local factory reps representing 30-plus manufacturers. They set up appointments with 40-plus competitors to visit with them, socially distanced, in our front parking lot to see new products. The reps set up their trade show tables displaying products from their trunks — fast and no expense to them. The day was blessed, it was sunny and in the 80s. They were busy and had a steady flow of competing distributors all day. Since the pandemic lockdowns started, they had been unable to visit customers to show new products. This gave them a venue to do so. We did it to help the industry — our good deed for the day.

P.S. – Looking back: One may question why we would help a competitor, the enemy. I looked at it as assisting our vendor partners who needed help. It may have even assisted us with a few of the competitors. Time will tell.

??? – Would you have lent a hand in this situation?

JUNE 27TH: POSTED AN OPINION ON SOCIAL MEDIA

I've never responded with an opinion on social media. I try to keep my posts apolitical, positive, and personal. Well, that day was a *first* as I responded to a friend's post to his simple question: *Mask or No Mask? Why? Love to hear your thoughts …*

His somewhat simple, innocent little question ignited a firestorm of debate that went all over the place. In 12 hours he generated over 600 comments and counting. There were both negative and positive comments. I've cut and pasted a few to show the debate, divide, misunderstanding, aggression, and in my opinion ignorance that evoked my *first* that day.

NO … *"No. It's stupid…."*

YES … *"Definitely mask"*

NO … *"No mask, here's why. They are a complete pain!"*

YES … *"Yes, not wearing one given the climate of everything is just selfish."*

NO … *"FUCK THESE MASKS … JUST BECAUSE … FUCK EVERYTHING!!!!"*

YES … *"It slows down transmission. Simple as that."*

NO … *"No mask, here's why. Freedom. "My body, my— choice' right?"*

These were the short and mild responses. I'll let your imagination take over. It was hard to believe and even harder to read the responses. To these responses and many similar others, I posted my first opinion in this setting with a quick back and forth with the author:

ME: *"I just don't understand. It seems simple. Wear a mask, wear a seat belt, don't text or drink when driving, social distance, respect others, be smart, be safe, not reckless, and get back to work YESTERDAY! Protect the elderly and those at risk. This is global, not a national political issue or conspiracy. Common sense with understanding and not hate. The negative discourse makes me sad … The way I see it there are no "sides," we are all in this together. But what do I know?"*

MY FRIEND: "*My man. Well said. Sad times we are in. Clearly, as you can see there's a huge divide on this. Hope it gets better quick.*"

*P.S. – **Looking back:** A sad commentary on the state of affairs. I never say never — but I will venture to guess that will be my last social opinion post. I do not need to expose myself to this. I'm one and done on this* first.

??? – How can such a simple question evoke such anger and hate? Why are we so mean, nasty, and ignorant? Would these people make these comments to your face?

CHAPTER EIGHT:
A BUCKET LIST OF FIRSTS

When I mentioned my year of firsts to others, they assumed it was a glorified bucket list. In some ways that is accurate. I went into the year with numerous bucket list-type experiences that I wanted to accomplish. At the top of that list was flying a plane. I had committed to do this in front of a room of people in December 2019. That is what started all of this. I achieved this goal in addition with many others, as you will see.

JULY 1ST: FLY A PLANE

I stood in front of a room full of people last December to commit to doing this *first*. Something funny happens when you commit to a goal, actually write it down, and put yourself out there by telling others. In various circumstances, in conversations with numerous people, I mentioned *my year of firsts* and my goal to fly a plane. I broadcasted this out into the universe, so to speak. Just by chance, I was talking with a business friend at a networking event who said he was a pilot. I never knew. He earned his license at the Northeast Philadelphia Regional Airport located adjacent to my business. He educated me on the possibility of flying a plane, explaining that an instructor pilot would have to accompany me for a one-hour flight, which who would allow me to fly. The puzzle pieces of this *first* started to come together. Next, I had to find a willing pilot instructor and a plane — minor details. Again, by happenstance one of my partners knew a pilot instructor named Adam. What are the odds? Adam flies out of Northeast Philadelphia Airport as a hired hand for the corporate jets housed at the airfield and worked there as one of the flight instructors. What a coincidence! I got the pilot's contact info, another piece to the puzzle. I had planned to do this earlier in March, but the pandemic forced me to shelve the idea. My kids had asked what I wanted for Father's Day and I said I wanted a gift certificate to the flight school so I could book this experience. Another piece in place. All I needed was to muster the courage and find an opening in my 24/7 schedule.

This *first* was a long-time typical bucket list item that I had given up on years ago. Flying a plane seemed out of reach. It would take too much time and too much money. I didn't know of a fast-tracked way to accomplish this first. That was until I committed to it and started to talk about and research it. The dream was starting to become a reality.

I contacted the flight instructor and told him about my *firsts*, and he was all in. I was to book the time and let him know. I stopped in at the airport flight school to check it out. My excitement grew.

I had done a great job of getting ahead of my schedule at work and was unbelievably open one afternoon. I usually spent afternoons on Zoom calls, but not this day! I decided that unless something blew up, which seemed to happen every day in the new normal, I was going to do it. At 10:30 a.m., with the day going amazingly smoothly, I called the flight instructor. It was my lucky day. He had just finished mowing the lawn and was free that afternoon. Adam flies a corporate jet out of Northeast Philly to make weekly runs to Florida for his clients. Despite the devastation of the airline industry during the pandemic closures, he was lucky. He had steady employment. Many of his pilot friends that worked for the commercial airlines were not as fortunate.

I booked a 3 p.m. flight time and *BAM,* it all fell into place. All I needed to do was work through the next few hours without some major issue materializing. My luck held out. Before I knew it I was in my car making the five-minute drive around the corner to the airport. The next vehicle I'd be operating would have wings — scary thought!

I met Adam at the hangar. We hit it off immediately. He snapped the obligatory tourist-type pictures of me standing next to the plane I was about to fly; one is pictured on the back cover of this book. We circled the plane to check various components of the green-trimmed two-seat Piper Archer aircraft. He took me through the fifteen-minute exterior preflight checklist. Next, we climbed into the cockpit for another set of checklists. We put on headsets and checked the communications between ourselves and the control tower. The myriad of instruments was mind-numbing, and Adam explained every one. His methodical process of checking the plane's instrumentation and systems put me at ease. Even though I had this desire to fly, I still had some apprehension. We buckled up and turned on the engine. I was now in charge! A slight panic set in. I turned the plane with the foot pedals. It seemed unnatural and felt weird. Adam assured me that if anything happened he could take over the controls, just like a driving instructor in driving school car. He was right next to me. There was no reason to be nervous, right? Guess again; I was. It was go time!

He had me lightly nudge the throttle forward as we taxied and lined up on the runway. As instructed, I hit the throttle. We picked up speed. When we were halfway down the runway, he told me to pull the yoke (steering wheel) toward me. Check. The nose of the plane lifted ... we were off! I was flying an actual plane for the *first* time in my life. There was some wind, which caused some bumps in the road, so to speak. I was petrified as the voice inside my head repeatedly screamed, "Don't crash, don't crash, don't crash …" We climbed to 2,000 feet and veered north toward the Doylestown Regional Airport 20 miles away. I was so fixated on keeping the plane level with the horizon that I didn't enjoy the scenery at first. The mechanics of operating the plane consumed my complete attention. Adam tried to interrupt this focus with a command to turn right. It was nerve-racking but I slowly banked … *left?*

Without panic but with increasing urgency, Adam repeated, "Right, right, your *other* right!"

I was still thinking "Don't crash, don't crash," when his change of direction command finally registered. I was turning left and needed to turn the other way — duh. I can only guess what was going through his mind. Eventually, I banked right and we turned in a circle to head to our destination. A typical drive of an hour by ground took five minutes by air — it was phenomenal. The wind jostled us from time to time, keeping me on edge. But it was cool, I was in control, and I was flying! It was by far a once in a lifetime exhilarating *first* experience.

We headed back to the airport and Adam instructed me on the approach, gradually reducing the speed and altitude. As we reached the runway, he had me look for the lights that needed to turn red signaling approval to land. This seemed counterintuitive, so I clarified by asking, "Red, not green, correct?" Yep — red, not green. We received the red lights from the tower, and I took it down. Terror-stricken, I steered and pushed the yoke forward to take us in. Astonishingly, Adam allowed me to stay in control through the landing. I touched us down perfectly. I had achieved another goal of not crashing and landing safely. There was never a doubt, except for the incessant skeptical voice in my head.

As we taxied down the runway, Adam suddenly took over the controls, hit the throttle again and we were off on another flight. I thought we were done; we weren't. My hour wasn't up and apparently my *instructor* *loved* to fly. Any opportunity to be up, he took it. There's something inexplicably liberating about soaring above the din and clatter of the Earth below. He didn't want my *first* to end. We flew over my building, quickly circled around the airport, and went back down for a second landing. I started feeling a little queasy in the stuffy cockpit and the bumping around due to the wind. We landed just in time for my stomach to calm and to achieve my thrilling goal. *I LOVED IT!*

P.S. – **Looking back:** *I committed to this goal and achieved it. It was one of the highlights of the year. It will be an experience I will always have. I'm proud of me.*

??? – Have you ever committed to a goal by writing it down? Do you have written goals?

JULY 6TH: QUESTIONS FOR UNCOMFORTABLE CONVERSATIONS WITH A BLACK MAN

For the *first* time in my life, I submitted questions for an "Uncomfortable Conversation with a Black Man." The Black man I was hoping to have the uncomfortable conversation with was Emmanuel Acho, a Nigerian-American former linebacker who played in the National Football League. Mr. Acho is currently working as an analyst for Fox Sports. He also hosts a weekly webcast called *Uncomfortable Conversations with a Black Man.*

The opportunity came through a local relationship group I belong to, BCA (Business Club of America). The members received a challenge to present questions to Mr. Acho. He would select a few members to be a part of these webcasts from the questions submitted. I was somewhat afraid to hit send on the email to proffer the questions. My younger self would never have had the courage to come up with, much less submit, the questions. I guess age does have a few advantages. At least it has with me. I felt honestly curious and wanted to learn.

I wrote most of the following questions right after I received the email. I slept on them and sent them to my wife. As a secondary counsel, I discussed the queries with the ordained minister in my sales department, who also happens to be a Black man. Both sounding boards boosted my confidence that I was on the right track. My discussions with my friend at work spurred some additional questions that I had not initially thought of. The following are my proposed questions.

1. *I recently saw Bryant Gumbel's* Real Sports *commentary of a "Black Tax" that he and most other Black people live their lives with. Did you see this? Is this "Black Tax" discussed in the Black community? Have you felt it personally? If so, can you provide a few examples that stick out to you from your life, to paint the picture for me and others? I want to better understand the angst and heartache caused by just having a different skin color. Mr. Gumbel said it was "exhausting." Is it?*

2. *As a white man who would like to be part of the solution and not part of the problem, what would you suggest I do personally? What should we be doing collectively?*

3. *I see the continuing racism in the world, and I know there is a ways to go. In my opinion, it has gotten better in my lifetime. Do you feel that it has gotten better over the last 20 to 40 years? Am I, or other white people, fooling ourselves in thinking this?*

4. **I believe racism is a learned trait, born out of ignorance, and passed down — do you agree? If so, how can we best educate to turn this tide and dilute this prejudice as time goes on?**

5. **If I gave the Black community a magic wand to fix this inequality, what would you use it on? Education?**

6. *There are applications and various forms that ask for a race designation. Do you find it offensive when it lists Caucasian, African American, Asian, etc.? What would you think if we did away with asking this and replaced it with one box to check that says, "Human Race?"*

7. *Do you think that sometimes there is reverse racism from the Black community? If so, what are your thoughts on it?*

8. **What do you think about hiring quotas, set-aside contracts for minorities, etc.? Does this help or hurt the cause?**

9. *What do you think about what happened in Charlottesville?* (The impending removal of a statue of Confederate Gen. Robert E. Lee was the reason white nationalists and neo-Nazi organizations came to Charlottesville in mid-August.)

10. *What is the correct term that should be respectfully used when describing a person of color — African American? Black? Something else?*

11. *How do we support the good police majority while addressing the small minority of bad ones and the system that covers for them?*

12. *How do you feel about the current Civil War statue issue?*

13. *What do you think about current state of politics?*

14. *I understand and empathize with the current protests, but not the looting and destruction of property. Do you agree? Am I missing something?*

15. *What do I as a white person need to understand most on this subject?*

16. *What question(s) should I ask that I did not ask? What question would you like me to ask?*

P.S. – Looking back: *The questions were well received, and I was selected to ask these questions directly later in the month on the 23rd. This would lead* *to another first. Three of the questions asked were mine. You can also find the video of this interview by searching BCA – Powerful Conversation on Equity in the search bar in YouTube. The conversation starts five minutes in. The panel I was on were able to ask Mr. Acho the questions #4, #5, and #8 (**in bold above**) from the 16 questions I submitted. The toughest question was mine — #5 shown above. This was the question about the "magic wand." The answer that was the most surprising. I would have never guessed Mr. Acho would answer it by saying that he would "travel back in time one hundred years to fix the foundation." It was an interesting and thoughtful answer. I thought the answer would have been education. This answer came into focus for me and made sense after I read the book,* The Person You Mean to Be, *by Dolly Chugh, which I finished in May of 2021.*

??? – Have you ever had an uncomfortable conversation with a Black man? A White man? An Asian man? An Indian man? A Hispanic man? Or any other man or woman that is not of your ethnicity to gain understanding and empathy?

<u>JULY 10TH</u>: LISTEN TO AN AUDIO BOOK (*THE FIRE NEXT TIME*)

I had never downloaded and listened to an entire audio book before. Today was the *first* time I did, and I chose *The Fire Next Time* by James Baldwin, a namesake. I specifically chose this book for a *first* due to the inspiration from the questions I had submitted four days earlier and the current racially charged climate. I wanted to learn. I wanted to understand the best I could. I did some research and settled on this book, considered one of the most influential books about race relations in the 1960s.

The Fire Next Time is a 1963 nonfiction book containing two essays: "My Dungeon Shook: Letter to My Nephew on the One Hundredth Anniversary of the Emancipation" and "Down at the Cross: Letter from a Region of My Mind."

I discovered that the book's title came from a couplet in "Mary Don't You Weep," an African American spiritual song: "*God gave Noah the rainbow sign/ No more water, the fire next time.*"

The first essay, written in the form of a letter to Baldwin's 14-year-old nephew, discusses the central role of race in American history. The second essay takes up the majority of the book, and deals with the relations between race and religion, focusing in particular on Baldwin's experiences with the Christian church as a youth, as well as the Islamic ideas of others in Harlem. Mr. Baldwin provides a lot of wisdom and insight about race, religion, and life.

*P.S. – **Looking back:** This book was a great choice, and I would highly recommend it. I wonder how the lives of Keith and James Baldwin would have been different if their places of origin had been transposed. I cannot imagine being born and raised in Harlem at the place and time that he had. Would I have made it out? Would he have written a book of* firsts*? Would I have produced* The Fire Next Time*?*

??? – Have you tried to travel in another person's shoes, or look through their eyes with an open mind?

JULY 17TH: MOON A FRIEND ON THE GOLF COURSE

For the past five years, I have been reconnecting with childhood friends for a golf weekend. At 62, I would venture to guess that I am fortunate to be in the minority to do so with people I have known since *first* grade. We all grew up in a small section of Northeast Philly called Birdwood Farms, populated with twin homes at the edge of Pennypack Park. We were all in the *first* fully graduated class of St. Albert the Great grade school. We shared those indelible experiences of youth and growing up together through high school and on the playground. It forged a lifetime bond of familiarity. We shared all the embarrassing, stupid, and sometimes illegal times. We shared the funny and tragic happenings of our lives. We recount and laugh at those times, sometimes trapped in those years, with an appreciative nod to our lifetime experiences that followed in our separate grown-up lives. We all made it through and out of the neighborhood. This get together was our trek back to the past.

The COVID-19 situation had put this up in the air for a while, but it stabilized enough as July got closer, and we kept the date. The COVID-19 challenge did produce a few casualties causing a few of the out-of-town participants to stay home. For various reasons, they could not fly in from the current "hot spots" at the time — Texas and Florida. That year's group contained the guy who was my inspiration for my *first* that day. Alan was the exhibitionist in the group who was the king of "mooning" while growing up. Our exhibitionist, unlike me, does not have any inhibitions, which is why we all love him so much, and why he is the source of many jokes and laughs. He was also a recent liver transplant survivor. The Gift of Life provided added perspective to these friendships. Oh, and he can sing and play a great acoustic guitar — just another treat for the get together. It is an eclectic group bound together by the common thread of youth.

When I received the invite for this annual jaunt, I had an idea for a *first* for this extremely shy and reserved writer. I was going to "moon" the king of moons from my youth when we got together. I know this sounds childish, and it is. I guess that is the point. I was looking for the opportunity for my first actual "mooning" of someone at the ripe old age of 62. I was going to move outside my shyness, my character, and put myself out there so to speak – or at least put my hindquarters out there.

That opportunity presented itself at the isolated par 4, 11th hole. As the four of us stood on the tee, our exhibitionist was setting up to hit. No one else was within sight. As he was hitting, I unloosed my belt. I was off to the side and behind the others. He hit one of his better tee shots of the day. As he finished his tee shot, I called out, "*Hey, great shot!*" With that, I turned and dropped my drawers and saluted the king with my *first*, to which he calmly replied, "I think I just saw Haley's comet," referring to the uniqueness of this less than momentous event. The others in the group laughed with approval. My *first* and my dignity were both behind me, literally and figuratively. Oh well.

P.S. – Looking back: *What made that so special in honoring my friend with my hindquarter salute was that I wasn't sure he would even make the trip. I wasn't sure if he'd be alive for the trip. I had told myself that if he made that trip, I would do this* first *for him. He had needed a liver transplant to live and had been on the waitlist for almost a year. He had a few false alarms leading up to the donation of a Gift of Life in March. His condition had been deteriorating prior to his gift. I write this a year later, after having just recorded a video for his family. They spliced a video from his friends and family to celebrate his one-year anniversary of his rebirth.*

??? – Do you know someone that has either been a recipient or a giver of the Gift of Life?

JULY 20TH: JUGGLE

This *first* was almost as hard as my *first* from earlier in the year, driving the speed limit for a day. I thought this *first* would take me just one day. I grossly miscalculated. I started by asking YouTube how to juggle and watched several videos. I then picked up a few tennis balls and thought, "I got this." I didn't. It was humbling. I started this *first* months ago. I progressed to buying a book and kit with special featherweight juggling props. I consider myself somewhat athletic. How hard could this be? (For me, *very!*)

I can't say I mastered it, but I juggled three balls a few times in a row and declared my frustrating *first* accomplished.

P.S. – Looking back: *I had intended juggling to be my* first *for countless days throughout this year. I put in numerous days of practice and had many failed attempts leading up to today.*

??? – Looking back: Have you ever tried something you thought would be easy, but turned out to require more patience and perseverance than you had anticipated?

JULY 24TH: PLAY PICKLE BALL

I have an ageless, retired friend in his seventies who still plays numerous sports. He had become hooked on Pickle Ball. I texted him earlier in the month, "*For my year of firsts, I want to play Pickle Ball one time. Could you help me accomplish this?*" He was gracious and agreeable in his reply. He sent a link to a video to help me understand the game prior to us playing. The video showed a paddle-ball sport (like a racquet sport) that combines elements of badminton, table tennis, and tennis. Two or four players use solid paddles made of wood or composite materials to hit a perforated polymer ball — much like a Wiffle ball, with 26 to 40 round holes — over a net. The sport shares features of other racquet sports: the dimensions and layout of a badminton court, and a net and rules somewhat similar to tennis, with several modifications.

I met my old friend John at 8:30 a.m. for my *first* Pickle Ball game at Masons Mill Park. I pulled up and I was the only one there. The courts were dotted with puddles from an earlier rain, which apparently delayed a number of the regulars. My friend showed up and my education began. We played singles until a few dozen of regulars joined us, filling the converted tennis courts with double matches. We threw our hats in the ring to play the winners. The regulars were mostly retirees. My friend had warned me that most of them were very skilled as he introduced me as a rookie. As an ex-tennis player, I surprised my friend and our opponents by how quickly I picked up the game. I made some rookie mistakes by putting my foot in "the kitchen" a few times, but we fought back. I played well enough that I had my *first* win, in my *first* Pickle Ball game. We won on the last point. I was ecstatic!

*P.S. - **Looking back:** I loved playing Pickle Ball and would enjoy becoming part of a regular group like my friend's. I was hooked.*

??? – Do you even know what Pickle Ball is?

JULY 29TH: GOLF 18 HOLES WITH THREE CLUBS

The setting for this *first* was Elms Golf Club in Sandy Creek, New York, just off Lake Ontario. I was there for another *first* the next day, my father and son Great Lake fishing trip. The course was a dog track, a term used for a beaten-up golf club. But it allowed me a *first* that I'd wanted to try. I played the 18 holes with just three clubs; a 9 wood, 8 iron, and a putter. I hit every fairway with my 9 wood, which I also used around the green for short chip shots. I couldn't reach a few of the long par 3 holes with the 9 wood. The longer chip shots with the 8 iron gave me trouble or I would have scored even better. I shot a pair of 44s on both nines for a total of 88. I had broken 90 using just three clubs. Sometimes less is more. By using just three clubs it made me more creative in order to improvise hitting the different distances required.

*P.S. - **Looking back:** If I try this again, I will replace my 9 wood with a 3 wood and replace my 8 iron with a pitching wedge.*

<u>JULY 30TH</u>: FATHER AND SON FISHING TRIP

The sun rose out of the water on the horizon. It was perfect as we motored out a mile to our *first* fishing spot. We had three sets of father and son combinations onboard, which made it even more special. My brother and one of my best friends also brought their own sons. I had taken a few family fishing day trips before to the Jersey Bay, fishing for flounder. I had never taken the time for a father and son overnight trip to one of the Great Lakes. We traveled five hours by car to Sandy Creek, New York, on Lake Ontario. We were spending a long weekend with two days of chartered fishing for salmon on a Great Lake for the *first* time in my life, with my 24-year-old son.

What an emotional treasure to share this *first* with my son. It was a *first* for both of us. There are certain rites of passage with a father and son. A fishing trip together is one. Some days stand out among the routines of everyday life. This was one of those experiences. I'd had handfuls of uninteresting *firsts*, which was okay — that's life. This, however, was special as I watched him pull the *first* fish out of the lake on his *first* morning on Lake Ontario; it was a lake brown trout weighing over five pounds (pictured above). His smile of accomplishment meant more than anything to me. He was so proud and happy. It is something we'll both always remember.

No one was shut out and we all caught something: lake bass, trout, or salmon. We lost a few salmon early on while we learned how to keep the line taut. If you allowed for any slack in the line the salmon would use this opportunity to shake out the hook.

*P.S. – **Looking back:** Despite the chaos of the time, I made the time. I've come to learn that giving money to children is not as valuable as time spent with them. That day was one of the best memories of the year.*

??? – Do you take the time to create special memorable traditions with your kids?

JULY 31ST: CATCH A KING SALMON

It was my turn next. I waited impatiently as I sat on our chartered boat on semi-calm Lake Ontario. My eyes were shifting from rod to rod looking for that telltale tug when the fish hits. Bang! I jumped up to grab the lucky rod of that moment. As I begin to reel, I kept telling myself, "no slack, no slack, keep the line tight." I wanted to land this warrior. A few of the anglers that preceded me had not. I could tell it was of good size as it jerked back and forth trying to escape. I remained focused and concentrated on the tip of the bent rod. I had to keep it taunt to keep him with me. That is what it is all about, a great fight to get him landed. Fifteen minutes of tension ended. I had landed my *first* 20-pound king salmon. He was in the boat, and he was mine. It was an awesome *first*!

CHAPTER NINE:
FUN(NY) FIRSTS

Fun is one of our company's ten core values. We define "fun" as: *"Keep things fun. Remember that the world has bigger problems than the daily challenges that make up our work. Stuff happens. Keep perspective. Don't take things personally or take yourself too seriously. Laugh every day. Celebrate Success. Catching people doing things right is more effective than catching them doing things wrong. Create and have fun while accomplishing goals."*

I tried to keep this in mind, despite the many challenges of the year, as I looked for *firsts* to experience.

AUGUST 1ST: KAYAK – ALONE

I had kayaked before one other time, but with a two-person kayak in the Channel Islands in California with my wife. I had never done so alone. That morning on the last day of our father/son fishing trip on Lake Ontario I was up early and ventured out alone. The place we were staying had a kayak which I grabbed and hauled a few hundred feet to the edge of Sandy Creek. I placed it in the cool, breathless, and calm morning water and jumped in. Sandy Creek is a little quiet cove that feeds into Lake Ontario. The sun had awoken within the hour and sat low on the horizon. I paddled through the waist-to-chest deep water to the mouth of Lake Ontario and back. It was a picture post card moment as I paddled with slow strokes to a serene and cathartic *first* for the next hour.

P.S. – **Looking back:** *The morning calm, beauty and solitude are more than one can imagine. Mornings like this provide time to reflect. It's easy during troubled times like these to lose perspective. Take opportunities like this to refocus your energy. Unplug. Decompress. Reflect. Then get back at it!*

AUGUST 4TH: FLOOD AT ONE OF THE SHOWROOMS

Remember the EF2 tornado that struck the Northeastern Philadelphia suburbs that I mentioned in the beginning of the book? Well, this was the day it happened, causing a river to run through the showroom located on what Philadelphians call the Main Line. That was the *first* time I experienced a flood in one of our showrooms, adding insult to the injury of the year. That was not on the schedule for today. Mother Nature could throw a wicked curve ball at times. In business and in life, you gotta know how to hit the curve ball. My turn at the plate — *swinggggggg batter*!

Apparently, our neighbor did some work the week prior to their driveway and adjourning stone wall which diverted the runoff our way. This and the combination of the excessive rain from the tornado produced our misfortune.

*P.S. – **Looking back:** So, when it rains it pours, both literally and figuratively! I guess I should have expected a tornado, right? What was next? All the flooring and most of the drywall had to be replaced in the flooded location. No-one was harmed, which is what really matters. Flooring and drywall can be replaced. People can't. I try to keep things in perspective.*

AUGUST 5TH: A 7-FIGURE SALE (SNEEZE GUARDS)

Every day has its surprises. Yesterday was a flood. Today it was a million-dollar sale. We received a signed purchase order for the *first* million-dollar order in our company's 90-year history. Unbelievable. The order was for sneeze guards for a school district, naturally. These sneeze guards were three-sided and would fit on the students' desks to protect them from one another — another PPE *first*!

The lesson: stay nimble and be prepared. There's a saying that luck is what happens when preparation meets opportunity. The business was prepared to take advantage of new opportunities in the marketplace caused by the pandemic. When the opportunity presented itself, we stepped forward to fill the need. This was not by chance. We created our own luck by fabricating marketing lists of schools and school districts. We partnered with a manufacturer to distribute these sneeze guards. We navigated a lot of hurdles this year.

*P.S. - **Looking back:** We had multiple large sneeze guard orders during that time frame as schools started to ramp up for the possibility of going live in-person. We had created our own luck, so to speak, by extreme hard work, creativity, relationships, and integrity in doing what we said we would do. There was some luck by being in the right place at the right time. Another saying is the harder you work the luckier you get. We lived this.*

AUGUST 8TH: LISTEN TO A CLASSICAL MUSIC STATION (SIRIUS 76 – SYMPHONY HALL)

Today started what I themed as weeks of listening *firsts*. I love all kinds of music. You will find an eclectic mix in my iTunes playlists. In the car, I have the following stations hardwired on SiriusXM: Classic Vinyl, Beatles, 60s, 70s, and 80s. I rarely venture outside of these stations while driving. The light bulb went off this morning as I turned the dial to listen to Sirius 76 —Symphony Hall, their classical music station, for the *first* time. My morning commute is a good 40 minutes. I was struggling finding time for *firsts* and thought this an efficient use of time in experiencing them for the next few weeks.

AUGUST 9TH: TODAY'S TRENDY HITS STATION (SIRIUS 3 – PANDORA)

I jotted some of the artists that I heard for the first time: Jonas Brothers, Cardi B, Harry Stiles. OMG, Cardi B's song "WAP," which happened to be at the top of the charts, was pornographic. It made me feel old. The Cardi B song caught me off-guard to some degree. I'm no prude and I've heard just about every four-letter word and compound variation that you can think of, I just didn't expect to hear something like this accepted as "mainstream" art. If unfamiliar, Google WAP lyrics as be prepared to blush. Is this what our youth listens to on a regular basis? Something to ponder, I guess. To be fair, I assume this is what my parents opined when they heard and saw the exploits of artists from the 1960s like the Doors, Janis Joplin, YES, Jimmy Hendrix, not to mention the whole Woodstock thing. I guess every generation's musical artists look to shock and challenge the established order of things.

*P.S. – **Looking back:** I'm old! Sometimes firsts can challenge you in ways you never expected.*

AUGUST 10TH: PHISH STATION (SIRIUS 29 – PHISH RADIO)

I heard a Frank Zappa instrumental that turned into Little Richard crooning — the broadcast was hosted by Phish drummer Jonathan Fishman. A strange mix.

AUGUST 11TH: HIP-HOP STATION (SIRIUS 44 – HIP-HOP NATION)

I listened to Drake, Lil Dirk, Kendrick Lamar, Lil Baby, French Montana, Jackboys, Migos (Stir Fry), and 21 Savage. I had only heard of French Montana because I think he dated a Kardashian — a fact that I'm almost embarrassed to admit! I could listen to this in the future, although sparingly.

AUGUST 13TH: ELECTRO DANCE STATION (SIRIUS 51 – BPM – BEATS PER MINUTE)

This station was torture that I somehow endured. It was horrible; nothing but constant pounding. Was this music? Did I mention I'm old? *First* and hopefully for the last time I've heard the following artists: Tiesto/Ilira, Cash Cash, Tritonal, Deacon, Deadmaus, Paul Woolford, Marshmallow, and Ivan Gough. Curiously I Googled "BPM" to find it meant "beats per minute." To me it was "beatings per minute!"

??? – Is this what my parents said when I blasted early Pink Floyd? Anyone have some Excedrin? (Extra strength please!)

AUGUST 14TH: BLUEGRASS STATION (SIRIUS 62 – BLUEGRASS JUNCTION)

Bluegrass was much easier listening than the Techno station. Following are some of the artists I jotted down and listened to: Alan Bibey, Ricky Skaggs, Missy Armstrong, Chris Jones, Bill Monroe, Special Consensus, Grascals, Antique Persuasion, Gina Furtado Project, Band of Ruhks, and Junior Sisk.

P.S. – Looking back: The Philadelphia Folk Festival is only a few miles from the farmhouse in Perkiomenville where my grandparents used to live. It's held at the Old Pool Farm in Schwenksville, Pennsylvania. This is hallowed ground to me. It holds some of my most cherished childhood memories.

This year will be the 60th festival at that venue, and I've never gone! Every notable Bluegrass and Folk artist in the country has played the festival at some point. I just checked the date for this year's festival in August. It is the same date as another planned first, *a South African Safari. Maybe I'll make it to the 61st?*

??? – Have you revisited places from your childhood? How did it make you feel?

AUGUST 15TH: SOUTHERN GOSPEL STATION (SIRIUS 65— ENLIGHTEN)

In moving up the dial from the Bluegrass station, I found enLighten, the Gospel Music channel. I listened to the following artists for the first time (I had never heard of any of them): Dottie Rambo, David Phelps, Cathedrals, Vestal Goodman, Homecoming Friends, Sue Dodge, Squire Parsons, Ivan Parker, The Trio, Janet Paschal, and Candy Christmas.

*P.S. – **Looking back:** Listening to the new diverse music throughout the week was interesting. I tried to listen and understand the lyrics. Boy there are lots of flavors on the dial. The different perspectives are amazing.*

??? – Have you ever ventured out of your comfort zone to explore other musical genres?

AUGUST 16TH: 1ST GRANDCHILD'S FIRST BIRTHDAY PARTY

I am so fortunate to have my first grandson Luke turn one in my year of *firsts*. Such kismet! The party was a typical family gathering for the celebration of a *first* birthday. It was hosted at my daughter's home and contained both sets of grandparents, the uncle and the aunt. My daughter produced a nine-inch round, six-inch high, blue frosted layered vanilla birthday cake that she plopped down in front of my grandson. After a healthy rendition of Happy Birthday Luke inquisitively probed the cake for a few minutes. With coaching from his parents, he dug in. For the next half hour his hands became a mosh pit of mangled cake. He explored the textures. He stuffed some in his mouth. He enjoyed. He had his fully immersed *first* birthday cake experience. A happy blue mess. It looked like so much fun. I wanted to jump in but didn't. As dutiful grandparents we cheered him on and took numerous pictures. All good things come to an end. The cleanup was not as much fun. The cake was everywhere.

*P.S. - **Looking back:** Priceless! In life we don't need much to be happy. Today all my grandson needed was a cake. A valuable lesson from an infant. Maybe this is how I'll celebrate my 65th?*

AUGUST 17TH: REAL JAZZ STATION (SIRIUS 67 – CLASSIC JAZZ)

Although I had not heard of any of them, I listened to the following Real Jazz (just more *firsts*): Wes Montgomery, Benny Green, Diana Krall, Roy Haynes, Steve Turre, Sonny Rollins, and Giacomo Gates. This was good background music to drive by, although not a favorite.

AUGUST 19TH: BLUES STATION (SIRIUS 70 – BB KING'S BLUES)

I turned on Sirius's Blues station this morning and listened to the following artists: Christine the "Kingfish", Otis Spann, Chris Cain, Slim Harpo, Taj Mahal, Corey Harris, Ruth Brown, and Albert King. I could listen to Blues all day. One of my favorite past memories is spending a night in Chicago at a non-descript blues club. I'll never forget the rendition of "Kokomo me baby" played that evening.

??? – Did you know that BB stands for Blues Boy?

AUGUST 20TH: OPERA STATION
(SIRIUS 74 – MET OPERA RADIO)

I took in the following on Met Opera Radio: Giacomo Puccini's *Tosca*, Wolfgang Amadeus, and Thomas Tompkins.

According to Wikipedia, *Tosca* is a three-act opera based on Victorien Sardou's 1887 French-language dramatic play, *La Tosca*. It is a melodramatic piece set in Rome in June 1800, with the Kingdom of Naples's control of Rome threatened by Napoleon's invasion of Italy. It contains depictions of torture, murder, and suicide, as well as some of Puccini's best-known lyrical arias.

P.S. – *Looking back:* *I had tickets for my* first *in-person live opera, which was canceled due to the pandemic. I was to see* Madame Butterfly. *(FYI — Met Opera Radio can now be found on Sirius 35.)*

AUGUST 21ST: JOEL OLSTEEN RADIO (SIRIUS 128)

I didn't know Joel Olsteen had a channel. Good guy but not my cup of tea. I listened to his Sermon 735. On Joel's website it is titled *The Twenty-First Day*. I copied the following overview from the site about what I listened to that morning.

> *The Psalmist said in Psalm 56:9, "The moment you pray, the tide of the battle turns." In the unseen realm, God begins to change things in your favor the moment you pray. But many times, when we've been praying for a long time for something, and don't see anything happening in the natural world, it can seem like God went on vacation and our prayers aren't doing any good. Joel wants to show you that even when you can't see behind the scenes, God is at work. He not only heard you when you prayed, but He took it one step farther; He put the miracle in motion.*

Just because you don't see anything happening doesn't mean the answer is not on the way. The people that see breakthroughs and promises fulfilled are the people that keep praying, keep believing and keep standing in faith. This message will inspire and equip you to be one of those people!

Hmm, who knows?

AUGUST 23RD: COMEDY STATION (SIRIUS 98 – LAUGH USA)

I ended up on Laugh USA. I listened to an hour of comedians and their jokes. It definitely was a welcomed change of pace. I listened to the following comedians (with their topic in parentheses): Grant Lyon (stalking online), DJ Demers (deaf — whisper down lane), Erin Jackson (online dating sites), Buddy Fitzpatrick (smart cars), Sabastian Manakowsi (Subway sandwiches, Craig's List, and parents), Russell Peters (Italians and Chinese), Jim Floerentine (phony call – construction), Andy Hendricks (Hamilton and sympathy cards), Brandon Vesta (Republicans in California), Josh Gondelma (walking the dog), Rob Patavonia (song on relationships — one-word answer), and Steve Simone (fat). Some funny stuff that put a smile on my face.

P.S. – Looking back: I wish I had the memory to remember jokes to tell.

AUGUST 25TH: AGRIBUSINESS AND WESTERN LIFESTYLE STATION (SIRIUS 147 – RURAL RADIO)

It is funny sometimes what committing to these *firsts* made me do and experience. Never in my life did I think I'd listen to a Rural Radio show. I didn't even know one existed. Surprisingly, there is one, which I discovered as I cruised up the dial; eye-opening. The following topics were covered while I listened — who would have ever thought? Topics: Ontario corn, soybean and wheat yields, bin temperature monitor, bean leaf beetles, stay on top of harvest time, nitrate poisoning, and moisture testing.

P.S. – *Looking back:* *I'm sure if I lived on a farm these would mean something but to me it was like listening to a foreign language.*

AUGUST 31ST: SENT INVITATION TO FILL A RESTAURANT

Inviting hundreds of my friends out to dinner all at once to fill a restaurant was a *first*. I belong to a number of relationship groups. I reached out to all of them to help a friend. My quest was to fill my friend's restaurant for his reopening after closing for months due to the pandemic. His employees had lost months of tips. The following is the email invite I sent:

> *I'm looking to see if you are interested in joining me in helping my friend, the owner of Cuba Libre, in their opening of indoor/ outdoor dining on the 8th, while joining me in a "first". The time has come for his reopening! Yea! FINALLY!*
>
> *I'm not sure if you are aware that I'm doing a "Year of Firsts" this year. I am doing something EVERY DAY this year that I have never done or experienced before in my life. The firsts have been diverse with a wide range of things. The current challenging global events have provided some unwanted firsts, which is okay. I started on January 1st. For this "first,"" I need your help. I have NEVER filled a restaurant with my own reservation before. I would like to do this on Tuesday, September 8th, at Cuba Libre. This will also be Cuba Libre's "first" reservation when they reopen indoor dining on September 8th. Can you help me with this "first"?*
>
> *Because of the restrictions on capacity of 25 percent and the social distancing requirements, there will be limited time slots for reservations. Attached are the time slots not filled yet and the number of tables available to fill. IF we fill the restaurant on the*

8th, Cuba Libre has agreed to open up a second and third night, if needed, on the 9th and 10th. I plan to fill the 8th and will be there as many nights as we fill to personally THANK everyone for their participation in my "first." I already have a few reservations for the 9th from friends that could not make the 8th. Hopefully, there will be family, friends, and business colleagues in attendance. I will be inviting a lot of other people, as you can see by the reservations already filled. Feel free to do the same.

For capacity purposes, the availability list is attached: ten tables of four, three tables of two, and two tables of six. The tables will turn every two hours and run from 4 p.m. until 9:30 p.m. We can accommodate 174 per night. I have attached the safety measures in place at Cuba Libre to keep us safe. The following link is the menu available.

FIRST COME, FIRST SERVED! Your Friends AND Family are INVITED! The more the merrier! If you have been looking for the opportunity to go out to dinner, sort of like the "old days"(remember them?) — here is your chance!

PLEASE REPLY TO ME with HOW MANY and WHAT TIME SLOT you would like. If the time slot that you selected is filled, I will reach out to you with the closest option.

I will let you know once we have filled the restaurant for Tuesday, September 8th, and we will open up the following night Wednesday, September 9th.

I know that some may feel uncomfortable in venturing out; that is okay, I'll catch you next time. Some may be on vacation or have other plans, I get it.

As you can imagine, the restaurant industry has been devastated. Cuba Libre is no different. If we can get them off to a GREAT foot as they open, I'm sure this will assist Cuba Libre *and their employees. Please let me know. Stay Safe! Hope to see you! Should be FUN!*

With much Love!

Keith

P.S. – Looking back: *As you can see, I leveraged my year of firsts shamelessly for my "why." Begging to help others was not beneath me. I wonder what those people thought when they received this crazy email out of nowhere?! I was still working a ton of hours, but I was starting to catch my breath in August and could do things like this.*

SEPTEMBER 5TH: HORSESHOE BEND PARK HIKE

I had traveled with my wife for over an hour to Horseshoe Bend Park for a *first* on this crystal-clear sunny Sunday. I'd never been there. It came highly recommended from a few couples who were hiking as a diversion from the seclusion of the pandemic. It seemed in the middle of nowhere. The park bordered secluded farmland and the Delaware River.

Over the next few hours, we got lost then found our way. It didn't matter; we had nowhere to go. Through fields, forests, ravines, and streams we hiked. We followed the hike with lunch on the water in Frenchtown, New Jersey. It was a great day.

P.S. – Looking back: *I carved out time for these COVID-19 inspired hiking* firsts *to spend special moments with my wife. We took a half-dozen similar hikes through the year to places we had never been. You don't need to hear about all the* firsts. *I published this one to represent all the others.*

??? – How did you keep from going stir-crazy at home during COVID?

SEPTEMBER 8TH: FILLED A RESTAURANT

I accomplished my goal of filling a restaurant with my reservation for the *first* time, even if it was for 25 percent capacity inside due to COVID-19 restrictions. There was a combination of inside and outside dining. I had over 100 guests that started with reservations at 4:30 p.m. and ran through to closing. This was the restaurant's first night reopening after being closed for over four months! I was running from table to table taking pictures and thanking everyone for their support. I felt like a father at my daughter's wedding. Everyone was so gracious — I was blessed to have friends support another friend, especially during those challenging times. As one of my friends texted me afterward: *"At least these few* firsts *created some much-needed uplift in spirits."*

P.S. – Looking Back: *I was told by my friend Larry — who is the owner — and staff that I helped give them footing and momentum to succeed to stay open and keep their people employed. The rest of the block of restaurants in Olde City Philadelphia were virtually empty that week with few people in them, while Cuba Libre was full. The staff made more tips with a higher check average than they had ever done in the past. They keep track of this, which I didn't know. They told me this on the third consecutive night I dined there. My guests were generous. I went every night I had guests, which was the rest of the week. The reservations spilled into three nights. They were able to bring staff back that they would not have otherwise, which was the purpose and my "why": saving jobs.*

SEPTEMBER 17TH: PICKED UP A MILLION-DOLLAR CHECK

I personally drove two hours to pick up the payment for our company's first seven-figure sale. We had made special arrangements for the expedited payment from the Board of Education and had just delivered the product a few days earlier. American Express was anxiously awaiting a payment that happened to be worth more than my home! The placing of over three-hundred thousand dollars on our company's AMEX card for a deposit for this sale was another earlier first for me a month ago. I could never have imagined doing this. It was nerve wracking. I learned to juggle more than balls during my year of *firsts*. I learned to juggle the unimaginable Monopoly money that I was now dealing with. It was the *first* and probably the last time I would have a $1.1 million dollar check in my hands.

We were not rich and still had many bills to pay. When you sell something for a million dollars, you don't make a million dollars. We made a small fraction of this. It was a little oxygen (cash) to help us breathe a little easier at the time. A lot of things could have gone wrong with this project, and I do mean a LOT. The manufacturer we had partnered with dodged hurricane Laura, for one. We got lucky.

*P.S. – **Looking back:** In the chaos of the year, we had stopped producing our monthly company profit and loss statements. They became irrelevant. We knew we were losing money, and lots of it. We had created and relied on what we called an "Oxygen Report." The report consisted of all the money we owed or had to pay out against the money we had coming in. Part of this was what we had left in our line of credit to borrow. I had taught our employees that cash is oxygen to a business. We are an open book management company and practitioner of the "Great Game of Business." Cash became our "critical number." Since March, we had tried to conserve and generate as much oxygen as possible to be able to breathe for another day to survive. The oxygen report told us how many months we had to live as a company. At that time, we had enough oxygen to survive six months. We monitored this weekly because we did not know when or if the business would return. We are still breathing, creating our own luck and oxygen.*

SEPTEMBER 23RD: VISIT THE VIETNAM WAR MEMORIAL

It was a glorious sunny, early fall afternoon. I had just finished an outdoor networking get-together about 90 minutes from my office. I debated traveling back to work but I had nothing on my calendar for the balance of the day. I figured that I could make the eight-hour round-trip drive to Washington, D.C. for my *first* visit to the Vietnam Memorial, and I took off south.

A little more than three hours later, I reached my destination. The number of names etched into the mirror-like black granite of the memorial was overwhelming. I downloaded an app that took me through the history of the memorial and the biographies of the names of the soldiers who had given their lives. I could not imagine what they had gone through as I read. I looked up my last name to see if I had any relatives among the 58,318 names. I discovered a number of Baldwins that had given their lives. I went through all of them. The best that I could tell, though, not one was a relation.

The fire for this *first* was lit on January 19th when I binge watched the series *The Vietnam War*. My last visit to the capital was a grade school class trip, which was before the memorial existed.

While in D.C., I took the opportunity to take in the National Mall just adjacent to the memorial. I spent the most time at the Lincoln Memorial. I read Lincoln's Gettysburg Address etched into one of the walls of the memorial. The words are still relevant today. I stood on the steps of the memorial overlooking the reflection pool of the National Mall and thought deeply about those words.

P.S. – **Looking back:** *If you get a chance to go, do it.*

??? – Did you know that there is a misspelled word etched into the white marble of the Lincoln Memorial? Do you know what word it is?

If you don't know and curious, Google it. Being in the engraving business, I had to ask. It happens to the best of us.

. . .

CHAPTER TEN:
GETTING BACK TO NORMAL?

As we rolled into the fall things seemed to start to drift back to some sense of normalcy. It really didn't. It just started to feel that way coming off the chaos and madness we had just lived through since March. The nouns associated with the word normal (which are: standard, usual, typical, average, the rule, predictable, and par for the course) still don't apply almost a year later into 2021. Things were different due to the pandemic. We were adapting.

OCTOBER 2ND: ACQUIRED A COMPANY DUE TO COVID-19

I just got off the phone with the owner of a local trophy shop that was closing because of the pandemic. I had put out word locally to our distressed industry the previous month that we were here to help. We did a deal quickly to take over the accounts. We had acquired several companies over the years, but never in one day. This was my *first* acquisition due to COVID-19 during that crazy year. This was bittersweet. My heart broke for my industry and the good people in it. My industry had been hit very hard.

*P.S. – **Looking back:** A week later, I found myself traveling over Manhattan Bridge for the "first" time to pick up the remnants of another fallen competitor in New York City. The deceased 65-year-old owner had successfully been in the awards business for 35 years. He succumbed to COVID-19. My heart broke. We assisted the widow in packing up a man's life work and legacy. This demonstrates the distress in our industry, so tragic.*

??? – Did you lose anyone to the pandemic?

OCTOBER 12TH: WATCHED *COLLATERAL BEAUTY*

I got up at 4 a.m. and couldn't go back to sleep. I turned on the TV and happened on the movie *Collateral Beauty* starring Philly native Will Smith. I had caught pieces of this movie in the past, but never watched it in full to really get the point and moral of the plot. That morning I did. It touched me. Perhaps the current troubles of the world made the movie strike my core. Will Smith's character loses his eight-year-old daughter to cancer? This resulted in his withdrawal from the world, as well as depression, divorce, and issues at work. He had become catatonic.

So, despite the business being in danger and the world gone mad around me, I was reminded of what was important. With everyone tense, anxious, angry, depressed, and fearful of the unknown, including their jobs and their lives, due to the virus, the movie highlighted how we must look and find the collateral beauty around us. *Collateral Beauty* highlights the three characters of life:

- **Death**, which is inevitable (no one is getting out of here alive), is not to be feared.
- **Time**, which is all we have in this life. Use it well. Live it and don't waste it. That year of *firsts* highlighted this fact for me. Life is too short.
- **Love**, is what it is all about. Love of others. Love of yourself.

I had goose bumps as the movie ended, and I realized that was what I had to continue to do. I know it was only a movie and these were not new ideas. But it was something I had to keep re-learning all over again from time to time. This may have been a stretch for my *first* that day, but it was the *first* time I watched *Collateral Beauty* from start to finish which helped provide clarity.

*P.S. – **Looking back:** Since I was expending so much energy in doing what I was doing, I was always looking for opportunities to refuel. Mornings like those filled me up.*

??? – Have you been inspired by a movie? If so, which one? Do you look for the Collateral Beauty in your life?

OCTOBER 16TH: RENT ABATEMENT

It was the *first* time in my life that I ever asked for, received, and accepted a rent abatement for one of our business locations — humbled and grateful. I wrote the owner of the Center City high-profile office building that one of our showrooms occupies.

I pleaded my case. We had been a low-maintenance, good-paying tenant for over 30 years. We had continued to pay our monthly obligations, in full, since the COVID-19 mess started in March, despite the business's hardships, and despite the closure of the location due to the pandemic and civil unrest in Center City.

We had been in business for over 90 years, since 1929, and I had been there for 45 of them. That was the *first* time I wrote a letter or an email asking for rent abatement.

*P.S. – **Looking back:** We have since graciously received an extension to this abatement which was a percentage of the rent. We continue to pay rent at the reduced rate despite not opening the doors. For the foreseeable future, we meet customers there by appointment only.*

??? – Have you ever had to humble yourself and ask for help? Have you had to ask for a handout to get by?

<u>OCTOBER 20TH</u>: MAIL-IN VOTE FOR PRESIDENT

(Unedited email entry)

...For the *first* time in my life I voted by mail today. This year of the pandemic has introduced this reality to me and many others. Mail-in voting had never crossed my mind before. I had always assumed I would head to the voting booth on November 3rd in person, as I had always done, to place my vote. Seniors would normally man the voting booths in our area. With COVID they did not want to expose them. I got it.

I received the mail-in ballot a week or so ago and read every instruction. I knew who I was going to vote for. I had made up my mind a little while ago. I consider myself apolitical and vote for the best person to lead and do the job. Sometimes that is a Republican, sometimes Democrat. This year the division seemed wider than ever. The sides were more contentious than ever in my lifetime. Honestly, I am disappointed in both "sides." There are so many challenges that need to be solved. The two parties need to get together to solve them and not just focus on selfishly getting themselves elected or re-elected, while creating a great divide. There seems to be no room for civil debate. Facts and reality are being distorted. Those alternate realities play out every day on either CNN or Fox. I watch fifteen minutes of each every day, and try to decide on my own. I don't take either as gospel. Is it mask or no mask? White supremacy or Antifa? Is Climate change real or not? Is the world flat or round? Pro-life or Pro-choice? I observe and try to live my core values that I practice in running my company: respect, integrity, fun, learn, win-win, dependability, hustle, smarter (not harder), and find a way to say yes to make a goal happen. I try to live by what is "fair and reasonable" with common sense. I have learned in business and in life there are three sides to a story: one side, the other side, and the truth usually somewhere in the middle. But what do I know? I thought I lived in the UNITED States? Recently I'm scared that we are more divided than any time since the Civil War. Compassion and understanding seem to have taken a vacation. Sad. I recently traveled to Gettysburg and experienced what a division like that produced. I'm afraid for our country despite who wins between President Trump and Vice President Biden. I hope and pray that we get through this time together, for the betterment of all.

I signed and sealed the election envelope. The drop-off point is 1.4 miles away at the local municipal building. I drove to the county Board of Elections to personally verify I had filled out my ballot correctly. I wanted to personally hand in my ballot for my *first*. I filled it out correctly! In handing it in I had to show my driver's license, which they checked against the ballot. It matched. Then I had to sign a piece of paper verifying I dropped off the ballot. I had to keep the inexpensive Bic pen I signed this with, due to COVID. Crazy times! I said a prayer for us as I walked out!

*P.S. – **Looking back:** I guess I was afraid of what would happen in January 2021?*

??? – Do you take the time to vote?

<u>OCTOBER 22ND</u>: SKYLINE DRIVE, VIRGINIA

Instead of lemonade from lemons, we made beautiful southern fall scenery and beaches out of pyramids, ancient temples, and the desert. My traveling group of five couples had planned another "trip of a lifetime" that was supposed to be on that day. We had booked a river cruise down the Nile River in Egypt to see the pyramids and ride a camel, with a side trip to Jerusalem. They were 12 days of *firsts* that I lined up that were not to be and had to be replaced.

Instead, my wife and the other couples that were to travel with us turned a flight overseas to the Middle East on an airplane into a rented van to drive south to visit Asheville, North Carolina, and then onto the beaches of Isle of Palms in South Carolina. On the way to Asheville, we traveled the breathtaking Skyline Drive through Virginia while stopping for a challenging hike to Dark River Falls, both *firsts*. It was fall, the perfect time to view the change of seasons and the palette of colors that nature paints at that time of year. The varying shades of yellows, oranges, reds, purples, and browns were spectacular on a beautiful, clear day. I wanted to pull over at every opening to fill my camera with the sights. Fortunately, my wife would not allow me to stop at every turn; I think I negotiated every fourth one. Skyline Drive is a perfect description of the winding road at the skyline of Shenandoah National Park along the Blue Ridge Mountains. We ended our day at sunset with a short hike on the actual Appalachian Trail. We had made lemonade out of the day and drank it all in.

*P.S. – **Looking back:** I made a photo book of the trip for each one of the travelers to view our shared memories. I pick it up every so often to page through and smile. Creating photo books for family and friends is a habit and passion of mine to document our travels.*

OCTOBER 23RD: BLUE RIDGE PARKWAY

The Blue Ridge Parkway was a continuation of the beauty of the day before as we drove through the Blue Ridge Mountains. I have picture after picture to prove it. The roads were windier. We had used this as the halfway point for the 10-hour trip to Asheville.

Besides the Blue Ridge Parkway, the day was chock full of *firsts*. We hiked Cascades Falls and Linville Falls before arriving at our destination of the aptly named Skytop Chalet at the top of Black Mountain outside of Asheville. All wonderful *firsts!*

*P.S. – **Looking back:** The Skytop Chalet had everything for vacation therapy to enjoy with friends — seclusion, views, hot tub, grill, fire pit, and more space than we needed. We each had our own floor. We supplied the friendship, food, and games. We played Code Names late into the night with glasses of wine in hand and lots of laughs for the next three nights. Did I mention it was the first time I played Code Names? Perfect!*

OCTOBER 24TH: STARGAZING APP

At 4:30 a.m., I grabbed my coffee and Googled "what is the best app for stargazing?" My friends had a conversation about this the night before as we reclined on the back porch overlooking the valley with the stars starting magically appearing out of the darkness. The app could apparently recognize the various stars in the sky by pointing your mobile phone at the location.

I loaded the SkyView app and walked outside into the abyss. I could not see in front of me. I headed up the road, at a steep angle, with assistance of my cell phone flashlight. After a few hundred feet, I was at the top of Black Mountain, North Carolina on vacation. I tilted my head skyward — it was incredible. The sky was covered with countless dots of light. I started to use the app to make sense of it all. As I scanned the sky, the constellation of Orion appeared on my screen. I had heard of it before. That was the *first* time I located it by identifying the three stars that make up the belt. *Thank you app!*

I then pointed the phone toward the brightest star in the sky. I never knew it was Sirius. The app provided detailed information. The app also identified the International Space Station as it traveled across the sky. That was very, very cool. I spent the next hour pointing and identifying stars for so many *firsts*.

*P.S. – **Looking back:** I came to learn through the app that Orion is located on the celestial equator and was named after a Greek mythological hunter. Again, I wouldn't have taken the initiative to do this without looking for something new to experience every day. My quest got me off my ass and into the sky.*

??? – Do you know the names of the three stars on Orion's belt?

OCTOBER 28TH: ISLE OF PALMS SUNRISE

It was 6:30 a.m. and I was sitting in a beach chair at the water's edge waiting for the sun to rise over the Isle of Palms in South Carolina on a picture-perfect morning. Just as the sun began to rise, I clicked away on my Canon EOS Rebel camera. The half-hour that followed provided a kaleidoscope of ever-changing colors. At *first* it started as soulful burnt oranges and dark grays, which proceeded to shades of deep purples with orange and light blue highlights. The sun hid behind a fortress of clouds protecting the horizon as it rose, producing a new mix of oranges, pinks, and blues. It was magical as the final transformation to bright yellows and gold against a crisp blue background with a smattering of pillow-like clouds concluded the show. It was inspirational and fulfilling.

I posted a number of the sunrise pictures from this magical morning on my Facebook page with the caption, "Sitting in a beach chair, on the Isle of Palms, camera in hand, watching the sunrise, talking business with my buddy, Charlie. Multi-tasking." One of these pictures ended up as the photo on the front cover of this book.

Later in the day, we took a carriage ride through historic Charleston led by Buddy the horse with our guide Dennis, an ex-preacher. After the must-see ride, we ate lunch on a pier where I had a blackened Tigerfish sandwich for the *first* time. It was a perfect day of multiple *firsts*!

P.S. – Looking back: Each sunrise is unique like a snowflake. Each day is unique in the same way with a first *to be lived for the* first *time in your life.*

??? – When was the last time you took in a sunrise?

OCTOBER 29TH:
LYING NEXT TO A LIVE ALLIGATOR ON A GOLF COURSE

On the ninth tee box of the Links course of Wild Dunes in South Carolina we ran into a twelve-foot alligator resting on the banks of the lake that the course weaved around. As I stepped up to the tee box, I got a brilliant (stupid) idea. This would be the *first* time, and last, I would lay down next to an alligator, who happened to be about ten feet away. I would do almost anything for a *first*. I proceeded to stretch out next to my resting, green-textured friend with big teeth while my other two-legged friends snapped away to capture the moment on their iPhones.

Later in the hole, which was a par 5, my ball came to rest on the very edge of the body of water that we had found the alligator in on the tee box. The only way to get a club on the ball to hit it was to take my shoes and socks off to stand in this alligator infested waters. I did. I believe this is the *first* time I had ever done that also. Two firsts in one hole. Or two reasons to question my IQ or sanity? I'm not the smartest author you have read.

*P.S. – **Looking back:** I did have a plan if the gator got agitated and approached me. I knew I could outrun at least one of the older gimpy-kneed friends in my foursome. Survival of the fittest. I am kidding.*

??? – Would you have taken a rest next to the gator on a dare or for a first?

NOVEMBER 2ND: SMOKE A CIGARETTE

This may be hard to believe, but I *NEVER* smoked a tobacco cigarette, not even a puff. I never bought a pack, either. Today, I did both. I purchased a pack at the local convenience store, shocked by the cost. *WOW – EXPENSIVE!* They were close to ten dollars a pack. I knew of the additional healthcare costs because of smoking from being an employer. I had no idea how much for an individual pack people spent daily to support this unhealthy habit.

I never smoked cigarettes because in my youth; I had a front row seat watching what smoking did to my father. He passed away from lung cancer. He had smoked three-plus packs of unfiltered smokes a day, beginning in his early teens. As a kid, I tried to get him to stop — throwing them away or pouring water on them. He was not a fan of my unsuccessful efforts. I eventually stopped trying and vowed never to smoke cigarettes — and I didn't, until today.

As I walked to my car after work, I pulled a smoke out of the pack I purchased and lit up in the parking lot. Yuck. I finished the cigarette. My mouth tasted like I'd licked an ashtray. I smelled of smoke when I entered my car. Just one and I was done. Never say never, but I am sure that I'll never have a cigarette again. I find no reason, between the cost, the health issues, the smell, the taste, and so on. I don't get it. I am not "cool," and at my advanced age I don't need to be.

*P.S. – **Looking back:** I'm thankful I never picked up this habit. My father quit cold turkey in his late forties. He told me more than once he would not have lasted as long as he had if he hadn't quit when he did.*

??? – If you smoke cigarettes — why? I could ask myself a similar question concerning my overeating – why?

NOVEMBER 3RD: ACUPUNCTURE

I woke up today and realized it was November and I was starting to run out of days. I would have to be more committed to planning if I was to complete a number of my planned *firsts*. I revisited my open list and selected *acupuncture*. I then Googled "acupuncture near me." I called and booked an appointment for 4 p.m. at $80 for my *first* treatment.

I showed up at the small neighborhood strip mall that contained the minimalistic office. There was a list of massages available in addition to the acupuncture…hmm. The hallway had three rooms on either side, with drapes in front of each doorway instead of an actual door. The decor had an Asian flavor. There were a few books in Chinese for reading material in the modest waiting room of four seats and the doctor's desk. I filled out the new patient paperwork and then was directed to Room #2. I walked through the draped doorway and was followed by the doctor who asked, "What do you need worked on?"

"My neck," I responded, and went on to describe the occasional stiffness and discomfort in my neck. He assured me that he could help. I shared the reason for my visit, my *first*. He proceeded to ask me a bunch of medical questions. "Do you have any medical conditions? Heart? Diabetes? High blood pressure?"

I replied "no" to all. He instructed me to take off my shirt and lay face down on the massage table. As the doctor started, I could smell the alcohol he swabbed on my neck. He slightly tapped the acupuncture needles to insert them into my body. I counted 14 needles that he placed on both sides of my neck and upper spine. He turned on a timer for 30 minutes and out he went. I took deep breaths and tried to relax as soothing Chinese music played in the background.

The doctor returned to check on me. He commented that I should experience a warming feeling in the areas where he placed the needles, which occurs from increased blood flow caused by the procedure. I said I felt it to be polite, but I really wasn't sure.

The timer went off and out came the needles and he asked, "Full body or just a neck massage." I selected the neck to be cautious. In walked my masseuse who I could not see. Looking down through the hole in the massage table, I could see small female sneakers. She proceeded to work on my neck for the next 15 minutes. Occasionally, she'd ask if she was applying too much pressure; she wasn't.

I was informed that acupuncture is not a "one and done" cure. Permanent, long-lasting results required continued treatment. "Another appointment?" They were looking for repeat business. I might have said yes if I was in debilitating pain and searching for answers, but I wasn't, so I politely declined. It was an experience.

*P.S. – **Looking back:** I now wonder if that acupuncture doctor's office also doubled as a "massage" parlor!*

NOVEMBER 5TH: VIRTUAL COOKING CLASS

The pandemic produced many *firsts* for many of us as we adapted our lives to conform to isolation. Caterers were also adapting to survive by trying many *firsts*, including virtual cooking classes. These new realities collided that night as I participated in my *first* virtual cooking class.

I had signed up to participate weeks before with one of my business relationship groups to support my friend in the catering business. She was supplying the food and instruction for this *first*. The prepackaged and measured out food supplies in a thermal, insulated bag were delivered to my house a few days prior. The Zoom class was to start at 6 p.m. I arrived home about a half-hour early to lay out and stage the ingredients, along with setting up my cell phone for Zoom. I opened a bottle of wine and was ready.

Each meal kit provided dinner for two. The menu consisted of candied Walnuts and Roasted Pears over Kale & Spinach, Heritage Barley Risotto, Oven-Roasted Chicken Breast, English Peas, Baby Carrots and Sautéed Cauliflower. The class was a little fast at the start. The 30 people virtually participating scrambled a bit at the beginning to keep up with the chef as she led us. The chef started with the candied, spiced walnuts and continued for the next hour and a half to our conclusion.

For me, who had fashioned myself as a self-taught gourmet cook many moons ago, it brought back memories of being in the kitchen. It was fun! When I was finished, I made two plates. I took one up to my wife to serve her dinner in bed. I *loved* the risotto, which took a little extra time to get al dente and required more liquid to stir in than was provided. But I figured it out and it was worth it. A delicious and fun pandemic-inspired *first*.

P.S. – Looking back: If you would like to view this class and experience the tastes by recreating this dinner you can view it on YouTube by searching "BCA Virtual Cooking in November."

??? – What did you do to socialize during the pandemic shutdown? Did you learn how to cook virtually?

NOVEMBER 6TH: DISC GOLF

I was both curious and excited as I drove an hour and a half through rush hour traffic for my 8 a.m. tee time for my *first* round of disc golf. This *first* emanated from a conversation with Ryan who is an avid disc golfer. He wanted to help me achieve a *first* and extended an invitation to join his five-some. It was a blue-skied morning. The 18-hole disc golf course was located at Kerr Park in Downingtown, Pennsylvania, which was free and open to the public. I didn't know that an 18-hole Disc Golf course existed. It was first come, first serve, with no one on the course when we arrived. My friend supplied the three discs needed to play. One was a "driver," which was the lightest disc designed to go far. The second disc was a "mid-range" disc. The third was a "putter." The putter was a larger and heavier disc meant to be more stable and to fly straighter for shorter distances. When I first heard the term *disc golf* I ignorantly assumed it was just throwing a Frisbee to a spot. Nope. I soon discovered that it was much more sophisticated and harder than I could have imagined.

The first tee had a 4-foot by 8-foot rectangle slab of cement "tee box" to throw your disc from. I was the only novice in the group. The others had played at least once before. My friend played all the time and was good. He could get distance, as he demonstrated when he led us off with a drive more than halfway to the hole. I stepped up onto the *first* tee with confidence. It was a par 3, 325 feet away in a wide-open field with a few trees to the right. The chain-linked basket on a metal pole off in the distance served as our target and *hole*. I considered myself a very good Frisbee thrower from my beach days. How hard could it be? With the driver disc in hand, I tried to emulate my friend. Flinging my driver as I would a normal Frisbee resulted in a severe slice into the ground less than 50 feet in front of us. Uh-oh! I picked it up for my second shot, another catastrophic result. Yikes! My confidence quickly evaporated. This was different. This calamity continued until I finally made it into the hole for a humbling double par 6. Not good or what I expected of myself. This ugly pattern persisted for a few holes. I could not throw the smaller and lighter driver disc straight or level to get any distance. I finally resigned myself to playing "old man golf," using my putter disc to tee off. I slowly progressed to using my mid-range disc off the tee later in the round. It was a humbling experience.

Most of the holes were 300 to 400-feet par 3s — there were no par 5s. On the short 300-foot par 3, hole #7, I achieved my *first* disc golf par. The hole was a dogleg left through heavy woods. I threw a perfect mid-range straight shot, threading the needle by cutting the corner of the woods. It gave me a good look at my targeted chain-linked metal basket. I made another similar mid-range disc throw to within 15 feet of the hole. I took out my putter disc, lined it up, and threw it. Bang! It hit the dangling chains. My disc fell into the basket. I had my *first* par.

The course ran next to a large, fast-flowing creek, through woods and open fields that we had to traverse. I parred one additional short par 3 on the back 9 for my only other par of the day. The round took about an hour and half to play. It was a very cool and fun *first*!

P.S. – Looking back: I'd love to go to the driving range so to speak, to work on my drives before I play again. You need good distance on your drives to have a consistent go at par or an occasional birdie.

??? – Have you ever played disc golf? Did you know that there were different discs for different distances and shots?

NOVEMBER 10TH: MULTIPLE STAFF TEST POSITIVE FOR COVID-19

That day was the *first* time that two of my partners tested positive for the Coronavirus. An unusual *first* that was not on my to-do lists at the beginning of the year. Others were awaiting test results. I was just notified that CVS's national testing was shut down due to computer issues. Another employee left not feeling good and was going to get tested. All the test sites were out of vaccines. Another employee, one of our sales reps, was home not feeling while awaiting test results from a few days prior. Crazy or what?

P.S. – Looking back: This apparently was the infamous "second wave" of the pandemic and we were engulfed by it as it spread. Fortunately, none of those that tested positive resulted in a trip to the hospital, although a few had a rough go of it for a while. Three out of the five on our executive team (controller, sales manager, and operations manager) tested positive for COVID-19 that week. I was feeling lonely at work. Everyone was either sick or home quarantining.

NOVEMBER 16TH: VISIT MY GRANDPARENTS' GRAVESITE

I don't know why, but as I thought of a *first* for today, my mind drifted to visiting my grandparents Nan and Pop Baldwin's gravesites. It wasn't on my *first* list. I don't know where the idea came from, but I decided to just go with it. I had never been and was not sure where they were buried.

I texted my brother and asked, but he didn't know. His wife went online to the site www.findagrave.com and found Memorial Park, where they were laid to rest. My grandfather was born in 1905 and passed away in 1976. I called the cemetery office, and the person who answered agreed to take me out to the gravesite. The site was relatively close to work, so I took my lunch to visit. Off I went by myself to Nan and Pop Baldwin's gravesites for the *first* time.

I walked out the front door of the Memorial Park office and followed my guide to the second row of tombstones directly outside the door to the left. One "Baldwin" stone marked the gravesite of my cousin. He had been a police officer that I looked up to as a kid, who tragically took his own life. I never knew he was buried a few gravesites down from our grandparents. Several of my aunts, uncles, and cousins on Nan's side were also there. I wondered why I didn't know this. Had I known it at one point early in my life and simply forgotten?

It was a brisk, sunny, late afternoon autumn day. I soaked up the surroundings as I stood in front of my grandparents' graves. I sprinkled a few of my father's ashes on their gravesite from the vial I carried in my golf bag in my trunk. It just felt right.

P.S. – Looking back: This meant so much to me that I visited my maternal grandparents' gravesites on November 27th for the "first" time — the Twiss family.

??? – Have you ever awoken with thoughts and wondered where they came from? Did you spontaneously act on them?

NOVEMBER 17TH: CALL WITH WARREN BUFFETT

I was on a Zoom call live with Warren Buffett this afternoon. I received this very cool *first* as an alumnus of the Goldman Sachs 10,000 Small Business program. I loved his down-home, human approach to life and business. His little truisms were the best. In learning to overcome his extreme fear of communicating his ideas in front of people, he took the Dale Carnegie course. I had done the same early in my career for the same reason. He then imparted his wisdom, "If you do not learn to communicate with people it's like winking at a girl in the dark — it will not matter, she won't see you." Another beautiful thing was his talking about being a little conservative with your money. He advocated having a little reserve (cash) for a rainy day. He relayed, "Only when the tide goes out is when you see who has been swimming naked." With a sly wit, he shared that the government had supplied a lot of bathing suits (PPP loans) in the last year.

When asked, "How do you find good people for your organization?" Mr. Buffet replied, "I never have looked at a resume. I like to talk to people."

Another pearl of wisdom was about learning and reading. He shared, "You can get to know Ben Franklin, or anyone else by picking up a book and reading about them." He proclaimed that knowledge is "Something no one can take away from you or tax — it is yours." He also commented, "The earlier the better," as far as reading to gain knowledge.

He started the talk by saying that our country is a "country of tail-winds, but we are currently facing a headwind like no other – a hurricane." He added that he wished he was born *now* and, in this country, because the tailwind that will follow will be great, eventually over time. He told about the first stock he purchased in March of 1942 during World War II, when there was a headwind. He bought it when the Dow hit $100 and now it is at $30,000. The same will happen in the future, over time, was his point. His position was that there is opportunity in the chaos!

PRICELESS – I had to share. These were the moments that picked me up off the mat and got me back in the ring to fight!

P.S. – **Looking back:** *I appreciated and admired the way Mr. Buffet lives his life humbly, grounded without pretense. I find his homespun wisdom and the way he dishes it out timeless.*

??? – Have you ever had the opportunity to meet one of your personal heroes? Were they everything you hoped they would be?

NOVEMBER 20TH: PLAYED HOOKY FROM WORK TO PLAY WITH GRANDSON

As my daughter began returning to work as a sixth-grade teacher, my wife went back to babysitting our grandson one day a week. We had watched him a few times earlier in the year pre-pandemic before he was mobile. My fifteen-month-old grandson Luke was now walking, animated and jabbering up a storm. My wife now travels to my daughter's house where he has all his toys. Prior to this he would be dropped off at our home. That day, she suggested I come over to assist her and play with him before work. I was never one to take the time like this to smell the roses, as they say. To me, for some reason it always seemed like I was cheating the business if I did things like this. I know that was crazy since I was the majority owner. It was a habit born out of over 45 years of driven and focused work. But that day for the *first* time I said, "Yes."

I hustled and got there by 7:30 a.m. He was in his highchair eating breakfast — eggs with broccoli, better known as *eggies*. He was all smiles, as always. He was stuffing handfuls in with his right fist, pausing at times to look at me grinning, with an occasional laugh. As he wound down, he started to perform. First it was: *SO BIG* – his tiny hands above his head, grinning and then laughing as I copied his actions. Then he'd clap and laugh as I imitated him. He was done and released from his chair. As his feet hit the ground, he was off to the living room, to his corner containing his toys. I joined in and we were off going through all his toys. First, it was spinning the wheels of a few vehicles. Next were his books. We laughed at the peek-a-boo book. We pointed at the lit stars in another book. The animal book made noises. We growled like a bear and roared like a lion. So much fun! We ended with the helium balloon left over from my wife's birthday party the week before. I would bring it slowly down until it was within arm's reach. He grabbed it and wrestled it, then let it go to drift to the ceiling as I cried out "*BALLLOOOOOON!*" It was step and repeat for at least 20 more times until he walked away. Then, it was time for me to get to work. The hour and a half flew by. He was rubbing his eyes signaling that it was time for his morning nap. As I left, he had one more trick up his sleeve. He started to blow me kisses – placing his hand over his mouth. I blew kisses back as the door shut behind me. It was the *first* time that I played "hooky" with my grandson. It won't be the last!

P.S. – *Looking back:* *This* first *started back on January 24th when I read to my* first *grandson for the* first *time. Having a* first *grandson fortunately provided the opportunity for many firsts. I have a new job — "Grumpa," my new handle as a* first*-time grandfather. Friday mornings are now the designated day my wife and I are responsible for his day care. I hold down the fort on the very early shift until my wife, alias Nini, awakes to take over watching our* first *grandson. Nini doesn't do mornings!*

Those Fridays have now turned into "Thursdays with Luke" as I write this in 2021. I now share these precious Thursdays with my grandson, as he experiences his own firsts. I post brief weekly videos of Thursday with Luke on Facebook of our time together to spread my joy. Luke's blonde hair, blue eyes, gorgeous face and infectious laugh are captivating. These posts are now in demand. Priceless!

As a recovering workaholic, I have used Thursdays in my rehabilitation to understand what is important in life. All kids want is your time and love. This may give me the title and content for my next book, if I ever get a chance — Thursdays with Luke — another book of firsts of sorts. It would be one seen through the fresh eyes of a child, Luke's firsts. I'm toying with the idea of something like Tuesdays with Morrie by Mitch Albom? Hmmmm.

??? – Do you make the time for things that are truly important in your life?

NOVEMBER 22ND: THE OPERA – *FALSTAFF* (VIRTUALLY)

As mentioned, I had purchased tickets for Madame Butterfly earlier in the year, but then the pandemic happened, the theatre shut down, and all performances were canceled until the next year. I donated the tickets back to the opera and wrote it off as a *first* casualty of 2020. My new speech coach, also an apparent opera devotee, spoke with reverence of Verdi and his last opera that he created at the age of 80, *Falstaff*. His passion for Verdi and *Falstaff* was contagious. A light bulb went off — YouTube!

I searched YouTube and found a 1-hour and 45-minute recorded performance from January of this year in Italy at the Teatro Minicipale Di Piacenza. It was in Italian with Italian subtitles. My search for a performance with English subtitles was fruitless. In order to have any clue as to what I was about to watch, I Googled "Falstaff." I then did my due diligence and read about the origins (a Shakespeare play), the plot, and the three acts for a few hours. I was ready.

It was Sunday and I had a 9:30 a.m. tee time, so I watched the *first* act prior to golf. I took in the second act after golf as I sat on a bench, iPhone in hand, at the edge of the Delaware River with a view of the Philadelphia skyline. After the Eagles game, I sat on the couch and watched the third act before dinner. I doubt Verdi had this type of viewing of his art in mind when creating it.

Even though I obviously didn't understand a word that was sung, I suspended my expectations and told myself to just take it in. I did. I felt the emotion. I got the drift of the goings on from my research. I absorbed the music. The plot revolved around the foiled, sometimes farcical, efforts of the fat knight Sir John Falstaff, to seduce two married women to gain access to their husbands' wealth.

I was proud for being persistent and creative and resurrecting this dead *first* to accomplish and experience an opera.

*P.S. – **Looking back:** I am still going to try and see a live opera once we are able to. Hopefully* Madame Butterfly. *I was inspired.*

??? – Did you know that the expression "He who laughs best, laughs last," is from Falstaff?

This is the message that comes at the end. Falstaff leads the whole company in telling the audience that man is born a fool, we're all deceived about who we are, and we're all taking ourselves too seriously. He tells us we need to lighten up because "the man who laughs last laughs best." Falstaff was deceived and made a fool of but laughs it off by singing these words in Italian with the cast as the curtain falls.

NOVEMBER 24TH: COVID-19 TEST – FOUR-HOUR LINE

I started quarantining for the *first* time the day before due to possible exposure. I traveled to a local COVID-19 test site at a Rowan University college campus for my *first* official COVID-19 test. I had tested myself a few times unofficially as a guinea pig with the fast test we were looking to distribute. When I arrived at the testing site, the line of people was literally a mile long, wrapping around and through the campus.

During the next four hours, as we zigzagged our way through the campus toward the testing center, my phone ran out of juice. I had been trying to complete my assigned reading from my *first* speech coach, the *TED Talk* book. I spent the next hour and a half speaking to and getting to know the two women in line in front of me through masks and at a distance. One was a very well preserved and good-looking grandmother of four and the other a horse breeder, with a passion for her four-legged friends.

I finished my test, which was a saliva test, at 1:55 p.m. I was told that I'd be notified of the results by email within 24 hours.

*P.S. – **Looking back:** I never did receive the emailed test results. Of course! I have no idea what happened with the results. I tried to contact the testing center without success. Maybe they typed in the wrong text number? I ended up quarantining for the required time anyway despite not having any symptoms. That was also the first time I had ever waited in a four-hour line for anything.*

NOVEMBER 26TH:
COMMUNICATED THANKSGIVING GRATITUDE AND LOVE

I have occasionally emailed a friend or family member to let them know how much I appreciate them. I never did this as a collective on Thanksgiving, so I decided to text my family and many friends from all parts of my life. I emailed my golf, industry, and numerous relationship and networking groups. I'll spare you the numerous text messages sent and just provide you a synopsis. I thanked them all for their years of friendship and love. I showed appreciation for the relationships, shared knowledge, and for the support provided throughout the years. Especially through a very challenging 2020. I was grateful as I wished them each a Happy Thanksgiving with much love.

I did all this early in the morning at 5 a.m. so they awoke to my messages of how I felt about each of them. Hopefully I put a smile on their faces in a very challenging year. This put things in perspective. Despite all the heartache, there was still much to be thankful for; I am. A rewarding *first*.

P.S. – *Looking back:* *Thankful!*

??? – Have you taken the time recently to tell your friends and family how thankful you are to have them in your life?

. . .

CHAPTER ELEVEN:
LESSONS LEARNED

This past leap year had impacted me. It changed me in some way. It made me appreciate what was important in life. It gave me insight. It put things in perspective. It reaffirmed things I already knew, but often lost sight of. The following *firsts* demonstrate some of these gained or rediscovered insights during that challenging journey.

DECEMBER 3RD: BIRDING

It was like rush hour at Chicago's O'Hare International Airport. Busy, with different birds coming and going in a flurry of activity: mourning doves, northern cardinals, purple finches, tufted titmice, European starlings, downy woodpeckers, black-capped chickadees, and a pine siskin. I wasn't at O'Hare; I was 20 feet from the bird feeder, with binoculars in hand, at the John James Audubon Center at Mill Grove in Pennsylvania. I knew the place well. Since it was the location of my daughter's wedding, it brought back memories. I was drawn to this spot that morning for my *first* experience in legitimate birdwatching. My guide and host Chris is an avid birder since his youth who would call out the birds as they flew in. I was impressed and could clearly see the different species. As I peppered him with questions, he introduced me to the Audubon app, which showed the birds. The app also played their different chirp sounds. I downloaded the app — another *first*. The *first* bird I "officially" watched was a dove. We viewed it as we wandered down the path by a few cages of owls (great horned owl, barred owl, and eastern search owl) and a broad-winged hawk on our way to the feeder. I'm not quite sure why these owls were caged since this was not a zoo?

My friend's love and vast knowledge of birding came from his mother. He sentimentally shared that his mom would stand in their yard with outstretched arms, birdseed in hand. She literally had the birds eating out of the palms of her hands — a human bird feeder. Interacting with the birds and identifying them formed their special bond. I could feel his emotion as he relayed the story. I had a similar bond with my father and golf.

My bird-watching friend was hosting a Cigar & Whiskey night and invited me to celebrate my birding *first* with this second *first*. I had never participated in an official Cigar & Whiskey tasting. I was in. While at the tasting, I took in a combined tasting of *firsts*. I lit cigars named Puro Dominicana and Arturo Fuente while sipping Uncle Nearest Tennessee whiskey, Wyoming whiskey, and a Glenmorangie 10-year single malt Scotch whiskey for the *first* time. A big day of *firsts*!

P.S. – Looking back: *This opportunity presented itself as I was experiencing an earlier* first, *playing disc golf, a month earlier. During the conversation that day, they asked me about my year of* firsts. *One of the players asked if I had ever bird-watched (officially). Never having bird-watched initiated the invite from an avid birder. Suggestions by friends provided a number of opportunities for* firsts *throughout the year. This was a cool by-product of these* firsts; *sharing of these experiences deepened my knowledge of many things and also deepened my relationships with a number of people. We shared time and I grew.*

Who names these birds? Tufted titmouse? I want to hang out with this person, or drink what they were imbibing at the time. I had to find out, so I Googled it. It was the first *time I ever Googled "who named the tufted titmouse?" I couldn't find who named the bird, but I did learn where the name came from. The name "titmouse" descends from two ancient Anglo-Saxon root words — "tit," from a word meaning something small, and "mouse," from a word applied to any small bird, as well as that little rodent. Aren't you glad I asked?*

??? – What activity creates an emotional bond of shared time with your friends, parents, and children?

DECEMBER 4TH: NITRILE (MEDICAL) GLOVE ORDER

This morning on my drive to work, I got a call from my partner. He informed me that we just received confirmation of our *first* ever nitrile glove order in our history! They were non-logoed medical gloves that would be used for the upcoming distribution of the vaccine. I had tears in my eyes when I received word. It was a large order, the largest in our history, again! We had lost more than half of our "traditional" sales and by all rights should be out of business. Somehow, we found a way to replace our lost sales with nontraditional PPE (Personal Protective Equipment) sales. We sold lots of masks, first blank, them logoed. We supplied face shields, hand sanitizer, hand-held thermometers, sanitary wipes, floor graphics for social distancing, sneeze guards, and now nitrile gloves. This just proved what I had believed all along. We were in the relationship business, not just the awards business. We were connecting the dots by supplying currently needed product to our many relationships in need. And half our staff was still taking unemployment calls for California and New York as part of a call center.

In writing those journal entries, I found that I mentioned my emotions or tears frequently. Please don't think of me as a cry baby. Maybe I am. I think it is tied more to passion. Sometimes I care too much. Having been raised in Philadelphia, I would witness Eagles coach Dick Vermeil's emotions overflow. I think I understand what he felt in those times. He cared about his players. He was passionate about them and the game. I knew that morning what this news could represent for my players in the game engulfing us — thus the emotion.

P.S. – Looking back: Little did I know at the time that supplying those gloves would become another odyssey of unthinkable twists and turns of strained logistics, container shortages, broken promises, product scarcity, and surging prices. The multiple bad actors in this new world had to be dodged and filtered out. Some companies took large deposits and disappeared. Some shipped sand, toilet paper, or less expensive products to fill the containers that were to be gloves. Some manufacturers took pre-payments to secure inventory, only to have the glove inventory sold to a higher bidder. This left distributors unable to fill committed-to orders. There were stories of container ships overloading causing containers to cascade off into the ocean to find their way to the bottom. There were cases of extortion to get containers loaded. There were many sleepless nights. In the end, we delivered these gloves in 2021. It was worth the trouble.

I forgot to mention that in order to fund those sales we had to take a temporary line of credit with our bank for twice what the company was worth. Like I said previously, there were a few sleepless nights.

??? – Have you had to create your own luck in tough times through hard work?

DECEMBER 5TH: SLEPT ON THE STREETS WITH THE HOMELESS

(Unedited journal entry)

... For some reason, I woke up this morning with a strange idea for a *first*: sleeping on the streets for a night with the homeless. I wanted to sleep on the streets as if I didn't have a home. I wanted to experience to understand. I had scheduled trap shooting this morning for the *first* time, but morning showers and bad weather postponed that until next week.

I grew up in my business on Race Street in Center City Philadelphia, near the homeless shelter where I had applied to volunteer to serve meals. I had targeted serving the homeless in a local soup kitchen, St. John's Hospice, as one of my *firsts* this year. The shelter denied me the opportunity to serve this year due to the second wave of the pandemic. I had dealt with the homeless constantly. They frequently lived on the steam grate in front of my old office. I had to ask them to move almost daily. So maybe this was what precipitated the thought? Or maybe it was the unemployment calls that my staff had been fielding? I heard the constant pain in the calls. One recent homeless caller (due to his job loss and difficulty in securing benefits) took his life while we attempted to assist. The news was showing the increasingly long food lines. In my interview with KYW News Radio, the reporter commented that he had done a piece on soup kitchens and how "regular" people who worked their whole lives now stood food lines. People like him and me. My heart bled. My current "why" and passion is to save jobs. I've become aware of the possible repercussions of not having one. The head of the Chamber of Commerce once said to me, "Save a Job, Save a Life." This stuck with me. It obviously was all around me and on my mind. I had written it on the easel in my office.

I was very familiar with the downtown area and the places the homeless congregated at night. I thought about it all day. With each passing hour, the experience of being homeless for a night was more and more intriguing, despite the possible risks. I wanted to understand the consequences of not having a job and losing one's home. I told my wife my thought. She obviously was concerned and not supportive. She questioned my sanity, and so did I. I get it. I wouldn't expect her to react any differently; it could be dangerous. She reminded me more than once of the potential peril and the many murders in the city that past year. She tried to talk me out of it numerous times, but I was steadfast. I can be hard-headed, stubborn, and not very smart. I kept wondering what it would be like.

I worked until 5:30 p.m. even though it was Saturday. I traveled home preparing myself mentally. I had not showered or shaved in preparation for the possibility that night. I layered myself in old torn pants, socks, and tops. I put on a beat-up knit cap. I grabbed a green trash bag. I stuffed it with an old torn sleeping bag and a tatty towel for my pillow. I looked homeless, although maybe a newly minted homeless person. My son also made a last attempt to talk me out of it. When he failed, he said he loved me and to be safe. I headed out toward downtown around 10 p.m. The temperature was slowly moving into the 30s with a slight breeze.

When I entered town, I cruised around for an hour, observing, looking for a spot to spend the night. I traveled up Callowhill and down Race

Street crisscrossing from 13th Street to 2nd Street. The concentration of homeless seemed to be around 5th and 6th Streets. There were mini-tent cities constructed under the highway overpasses. I spotted an opening in the fence between the overpasses on 6th Street, with a grassy knoll and some boulders for protection. There was one tent in the middle of the top of the knoll. I parked on Callowhill between 5th and 6th in order scout the neighborhood. I took a stroll around the block without my bag. I wanted to get the lay of the land. The one section of tents under the adjourning underpass seemed like everyone had already called it a night. There were a few people in front of the other condo-like tent section. They were reserved, catching a smoke together. They were polite and nodded their approval as I walked by. I was one of them. I walked up onto the grassy knoll and felt the ground. It was a little wet from the morning rain, but I thought I'd be okay if I placed the green trash bag under the sleeping bag to keep it dry. That was the spot! I walked back to the car for my trash bag with my bedding. I took my driver's license and a $20 bill and stuffed it in my right sock. I wanted some form of ID on me. I did not want to carry a wallet or anything of value. I placed my car key in my left sock. I was trying to take any precautions for any unknowns. I decided against bringing any weapons of any sort. I left the Swiss army knife in my car. I did take my cell phone as my one precaution. While at the car, I texted my wife my location as I promised, just in case something went awry. She was worried. I understood. I locked the car and was off on this uncertain adventure.

When I returned to the spot I picked to spend the night, it was midnight. I laid my sleeping bag over the green plastic trash bag between the rocks and got in. As I lay there gazing up at the half-moon and a few stars above I couldn't help but notice the constant noise of the highway. At first, it was distracting. Then, over time, it blended into the background. Occasionally, a car without a muffler disturbed the inconspicuous hum. There was dim light from the many streetlamps across the street. I found myself frequently checking my surroundings and listening for anyone approaching, but no one did. That didn't quell the occasional check with one eye open. At 1 a.m., it was time to try to catch some shut eye.

Somehow, I fell asleep, but not deeply. The increasing cold would wake me up with a nudge of a breeze. I could feel the cold come in through the zipper of the sleeping bag. The cold was incessant and seemed to grow like a fungus. I found myself moving the placement of my body every so often to give the part of my body I was laying on relief from the hard ground. Occasionally, I would look at my cell phone that I had tucked away in my pants to see the time — 2:30 a.m. ... 3:45 a.m. ... time seemed to stand still. I wondered how anyone could do this night in and night out, for weeks, months, and sadly, years. I was struggling with just hours. Where would I go if I had to go to the bathroom? Where would I shower? How often could I shower? How and where would I get food? How do they do this? How do you ever get out from under this? How do you get a foot-hold back into society — is it even possible? The homeless must "work the problem" EVERY DAY just to survive. They must be resilient, resourceful, brave, strong, and smart just to live without a home. So why and how did they get to this place? Did they lose their job? Did they lose a battle with drugs? Did they slip through the cracks of the mental health system? So many questions! With it being so late I had minimal interaction to ask or have conversations to obtain any answers. Other than head nods of acknowledgement to a few gathered outside their tents catching a smoke I did not have dialog. I was cautious and wasn't sure if starting conversations would be intrusive. I mimicked the behavior I observed and kept to myself.

I normally get up without an alarm around 5 a.m. every day. That day would be no different. I woke up at 4:45 a.m. It was time. I packed up to move out. The bottom half of my sleeping bag was soaked and partially frozen.

A memorable, humbling perspective-packed *first* as I slept with the homeless, unprotected, under the stars on the streets of Philadelphia on a biting winter's night. Wow. I survived unharmed, but somewhat changed from the experience. It provided me additional understanding and gratitude. It made me appreciate, more than ever, the roof over my head and the many things that come with it that I take for granted. I feel fortunate and blessed. I feel and empathize for the people I left behind on that street. I feel torn.

P.S. – Looking back: I think about that night often. I have come to appreciate what the homeless go through.

??? – Have you been homeless before? Do you know someone who is homeless? Have you been close to losing your home? What would you do? Can you imagine?

DECEMBER 7TH: ASSEMBLE BIKES FOR CHARITY

I traveled an hour and a half down the Atlantic City expressway late this afternoon from Philadelphia to my destination in Atlantic City for this *first*. I had signed up weeks ago as I had never volunteered before to assemble bikes for a good cause. In submitting my donation, which bought a few of these bikes, the opportunity to help assemble them presented itself. Due to COVID-19 restrictions, the charity needed assistance in unloading and assembling the bikes.

Putting a wrench in my hand can be dangerous. I'm not the most accomplished assembler. Luckily, the Annual Jaws Bike Drive to benefit the kids of the Boys & Girls Club of Atlantic City was staged well. I had signed up to be part of the assembly team to assist in putting together over 200 bikes to give at-risk youth the freedom that a bike brings. There were only a few other volunteers in this huge gymnasium. It made it easy to socially distance, yet we all wore masks anyway. The volunteers were a mixed bag of a few businesspeople and staff from the charity. I was directed to tighten and straighten the handlebars on the bikes after the assembly team stood up the bikes. From there, my responsibilities became lining the bikes up in a huge gymnasium while pairing them with the donated helmets and locks. They found something I could do.

When I left hours later, all 250 bikes were done, lined up, and staged for the next day's presentation — a satisfying *first*.

*P.S. – **Looking back:** I viewed the video of the kids walking through the door the next day to receive their "first" bike. The look of pure joy was everywhere. The namesake of the event, Mr. and Mrs. Jaworski were emotional in taking it all in. It made it all worthwhile.*

??? – Do you remember receiving your "first" bike? Do you remember the anticipation and the joy? What have you done to give back and make a difference? Can you do more?

DECEMBER 8TH: WATCH A MOVIE WITH SUBTITLES

The movie *Parasite* appeared on my radar when it won four Oscars at the Academy Awards in February. The four awards included Best Picture, Best Director, Best Original Screenplay, and Best International Feature Film, making it the *first* non-English language film with subtitles to win an Academy Award for Best Picture. How did a movie with subtitles win Best

Picture? My curiosity was piqued. Since I had never watched a movie with subtitles, I had added it to my list of *firsts*.

I didn't know anything about the movie, so I Googled it. Described as a South Korean black comedy thriller, it seemed to fit right in line with 2020. Of course, I had no idea what that meant, and my curiosity grew more.

For the next two hours and twelve minutes, I watched and followed the dialog by reading the subtitles. The movie is about a poor family that schemes and secures employment from a wealthy family to infiltrate their household by posing as unrelated, highly qualified individuals. The ending was a bizarre bloody mess. I thought the movie was good, and it held my interest... until the end. I could have done without the unhinged blood and guts.

*P.S. – **Looking back:** I would watch a subtitled movie again. It wasn't as hard to follow or uninteresting as my preconceived ideas had led me to believe. My perception of subtitled movies had changed.*

??? – Have you watched a movie with a subtitle?

DECEMBER 9TH: GUITAR LESSON

I have friends who have learned to play guitar later in life. They have taken it to the point where they occasionally play out. While watching them play, I simultaneously admire and envy them. I'd love to learn to play the guitar. I just never took the time to pick one up. They make it look easy. So, I thought I'd take my *first* guitar lesson to see what it was like. The previous extent of my attempting to play an instrument was a sole failed attempt at trumpet when I was eight.

Since our office building is the home to a few groups for rehearsals, there is always a guitar or two hanging around the building. After work, I ventured downstairs to grab one. I clicked on the site: www.theGreatCoursesPlus.com, and searched *guitar lessons*. I settled on "Guitar Basics: Play a Song in 60 Seconds." This video course touted: *"Discover how you can play a simple song on the guitar in just one minute. Then study the parts of the guitar, and how to hold the instrument. Play G and C major chords and review the classic bass line from the song you learned. Finally, practice your song, combining your bass line with a four-note melody."* I clicked on it — the *first* lesson was 31 minutes. I guess the instructor never had me as a student. I watched and attempted to follow the instructions.

As I went through the lesson, I tried to follow along with where to place my fingers on the frets to play a G, C, or D chord. It was a disaster. I looked deformed as I tried to get my fingers to land where they were supposed to be. The instructor went slowly, but it was not slow enough for me. I stopped and replayed a number of sections in the lesson. I did pick the guitar for the *first* time. I could do the I-IV-V progression! It was my one accomplishment, because it was so simple. In conclusion, I am NOT a natural when it comes to the guitar, but I tried.

P.S. – *Looking back:* I *know that like anything, if playing guitar became a written goal and I put in the time, I'd learn and maybe become passable. It is just not that important to me to dedicate and invest the many hours needed, especially since I can't carry a tune to save my life. I'm currently putting those hours into writing this book.*

??? – Did you use the spare time that COVID afforded us to learn to do something you had always wanted to do?

DECEMBER 11TH: WRITE A SONG (TWENTY-TWENTY)

I've always wanted to write a song, so it had been on my initial wish list of *firsts*. I finally got to it and wrote my *first* official song today. I'm not saying it is a good song. I sent it to my musically gifted partner to see if he could put a tune to my words. His band, the Warehouse Winos, is one of the groups who rehearse in our warehouse.

My process was to list all the events of the year, which I did below. The list was part of the letter I wrote to my employees for my annual holiday message to the staff. Once I had the list, I started putting lines together, trying to turn a phrase and have them rhyme. I also wanted to capture this unique and unforgettable year of *firsts* for many of us. *First* time we have lived through a pandemic as one example. Hopefully I captured it? If not, oh well, at least I had my *first* for the day.

A song for Twenty-Twenty

Twenty-twenty pandemic like '18

... Hundreds of thousands no longer seen

Twenty-twenty depression like '29

... Businesses closed, unemployment & food lines

Chorus:

We're in this together

United we stand

We're in this together

With love to lend a hand

Twenty-twenty social unrest like the '60s

... Black Lives Matter, protests & uncertainties

Twenty-twenty an election we had

... Brought back thoughts of our Civil War years, so sad

CHORUS....

Twenty-twenty survived generations in a year

... I don't know where to start, many tears

Twenty-twenty dark went Broadway

... No history or playbook to find our way.

CHORUS...

Twenty-twenty produced shortages of PPE

... Hello from a distance and Quarantine

Twenty-twenty are you kidding me?

... a world placed on pause, went virtual to see

CHORUS....

CHORUS...

P.S. – Looking back: *Bob Dylan has nothing to worry about. Where is my Lennon to my McCartney? My Keith Richards to my Jagger? My Carole King to my Gerry Goffin?*

??? – Have you written a song or a poem?

DECEMBER 12TH: FREE-FORM WATERCOLOR PAINTING

(Unedited journal entry)

... I had taught myself watercolor (poorly) many years ago. With the exception of my live model drawing experience earlier in the year, the last time I picked up my watercolors was over 20 years ago. I itched to pick it up again at some point but was honestly afraid to do so. Afraid that I was not good enough, afraid of making mistakes in the drawing. This is what made me put down the brushes, fear. When I took the online guitar lessons on the *Great Courses* website, I had noticed courses on watercolor and made note.

Today, I watched one of the watercolor courses. The course covered making something out of nothing in order to free you up from any caution, concerns or thoughts. The concept was to take just four complementary colors of paint, wet the paper, and splash the colors on randomly. While wet, the instructor sprinkled salt on the paint to give it a star-like effect where the paint and salt combined. Once dry, she scraped off the salt and said to take a step back. Then turn the canvas sideways and upside down to see if you could see something to work with in order to turn the blob of colors into something. In her painting, the instructor saw the makings of a lizard (which I did not see at first). She then proceeded to bring the lizard to life by highlighting parts and framing others. Wow — I was hooked. I had never done free-form watercolor painting before. I had always worked from a photograph or drawing. This seemed like a great vehicle to remove the chains of my lack of self-confidence. It was nothing to start. I couldn't make it worse — or could I? I had nothing to lose. I went in search of my old paint supplies buried in the basement.

I chose the colors: Ultramarine Blue, Intense Green, Windsor Yellow, and Turquoise. I wet the paper and did as instructed. I took a one-and-a-half-inch wide brush, added water to my paints, and just went at it. I swiped one way with one of the colors, and then splattered the paper with another until I covered the paper with color. There was no rhyme or reason, just a haphazard mix of the colors from the palette. I sprinkled the salt and waited for the paper to dry.

An hour later, I came back to see what gift of an image would be presented to me. It was like opening a box of Cracker Jacks in anticipation of the special gift inside. (Many of you may not be old enough to get his reference.) At the very *first* landscape glance, I saw a pair of eyes and the making of a nose. Not human, but some sort of animal. I turned the paper vertically — *NOTHING*. I saw nothing as I looked and looked, inwardly chastising myself for my lack of creativity. I flipped it again, this time vertically again, then upside down, again nothing, as hard as I tried. One more turn to vertical. Nope, I didn't see anything there. I walked away briefly to clear my head, and then came back for another stroll around the creativity block. This time I turned it in the opposite direction from the *first* time. This produced the same results. All I saw was the one initial landscape view of a start to an animal face. That face became clear on the second view. To me, it looked like the face of a leopard. I Googled "face of a leopard" to get some perspective. I settled on one of the images on my iPhone and started in.

After about an hour, the leopard appeared from the paper. Slowly it revealed itself like coming out of the tall grasses of the savanna into an open space on the range. I could see it. I could paint it, as imperfect as it was, I had done it. It isn't going into the Louvre anytime soon. but for the *first* time painting free-form, I was proud of what I had created. I think I would do this again, just using different colors. Maybe some brighter colors, some reds or oranges.

??? – Have you taken a chance and addressed one of your fears?

DECEMBER 13TH: PERFORM A MAGIC TRICK

"See this deck of cards that I am pulling out of this black case? I'm going to make it disappear," I told my wife. The poor, tortured soul had to endure my *first* magic trick today. By the look in her eyes, I think she would rather I had made myself disappear. I had practiced and practiced until I felt comfortable enough to perform.

I pulled a card out of the deck and had her kiss the card goodbye (a little showmanship). I inserted it back into the deck and allowed her to handle the deck holder I was going to use to make the deck disappear. I placed the deck back into the black case. I asked her to tap it three times for theatrics, torture, or both as she rolled her eyes. I then made the deck disappear magically! She was mildly impressed and asked me to do it again but slower so she could see how I did it. I did it again, but she couldn't figure it out. I'm a magician! But I won't be headlining in Vegas anytime soon.

P.S. – Looking back: I have a kit of other tricks that I ran through with success. I performed these tricks for my kids, siblings, nephews, and nieces in the months to come. The idea of this first was inspired by my deceased dad. I wanted to carry on a tradition of bringing wonder and joy to the youth in my family as he had done. The younger they were, the more they loved it. They kept asking me to perform the tricks over and over as they tried to see or guess how the trick worked. My "signature" and go-to trick is still the disappearing deck of cards, although I'm not giving up my day job.

??? – Have you ever performed a magic trick?

DECEMBER 18TH: WRITE A SPEECH

"Who am I to give a speech?" screamed my self-doubting mind. At the bequest of my *first* speech coach, who had me read the Ted Talk book, I put together an outline of my *first* speech. I had to write it before I would be able to give one. We discussed the different techniques. I could write it longhand and memorize the whole speech. (With my memory, this was not an option. Plus, when I tried it, I came across as robotic and boring. The same applied to reading from a script — terrible.) We settled on reducing the speech to an index card with bullet points that I could use to spark my bad memory. I felt sure it might morph and improve over time. The following is my *first* official motivational speech, which I intend to give someday — scary.

In my early twenties, I had written the goal to write a speech as I took the Dale Carnegie course. I added it to my to-do list of possible *firsts* for this year. As the universe does with written goals, a friend referred me to a speech coach. I hired my *first* speech coach on November 21st.

I started with pages of notes that I would need to reduce to an index card. My natural tendency, which I had to fight against, was trying to fit 10 pounds of stuff into a 5-pound bag. These are my notes for a 30-minute speech. Yes, I know the minutes listed below do not add up to 30, but I left some time for wiggle room. I had to write very small to fit it onto the index card.

START – A LEAP YEAR OF FIRSTS (5 MINUTES)

- Started **Leap Year of "Firsts"** doing something EVERY DAY I had never done (e.g., bow tie, drive race car, religious services, drive speed limit) — a few pics?
- Standing in the shower on **Friday, March 20th, early morning crying** about an unwanted *"first"* I was to do that day — **lay off employees (all of them)**
- **Hired back same day = call center.** Problems to work: technology, training, laptops, headphones for employees

WHAT I LEARNED – "HOW TO WORK THE PROBLEM" (15 MINUTES)

1. **Limit your Pity Party – 24-Hour rule.** Sometimes life just SUCKS! What are we going to do about it? 24 hours to grieve the possibility of losing the business, a loved one, a relationship, etc. Worrying or beating yourself up is NOT productive or good for you. It doesn't solve anything and cripples you from finding a solution or moving forward.

2. **Share — Ask trusted others.** When stuck, reach out to others. Share the problem. Talk about it. Don't PANIC = Gather Facts.

3. **Ask yourself good questions.** If I gave you a magic wand to grant you THE perfect solution, what would it look like? Look at your gifts and blessings.

4. **Depend (or identify?) your core values**: Integrity, learn, hustle, LEAN (efficiency), yes, fun, dependability, respect, care, and win-win.

5. **Sleep on it** when all else fails. When I am "working a problem" and done all of the above, after sleeping on it, I wake up with ideas and solutions that I scramble to find a pen to write down

Why work the problem? Because: "I gotta keep breathing. Because tomorrow the sun will rise. Who knows what the tide could bring?" (From the movie *Castaway*)

END (3 MINUTES)

This helped me **find my "WHY"** – **Saving Jobs:** Woke up one morning drove 115 mph on 95 to write on easel in my office / adrenalin / focus / lost in the moment / passion

Q&A (5 MINUTES)

I shared with my coach that my greatest fear was containing my emotions during my speech. He stopped me and implored me not to apologize for the emotion. He said that emotion is what is compelling and brought a tear to his eye as I shared a number of my *firsts*. He counseled that I have multiple stories and lessons to share. He commented that he has helped hundreds, if not thousands of people with books, speeches, etc., and never witnessed someone make a TV host come to tears like I had in my QVC appearance. I'm still scared.

P.S. – Looking back: This proves I needed a speech coach. This has evolved so much since I first wrote it with practice and coaching. Instead of bullet points with copy, I now use one page of sequenced pictures or pictograms, which represent my thoughts. My coach perfectly described it as "playing jazz." The pictures are my starting notes that I riff off of, just like a jazz musician. I use a stopwatch to keep time. So many things have changed and continue to with each speech experience.

I gave a few versions of this speech virtually to a few of my relationship groups. They served as my test pilots. I performed my "first" live speech based on my unpublished book in September 2021 in front of my industry group. I humbly received a standing ovation. What was more important to me were the people who came up to me after to thank me for being so vulnerable. It had helped them. They thanked me. I had achieved my goal to help others

??? – Are you afraid of sharing your emotions in front of a group? Have you done something that mutes your own self-doubting mind? Something that stretches your internal boundaries. Will you try (pretty please)?

DECEMBER 19TH: TRAP SHOOTING

(Unedited journal entry)

… Third time was a charm. I had planned this *first* for the past three weeks. Two weeks ago, it rained, which led to me sleeping on the streets of Philly. Last week my host, the head of the club, couldn't make it due to some last-minute family duties. Today when I awoke, I emailed him to discover that we are on — so excited.

I had never shot trap. Heck, I had never shot a gun before. Shooting a gun was on my bucket list.

What does one do when they don't own a gun and want to shoot one? Or wants to trap shoot and does not belong to a club or know anyone that can take him? I didn't have a trap shooting connection, just my desire to experience it, so I had to get creative to accomplish this *first*. I Googled "trap shooting near me." The club I settled on, Pine Valley Trap Club, was 40 minutes away. I emailed the contact listed on the club's site to see if I could shoot one time as a non-member. They emailed me back saying that they did not rent guns. I took a shot (pun intended) and figured you never know until you ask. I explained my *firsts* and that I did not own a gun. I asked if somehow, they could assist me in achieving this *first*. The head of the club promptly replied. At *first,* he said he was sorry, but they couldn't help.

He must have quickly reconsidered as he followed up shortly thereafter — motivated to help with my *first.* He offered to personally host and teach me, as well as lend me his gun. *Poof* –something came out of nothing, the power of the quest of a *first.*

I pulled into the club lot and walked inside. Lew, my host and instructor, was giving a lesson to another newbie. I wandered outside and took a seat on the bench behind him and his student. I was all ears. It was cold, below freezing with snow on the ground, as the sun peeked through the slightly overcast sky creating a glare. My newfound friend noticed me and signaled he'd be done shortly. Listening to the instructions helped. After a dozen more shots, he walked over and led me back inside.

He confirmed again that I'd never shot a gun before. I sheepishly admitted that I had only ever shot a BB gun as a teenager. My cousins and I used to shoot bats at dusk when they flew out of the top of the barn in "the country" at my grandparents' house. My host Lew grabbed a 12-gauge shotgun out of a storage locker and said, "Eight dollars for ammo and another three for earplugs." I had expected it to be a lot more. I tried to hand him more for the club and the favor he was doing for me, but he wouldn't take it. With 25 shells in hand, we strolled back outside to the range. He reviewed gun safety and the finer art of trap shooting. I went down his following mental checklist as he prepped me for my *first.*

"Look down the barrel."

"Place your cheek on the gun handle and keep it there. Don't pull away."

"Make sure the handle is snug against your shoulder" (to prevent the gun kick).

"Be smooth in following the disc."

He showed me where to aim. It was time. He then said, "PULL!" As he did, a 12-inch round clay orange disc flew out of this little green shed about 20 yards in front of us.

I did everything wrong! I was NOT smooth and jerked the gun as I tried to locate the disc. My cheek came off the gun handle as I shot and missed. The disc was on its descent — bad. Okay, my *first* time shooting an actual gun and my *first*-time shooting trap was not a huge success. I had to learn quickly; I only had 24 shots left. I was expecting a big kick from the hype I'd heard from friends. I didn't feel the kick, though, and the instructor explained that this was overrated, although there are some guns with a big kick. This was not one of them, as long as the handle was firmly against my shoulder. I did not want a sore shoulder the next day, so the handle became glued to my shoulder. I hit my *first* trap on the fifth pull. I had accomplished my goal. I wanted to hit one to say I did it.

As I continued to shoot, so did the mentoring. "Did not follow that one," or "You waited too long — you can't hit it as it is descending. You have to lead and hit it on the ascent." He asked if I was shooting with one eye or both. I wasn't sure, I really hadn't paid attention. I did on the next shot — I was a one-eyed shooter. My coach said he was also, but shared it was a bad habit he learned as a kid. Apparently, the better shooters use both eyes. I asked what defined being proficient at trap shooting — I wanted a measuring stick. I asked how many he could hit out of a box of 25 shells. He said that a good day for him was anything in the twenties. The good shooters at the club could hit 25 out of 25. I obviously was not in that class. At the end of my session, I had hit five out of 25. I was ecstatic with those results. I hit four of 12 with one-eye and one of 13 with both eyes. I could not get the hang of using two eyes. I was happy that I at least hit a few, and that I didn't hurt my shoulder OR anyone else.

**P.S. – *Looking back:* ** *I loved this* first. *I would have never had this experience without my quest to make this a* first.

??? – What is one thing that you can jot down right now that you'd like to experience but do not know how you'd ever do it? How can you accomplish this? Who do you know that you can ask for help to find out?

If you are stuck and can't figure it out, please reach out to the author: keith@GoSpikes.com

DECEMBER 21ST:
GAVE MONEY TO A HOMELESS PERSON AT A STOPLIGHT

As I stopped at a red light, a homeless person stood holding a sign asking for money. Earlier in my life, I had become callous to this. I always thought that if I gave money, it was just funding alcohol or drugs. I would occasionally offer to take someone to a place to eat or buy food and was always turned down.

With my recent *first* experience of sleeping on the streets, I took a newfound interest in the person asking for money. He was a middle-aged gentleman, dressed in a soiled yellow ski jacket. Most of his teeth were missing. I went into my pocket for some money, rolled down my window, and held the money out until I caught his attention. He approached and I asked him, "Why are you homeless?" I had never asked that before.

He was polite and answered, "My mother died when I was in jail and when I got out I had no place to go."

I didn't ask him what he was in jail for, but I did ask where he slept at night.

He replied, "I'm lucky. I live in an abandoned house and this guy allows us to plug in an electric heater to use his electricity for $5, so I'm all right."

Wow, I hadn't expected that answer. I handed him the money, he thanked me, the light turned green, and I was gone. My *first* time giving money to a homeless man at a stoplight was worth it.

*P.S. – **Looking back:** I wish I had given him more than twenty dollars. I wish I could have given him his dignity. I wish I could have given him self-worth. I wish I could have given him a job.*

??? – Have you given thought to having a conversation with a homeless person, or someone less fortunate than you?

. . .

With the gift of the pebble tossed on March 20th, I looked for every opportunity to help others to make it through the challenging year. My arm got tired at times from throwing pebbles. Many didn't make my *firsts* and will gladly go unpublicized. I'd rather it that way. I had my 15 minutes of fame. No more minutes needed. No matter how hard I might try, I will never be able to do enough to repay what was provided to me that year.

DECEMBER 25ᵀᴴ (CHRISTMAS DAY): WATCHED *IT'S A WONDERFUL LIFE*

I had obviously heard of and maybe caught a few scenes here or there over time of the movie *It's a Wonderful Life*, but I had never watched the entire movie. That day there was an *It's a Wonderful Life* marathon on TV. It was on all day. I took advantage and watched the entire movie for the *first* time. As I watched, with the challenges we faced in 2020, I felt a strong affinity to George Bailey.

I was touched by the closing scene. Who wouldn't be? I took a picture of the moral of the movie that was written to the central character, George Bailey (James Stewart), by his guardian angel Clarence that said… "*Dear George: Remember no man is a failure who has friends! Thanks for the wings! Love, Clarence.*" I then posted it to my Facebook page with my wishes of Happy Christmas and Merry Chanukah — a perfect *first* for that Christmas Day.

This day, Nashville was hit by a suicide bomber/terrorist on Christmas morning.

*PS – **Looking back:** I not only watched It's a Wonderful Life for the first time, I watched it back to back. It has been a wonderful life so far. I am going to continue to work hard to keep making it that way. I was given a gift by my father on his last days on this Earth. I spent his last dying days by his bedside. I held his hand as he took his last dying breath. The gift he gave me was the gift of the appreciation of life and not fearing death. He freed me somehow that day over 10 years ago. When it was determined that there was nothing that could be done for him, he was placed in Hospice care in my dining room, which we converted into a makeshift hospital room.*

He told me, "I'm ready to go; I've lived a good life." This was from an "old-school" guy who was not free with his feelings. I believe one of the few times, if not the only time, he told me he loved me was during that last month as I took him to and from appointments and treatments while running my business from his hospital room at Fox Chase Cancer Center. To self-analyze, maybe that is also why I now try and make it a point to express my love and feelings more freely as I age. He passed away the next day. My goal is to say the same thing on my way out that he said to me, "I'm ready to go; I've lived a good life." My firsts have helped me in part in achieving the living a good life in order to be prepared for the exit when it comes. Hopefully by me sharing these firsts it will help you to achieve the ability to say the same someday.

??? – Has the loss of a dear loved one changed your perspective on life and death?

DECEMBER 26TH: KWANZAA (LEARN ABOUT)

(Unedited journal entry)

… Today is the first day of Kwanzaa. I knew that it was some sort of holiday celebrated by the African American community, but I had never taken the time to find out any more details. I felt ignorant and wanted to learn about my first today. I used Google to learn and YouTube to experience

the meaning of the word and the holiday. The first *day of Kwanzaa starts on the December 26th, the day after Christmas.*

In doing my research, I discovered that American political activist Maulana Karenga created Kwanzaa in 1966, during the aftermath of the Watts Riots, as a specifically African American holiday. In 2020, with the civil unrest caused by George Floyd's death, it seemed appropriate learning material.

According to Karenga, the name Kwanzaa derived from the Swahili phrase matunda ya kwanzaa, meaning "first fruits." How appropriate! First fruit festivals are common in Southern Africa, celebrated in December or January during the Southern Solstice. Karenga's inspiration came in part from an account he read about the Zulu festival — Umkhosi Wokweshwama.

Kwanzaa celebrates what its founder called the seven principles of Kwanzaa. Each of the seven days of Kwanzaa is dedicated to one of the following seven principles:

- *Umoja (Unity): To strive for and to maintain unity in the family, community, nation, and race.*
- *Kujichagulia (Self-Determination): To define and name ourselves, as well as to create and speak for ourselves.*
- *Ujima (Collective Work and Responsibility): To build and maintain our community together and make our brothers' and sisters' problems our problems and to solve them together.*
- *Ujamaa (Cooperative Economics): To build and maintain our own stores, shops, and other businesses and to profit from them together.*
- *Nia (Purpose): To make our collective vocation the building and developing of our community in order to restore our people to their traditional greatness.*
- *Kuumba (Creativity): To do always as much as we can, in the way we can, in order to leave our community more beautiful and beneficial than we inherited it.*

- *Imani (Faith): To believe with all our hearts in our people, our parents, our teachers, our leaders, and the righteousness and victory of our struggle.*

I thought the first principle on that first day of Kwanzaa, Umoja (Unity), was so appropriate in this challenging year when unity was what we needed the most. I found this such a fortunate coincidence of my firsts and was glad my search led me to take the time to learn something new.

P.S. – Looking back: Kwanzaa is not a religious holiday, but a cultural one with an innate spiritual quality. Thus, Africans of all faiths can and do celebrate Kwanzaa, (i.e. Muslims, Christians). This is something I would never take the time to learn about if I was not looking for a first that day.

This concluded the part of my year of learning religious perspectives. I had attended a Bible study group in April. I picked up the Bible last week for the first time as an adult to read John 3:16. I Googled "most popular Bible verses." John 3:16 was it. When we are able to congregate again, I'll pick up where I left off. I'll explore the religious services still on my list that I was unable to attend in 2020 due to the pandemic.

<u>DECEMBER 27TH</u>: CAST A SPELL

I'm not sure where the thought came from, but casting a spell came to mind out of the blue today for a *first* to try — witchcraft? For the record, I do *not* believe in this stuff, but my mom has always had "feelings" from the beyond. She had used the Ouija board ages ago for friends and family. She would predict things through her "feelings." I always rolled my eyes. I was skeptical earlier in the year during my *first* Tarot Card reading.

Having never cast a spell before, I Googled "how to cast a spell." I clicked on the various sites to read as I looked for something easy that wouldn't take a lot of time. I wanted a spell where I could use things that I had around the house. I had made up my mind that I wasn't going shopping for any special crystals or ingredients that were part of a number of the spells online. There were many of those. There were many types of spells for many reasons. I settled on a spell from one of the articles I read. The article was dated February 2020 and titled, "How to Get Lit (aka Manifest

Whatever TF You Want) with Candle Magick. Please Don't Burn Anything Down, k?" by Kerry Ward.

The instructions read:

Casting a spell is a great way to focus on what you want in life and set your intentions towards your goals. Witchcraft is about embracing life and trying to make the world a better place for everyone, no matter what their faith, religion, color, creed, or sex.

That is what the year was about for me. It was what I tried to do in my own small way. I tried to make the world a better place. Why not add a spell to it to try to accomplish this? What did I have to lose? What could it hurt? It would be my *first* spell cast and it would be a positive one for hopefully the right reason. I now had to decide and focus on that right reason.

After some thought, I wrote the focus and reason for my spell onto a yellow post-it note as I sat on the couch early that morning. I wrote: *Create profitable win-win situation for my employees, my partners, and myself in my transition into semi-retirement in selling the business someday.*

I don't think I will ever retire. Knowing me, I have to be doing something. I love what I do but I'd like less responsibility and more freedom to travel. So that was the mind-set I searched for in my spell. In reading about spells, it read that doing it in the right frame of mind and for the right reason were important components. I thought I was at that place and time, so I proceeded. These are the steps I followed:

Step 1: What are you trying to manifest? Establish your goal and what you would like to accomplish or affect.

Step 2: Create your spell. The most basic candle magic spell is to simply visualize your goal, say a sentence, and light the candle to release the energy. Choose the candle's color carefully. Pick one that corresponds with the nature of your goal. Green helps bring your ideas to life and amplifies prosperity.

Step 3: Dress the candle. This is important. You're aiming to forge a psychic link among the candle, you, and your goal. This is called "dressing the candle." First, rub the candle with oil. Inscribe your wishes into the candle.

Step 4: Get lit (light the candle). Okay, you're ready for magic. Take a few deep breaths, release tension, and visualize your worries or thoughts drifting away from you. Clear your mind. Then start to visualize your goal as if it has already happened. Imagine how you'd feel and what life would look like. When you have a clear mental picture, repeat your chant/song/poem or say your intention out loud. When you feel almost full of your goal's energy and positive vibes, light the candle. Focus on the candle's aura (the light right outside the flame) and visualize it getting bigger and bigger until it fills the room. Then imagine it expanding beyond the room into the universe, beaming out and sending a signal to bring your intention to you. Hold this vision in your mind as long as you can. When you feel your energy waning or you start getting distracted, blow out the candle.

I did as the instructions read. I found the perfect green candle in my garage. It was the *first* candle I came across; a sign? I then found a brand-new unopened bottle of my favorite olive oil. I rubbed the candle with the oil. I carved a number of things into the candle using the end of a Phillips head screwdriver I found in my desk drawer where I was sitting. I carved the number "3" to represent the three years it would take. Then I placed the initials of my partners and me within a heart, a dollar sign, and my business's address (2701).

I envisioned my spell and the many things attached to it (transitioning the business, travel, experiencing more life, etc.), then lit the candle as I recited what I had written as my spell. I took in the light and visualized for a number of minutes. Although not part of the instructions I tilted the candle to have some of the wax drip onto my thumb. I rubbed the wax onto the spell I had written to close the circle. I then blew the candle out. My *first* spell was completed.

*P.S. – **Looking back:*** *I'm not saying there is any correlation, but the* first *half of the year of 2021, as I write this in March 2021, has been the most profitable win-win situation for my employees, my partners, and myself in my lifetime. For context, remember back in March 2020, the pandemic should have put us out of business. Magical?*

??? – Have you ever cast a spell? Did it work?

DECEMBER 29TH: BEING BLIND (SIMULATED)

(Unedited journal entry)

… I stumbled into my kitchen, feeling my way from the garage door entrance after work at 6:30 p.m., with my wife commenting, "What the hell are you doing now?"

I had a black cloth earmuff wrapped around my head, covering my eyes. I replied, "It's my *first* for today. I want to experience what it's like to be blind." I could hear, but not see, her expression as she let out a big sigh of disbelief.

I had driven home thinking about being blind for the night. It had been on my list. I remembered that I kept black earmuffs in my golf bag — *perfect.* They worked just fine; I could not see anything. During the next few hours at home, I was blind. I shuffled my feet from my car to the little concrete edge at the start of the garage. I could picture where I was. I knew my son had brought his new birthday present in from the backyard — a golf net. That was my destination. Once I had felt my way to the net, I followed it along the edge and turned to the door to the kitchen, which was when I made my clumsy entrance.

It was dinnertime for me as I had worked late. I heard my wife and son in the living room laughing at me. They had already eaten. I felt around using the countertop to find my way. My wife had cooked. She offered to dish dinner out for me so I wouldn't burn myself. I figured out where the glasses were and filled one with water from the tap. I felt my way to our home office and plugged in my cell phone, and then went upstairs to change clothes. I figured it out. I could visualize the house and knew my way. As I made it down the stairs to eat I was jabbing with either my foot or hand to get my bearings. My wife placed my plate on the kitchen table. It was comical as I tried to cut my chicken, twirl the pasta, and poke at the carrots on my plate. Locating each food on the plate was harder than you might think. It took me a little extra time, but I finished. I found my way to the dishwasher to make my deposit. I could hear the Sixers in the background. I went to the living room to listen to the game. While stumbling to the recliner, my wife snuck in front of me and spooked me with a loud "*BOO!*" as she touched me.

OMG! I nearly jumped out of my skin! She and my son were laughing HARD as I protested the cruelty of taking advantage of the disabled. I proclaimed, "That is just not right!" (But I have to admit, it was funny.)

I traveled down the hallway to the commode; I'd been to the bathroom at night, in the dark, virtually blind before, so I kinda had that down. I didn't miss!

I found my way back to the living room and to the couch. I fumbled to find the remote. I was a pro after years of changing channels — it came naturally.

After that, it was off to some real shuteye.

P.S. – *Looking back:* *When I woke to type this, I thought of the many things I couldn't do or would need to modify to get by if I was blind. I take so much for granted. Without sight I couldn't drive. I'd have to use the computer in a completely different way. I'd need a new type of cell phone. I'd have to make major adjustments to equipment. I'd need to learn a new language to read, Braille. Having already had eyesight, I could visualize my surroundings that I was familiar with, but I pondered how different it would be if I had been born blind without any frame of reference. I would have never seen a blue sky. Hell, I would not know the color blue. I can visualize a sunset since I have seen one, but what if I had never seen one? Again, as with a number of these firsts, it left me with many questions and much gratitude for what I have. I became more appreciative of my eyesight and gained a little better understanding of a life without it.*

On a funnier note, I came to find out after the fact that my brother caught wind of my first somehow. Maybe he called in to check on mom. Apparently, he spoke to my son to plead with him to rearrange all the furniture in my house. He wanted to throw a monkey wrench into my visualization of my home surroundings. I'm grateful that my son had more compassion than my brother. For the record, I would have done the same to my brother if the shoe had been on the other foot. Love can be funny in that way!

??? – What if you were born blind, and never saw a sunrise or a sunset?

DECEMBER 30TH: FLY A DRONE

The year 2020 is going out with a bang! A power surge great enough to blow out our server caused the remote showrooms' computers, as well as those of our employees and graphic artists, to shut down. Our full-color digital printers also went down at the same time. This was a *first* for our business and the manufacturer of the machines. We spent thousands of dollars to overnight new printer heads and ink in order to get everything up and running by the next day. There was a backlog of full-color personalization orders to do. This was just the morning. I wouldn't expect anything less. However, these problems were not the way I was going to end my *leap year of firsts*.

I headed home late and texted my wife: *On my way home – any ideas for my next to last* first *tonight?* I'd already decided what the official last *first* would be tomorrow, New Year's Eve. I planned to stay at work and complete my manuscript outline for my *first* book.

She texted back: *You could not speak, to see what it's like to communicate without words.* Hmm, I thought it might be a good idea or was it her polite way of asking me to shut up — I wasn't sure.

In the meantime, my brother-in-law Jeff had just posted: *First flight of my new toy! I have a long way to go* with an uploaded video he'd taken from his new Christmas present — a drone. Bingo! I had my *next to last first*, flying a drone.

I quickly texted: *Can you fly your drone at night? Is it too late for me to come over and fly it with you? Just got off work and I'm looking for a "first" for today. I have never flown one. If it's too late – no worries. Let me know.*

His response was quick: *Sure. Come on over.*

Wow! Perfect! I *was so* excited. I had always wanted to fly a drone. I texted back: *THANK YOU! You'll make my book (of* firsts*)! And I'm coming with gifts.*

I stopped at home for a second for a quick bite and picked up the Christmas presents for my nieces and nephew. I was off. I love when a plan falls together.

This was a fitting end to the *firsts*. It was very spontaneous, last minute, and something I would have never thought to do when I woke up today. It came about due to my daily quest to do or experience something new. When I arrived, I handed out the gifts. Once done with the formalities and a little catching up, we left.

We walked under the dimmed streetlamps of Haddonfield, New Jersey, to a small soccer field a few blocks away. The airspace over the soccer field was clear. He showed me the two components — the actual drone and the hand-held piloting control. My brother-in-law took out his cell phone and swiped to the drone app. He then plugged the phone into the controller and asked me to hold it. He held the drone and twirled it next to the controller, explaining that this set the GPS coordinates between the drone and the controller, which was confirmed on the screen of the controller. This allowed for an autopiloted landing in the exact place from where the drone took off — amazing! Earlier in the day, on his *first* try he said it was difficult to land the drone without the autopilot function; it kept bouncing off the ground instead of landing successfully. It took practice, and I didn't have that kind of time. Therefore, I would utilize the autopilot landing function that was activated by hitting the home button on the controller. Cool.

He got the drone to take off with its distinctive buzz and handed me the controls. As it hovered above us, he schooled me on how to work the two joysticks. The left one made the drone travel up and down, while the right one made it go forward or backward.

I watched as the droned buzzed over the dark field; the only lights were from the town in the near distance. Despite the darkness, the two red lights and one white light at the bottom of the drone allowed us to follow it. I was flying a drone. I sent the drone up and down, back, and forth, navigating it to hover roughly a few feet above our heads — too cool. After about 15 minutes, I hit the auto-land button and took my hands off the controls. The drone traveled back and forth, retracing its steps to orientate itself to its initial take-off GPS coordinates. The process took a few minutes, but suddenly it locked in. It traveled to about 10 feet above the spot and then slowly proceeded to descend. It lightly touched down and shut itself off. It may have been more exciting taking video from the drone or exploring more of the surroundings, but it was too dark. My maiden voyage was complete — perfect for me and my *firsts*!

DECEMBER 31ST: WRITE A BOOK (FINISH MANUSCRIPT OUTLINE)

(Unedited journal entry)

... It is the last day of my *leap year of firsts*. As I headed into work, driving on Route 38 in South Jersey, with a classic rock station blasting, my mind drifted to today's *first*. I had to write this final journal entry and write an epilogue to wrap up my book. I didn't want to lose the ideas bouncing around in my head, so I pulled to the side of the road *twice* and typed away clumsily with my thumbs on my iPhone. I was thinking about the many diverse *firsts* I'd lived. It was a fun, exhilarating, and very emotional journey where I learned so much. The *firsts* had been my thread of sanity to get through the insanity.

It is New Year's Eve and I'm sitting at my desk typing this last journal entry documenting my *first* for my *Leap Year of Firsts* — 366 of them. The emotion as I type is crazy with so many things running through my mind. I will define this last *first* for the year, writing a book, completing my outline, filled with the printed daily journal entries. I blocked out my day so I wouldn't have to work, although of course I did. I sent one last email to my staff wishing them a Happy HEALTHY New Year and confirming that they could head out early. I was then off on a day of writing, compiling the already written copy and finishing the *first* draft of my manuscript for the book.

I started painstakingly printing all the emailed journal entries. I placed them into a three-inch D-ring binder. The writing on each of the dividers represented the intended fourteen chapters. I planned to do a chapter for each month, with additions of a prologue and epilogue to wrap it up.

I had already done a *first* draft today of my prologue and still needed to write the epilogue. Once I write, print, and place it in the binder I will consider this *first* complete. That does not mean that there is not a lot of work ahead to get this published; there is. Tomorrow I will start on the quest of editing it and polishing it up to send the manuscript to a publisher for publication. Everything I have is fluid. I have the working manuscript, a working title and some preliminary cover mock-ups put together.

As I travel down the road to publication, I will go through each email, reread, edit, and place it in a Word document, which I will eventually upload the manuscript to my publisher Book Baby. I'll be self-publishing. I can't wait to get to this. I have forgotten half of the things I did. It will be interesting reading them over; I'll probably scratch my head and wonder what the hell I was thinking at the time. I'll have to read and reread for the grammar. I'm amazed that I kept doing this. As I communicated to my staff and others, this year we lived a generation in a year. It is 5:45 p.m. on New Year's Eve and I'm still in my office putting the finishing touches on this manuscript. I am about to hit send to email my last *first* to myself to complete the book — *DONE!*

In searching my database of resources for stuff to include in the book, I came across my "Personal Constitution," which I created some 40-plus years ago. It is a typed Word document that I transcribed from a handwritten memo after reading some business book to try and educate myself. I remember writing most of the things that I did NOT believe I would be able to accomplish. I had tried to project the person I wanted to be some day. I printed the document and read it. Although I'm still working on some of those things, I fast forward to today and realize I didn't do too badly. This exercise of writing a personal constitution showed me the power of writing and visualizing goals.

If I sell one book, or help one person, I will consider this effort in writing a success. The *firsts* this past year have made me richer in so many ways that I ever could have dreamed. I feel blessed and forever grateful for the experiences.

P.S. – Looking back: *I only finished the complete outline of the book with all the chapters filled with the individual daily firsts on that day. It had to be rewritten and edited, which would take me months. The working cover would be re-designed. I would spend every free moment I had writing this* book. Many times, my day job got in the way. My weekends became 16-hour writing sessions. My new commitment for 2021 is to do something every day in writing, editing, publishing, and marketing this book.

I have been through three rewrites with two editors. I first turned what I thought was my completed manuscript into my publisher for editing in May 2021. It was well over four-hundred pages. I rewrote it to reduce it by one hundred pages, cutting out boring firsts and taking it out of chronological order and into themed chapters. My independent editor convinced me to place it back into chronological order, as you now find it. I was warned by the publisher that the editing process would take longer than I would expect. They were correct. I had planned to have it published by September for my first live speaking engagement based on the book. I missed that target date and am now feverishly looking to get this over the goal line in late October 2021 with the hope of getting it published by the end of this year 2021. This too has been a journey. I hope you like the results. I'm looking forward to a new year of days that will contain many more firsts for me and hopefully for YOU!

??? – Do you have an inspirational story within you?

We ALL have a story.

. . .

WHAT I LEARNED FROM 2020

As my coach and I prepared for my *first* virtual motivational speech in 2021, he had me focus on the message: *What I learned from 2020.* He suggested that I distill these into four things that would be easy to communicate and remember. I had obviously learned much during the year that had changed me. I'll cover those in the next chapter. What I learned dealing with the adversity that year when disaster struck was ...

Limit your pity party

Ask yourself good questions, as well as trusted others

Rely on your core values

Sleep on it

This was the formula I developed and applied in working out the many problems that 2020 presented daily. I rinsed and repeated this throughout the year. I was tempted to throw an epic pity party that could have engulfed me for months. At times, I was enticed to ask myself some negative questions like: *Why is this happening to poor me?* Sometimes it seemed that following our core values was not easy or expedient. Often, I went to bed without any answers. But by staying the course of this four-step process, my business and I not only survived, we thrived. That and doing something new every day kept me unstuck and moving forward in understanding what was truly important — living life to the fullest.

.   .   .

I spared you many of my golf *firsts* that were fun for me. This also goes for the food and drink *firsts* I enjoyed. Here is a sample mix of these fun *firsts*:

- Three birdies in a round
- Foam bumper golf
- Shot 38 on nine holes
- On-course golf lesson
- Golf in Vegas
- Ocean Course — Palm Coast, Florida
- Ate/drank a Dirty Cookie shot
- Micklethwait, Austin, Texas BBQ
- Gator bites
- Sammy Sosa drink
- Chocolate covered coffee beans
- Pickle juice-infused vodka
- 5-Hour energy drink

- Ate a prune
- Belgium Gelato in a blue cone
- French Press coffee
- Built a gingerbread house
- Blue Chair Bay Coconut Rum

THERE WERE ALSO OTHER FUN *FIRSTS* **THAT I DID NOT FEATURE:**

- Wearing crazy heart socks
- Singing (poorly) as front man to a band
- "House call" as Dr. Baldwin (we tested the possibility of distributing COVID-19 fast tests)
- Emailed a golf joke
- Created a photo book of my grandson's *first* year
- Tried a massage chair during work
- Smelling salts
- Painted wine glasses
- Pedicure
- Played Farkle
- Wore ugly Christmas sweater

. . .

As an elder who did not grow up living and breathing technology, I did not want to bore everyone with the technology *firsts* I learned and accomplished this year. Some will seem silly or stupid depending on your viewpoint. Without attempting *firsts*, I would have not done these things. I would have blown them off or asked someone much younger to do it for me. You'll find a number of these listed in the back of the book. Here are a few of these *firsts* to give you an idea of how technologically challenged I once was:

- Ordered from Amazon
- Tweeted

- Re-Tweeted
- Used Venmo
- Used Slack
- Skyped
- Zoomed
- Converted a CSV file to Excel (A CSV file is a comma separated values file commonly used by spreadsheet programs)
- Used Asana program (Asana is a web and mobile application designed to help teams organize, track, and manage their work).
- Asked Siri a question
- Used FaceTime

Maybe you *can* teach an old dog new tricks?

. . .

CHAPTER TWELVE:
EPILOGUE – HOW IT CHANGED ME

It was early morning on Sunday January 24th, 2021, and I found myself on the couch at home drinking my *first* cup of coffee to get going for the day. I was reflecting on the past year as I started work on my *first* book. My mind drifted to how it all started and my inspiration for all of this. I felt compelled to reach out to LuAnn, the initial inspiration for my year of *firsts*, at that moment to inform her of the result of her inspiration and to thank her. So, I typed an email and sent it to her. After the email exchange, I reflected on the question she posed:

So, I need to know — how has your life changed? You may not know exactly yet. Time will give you different perspectives. But obviously, life has changed and evolved and during your year of firsts there have been dramatic changes all around us. I'm so curious to know how you got through it all.

Hmm…great question! It got me thinking deeper. I got emotional thinking about the answer as I replied. The following raw thoughts came pouring out that Sunday morning in January.

The list is probably long on how it had changed me. She was probably right, that time will add additional perspectives. Off the top of my head, these were the things that came to mind:

1. *It made me take chances and experience many different things. It gave me courage. I spontaneously took on new adventures. I would have NEVER slept on the streets of Philly, or many other things with my quest to find a first every day. I quenched the thirst of my curiosity for many things. I tackled a bucket list of goals. I lived life more fully.*

2. *It made me find ways to learn differently. I typed "how-to" into YouTube numerous times to learn new things. I learned so much.*

3. *The experience provided me with an appreciation, empathy, and understanding of many things. I would have NEVER crashed the religious services in a quest to learn and understand better.*

4. *There were a number of emotional and sometimes unwanted firsts which were profound and turned the experience into something that might hopefully help others. This helped me document the journey of a small business owner, that by all rights should have been out of business, find his "why" — saving jobs.*

5. *"First" time experiencing 15 minutes of fame. Apparently, the world was looking for a feel-good story during a tragedy and our company happened to have one. We didn't go looking for it; it found us.*

6. *"First" time we as a company received the largest order in our history. We received multiple and replaced our lost traditional business with PPE sales.*

At times, I wondered if I was writing a non-fiction book. It sometimes seemed fictional to me — The Twilight Zone! And I did this for most of the year for free. First time in my life I stopped paying myself for months. First time in my life I worried about my life's work ending, due to no fault of my own. I shared with my wife: "I did the best job in my life for free." But I was paid more than I have ever been paid in my life in so many other ways. That was life changing.

I obviously had no idea when I started this innocent and fun quest of *firsts* that it would also be a view into the chaos that the year became. In many ways, it provided threads of sanity for me in an insane world. For that I have these *firsts* to thank. There you have it, the overview of my book and my *leap year of firsts* in one brief conversation via email with the person who was my inspiration. This book, which started as something fun and challenging for me personally, took a dramatic turn a few months in. Did anyone at the beginning of 2020 think that professional sports leagues would shut down? That March Madness would be canceled? That schools would close? That Broadway would go dark? That you couldn't go to a restaurant or a bar to eat or get a drink? The world hit the "pause" button, with new terms like social distancing, self-quarantine, COVID-19, and pandemic. People walked around in public with masks for the *first* time — which was at one time unthinkable!

There was no playbook or history to draw from in making decisions. Everyone was making it up as they went along. Personally, in my business, like many other small businesses on the wrong side of this, we tried our best to survive a year like no other. We did this by *working the problem* every day to come up with solutions. It was not glamorous. I'm grateful every day. I learned to live life fuller amid the challenges.

P.S. – Looking back: The journey of the past year also changed my waistline. The one vice I have is that I binge eat late at night when dealing with extreme stress. Like many, I put on weight during the pandemic. From March 20th through the end of the year I gained 25 pounds. I'm not proud of this fact. Unfortunately, this was NOT a first.

As I turn this manuscript into my publisher, I have refocused on my health now that our employees and company are safe. My plan is to make the girth I gained disappear by the time the book is published.

??? – Did I inspire you to do a first that you had always wanted to do? Did I provide some additional understanding and empathy of others? Did I help you learn something? Did I make you appreciate life a little more? Did I make you think? Did I challenge you in some way? Will you do a first?

POSTSCRIPT – *TWILIGHT ZONE*: PART 2

A "perfect storm" swamped our industry in 2021, as well as many others. A combination of pent-up demand, the loss of competitors that didn't make it through the pandemic storm of last year, and an employee shortage has put a strain on many businesses.

One of my *firsts* from a year ago was walking through the company's production department in mid-May, mid-day, mid-busy season when *no one* was there. There were no machines running because there were no orders. We were out of business. Now we have reached overcapacity with too many orders with supply chain issues in getting goods — feast or famine. I'd rather have the feast. I found myself returning to my roots and working in production to lend a hand, but I'm not complaining!

After a year that should have put us out of business, we ended up becoming a debt-free company because of the sales "luck" we created. We were able to pay off our bills due to our hard work and some good fortune. Please do not wake me from my dream. Sometimes life is stranger than fiction — *My Leap Year of Firsts* was.

.   .   .

ACKNOWLEDGMENTS –
IT TAKES A VILLAGE

In closing, I would like to end by saying THANK YOU to the many people, the village that supported me during this journey. Many of you made it into this book. Others kept me afloat, giving me the opportunity to be here to write this while many others inspired or suggested a number of these *firsts*. You will know who you are if you read this.

THANK YOU TO ...

My wife Beverly: God bless her for putting up with my antics. I love her more than she will ever know. I thank the good Lord for that fateful night when I met this Indiana Hoosier at the Hard Rock Cafe in New York City almost 35 years ago. I couldn't have done ANY of this without her unconditional support. As my brother puts it in football terms: *I out kicked my coverage.* I did!

My family ... my kids: Kasey and Jake. *My siblings* Greg and Lynn. *My mom* for participating in many of these *firsts* — your love and support inspired me. I'm blessed.

My partners: Chris, Ted, Glenn, and Gary. I could NOT have done it without them. When the going got tough, the tough got going — incredible teamwork, love, and support. I am forever grateful.

My employees (or should I say, my other family): I'm SO proud of them. They may never know how much. Following our core values led us to the many good decisions we made together. Special thanks to our controller John who spent countless hours gathering and filling out financial information for loans and lines of credit needed to keep us afloat.

My many friends: You make me richer beyond my dreams because of your friendship.

My Penn National Group golf family: I live for my time with you all. SO much fun — the trash talking, games, and infamous nicknames enrich me so. There are: *The Commish, The General, Professor* and *Coach, Hollywood* and the *Kid, Slice,* the *Weasel, Suds, Kong,* and *good shot Howard.* Thanks for participating in a number of my *firsts!*

My old neighborhood Birdwood Farm boys: Too many laughs that take my breath away. I'm blessed to have reconnected after so many years. We picked it up where we left off, like we had never been apart.

My Cherry Hill — Maine Avenue posse: My heart never moved away!

My past Gold Medal Sporting Goods brothers and sisters: We went through many wars together while young. It is amazing you are still in my life after all these years. We learned so much together. We share a special bond. And especially Brian — thanks for being my sounding board and outlet during the year.

My industry, especially my brothers and sisters in Award Associates: You were in the foxhole with me as we made it to the other side of the gale force storm that hit us. Your encouragement, support, knowledge, hard work, friendship, and care leave me speechless and indebted.

My numerous vendor partners: Your understanding in assisting us in conserving "oxygen" during the worst of times will never be forgotten.

My many business relationships: Without their sharing, sage advice, and support I would not be writing this book.

AnswerNet, who provided my "Manna from Heaven": Especially Gary Pudles who I finally met after almost a year of friendship. We will break bread soon my newfound friend — God willing.

All the people at Firstrust Bank: Mr. Green, Tim, Beth, and the many others. The referral of a lifetime! I'm sure the support you provided us and so many others in the community during those Great Depression-like times, would make your Founding Father so proud.

My Business Club of America (BCA) "relationships": Invaluable, so special — priceless!

My DVIRC fellow CEOs: You added the IQ points I so sorely crave and miss.

The Philly Chamber's Excellence Awards committee: An inspiration!

My Philadelphia Business Executive (PBE) group: You are ALWAYS there for me!

The JerseyMan/PhillyMan crowd: I so appreciate the camaraderie.

My Goldman Sachs 10,000 Small Business alumni: For wisdom and friendship. Cohort 16 forever!

The crew at Executive Leaders Radio: I could spend the rest of my life sitting in the "green room" listening to story after story of the amazing and inspirational leaders who shared tales of their journeys in life. Most from very humble beginnings to much greater heights than I will ever achieve — awed and humbled.

My Philly Sports Hall of Fame gang — all HoFers to me! We'll get your museum built someday. You as well as the many inductees deserve it. Your passion will prevail!

My mentors and business coaches: Cliff, Russ, Ciab, Albert, Cheryl Beth, Marc, and Doug — your guidance, shared knowledge, accountability, and unique perspectives shaped and molded me, contributing to my success. My apologies: I never paid you enough for services rendered.

My AWESOME beta readers of this book: You took what I sent you and returned it to me 10 times better! To Brian, Rick, Geoff, Greg, Ted, Amanda,

Teresa, Paula, and Michelle — your honesty, care, and level of detail in editing my manuscript made me better than I am.

My fellow small business owners: Those who were on the wrong side of this challenging year of 2020. You put fuel in my tank every day as we banded together to help each other through to the other side of this calamity. Michelle: My sweetheart at 12th Street Catering. Larry at Cuba Libre Restaurant: The BIGGEST-hearted person in my world. Steve of Advanced Staging, Karen of Embarq Creative, and the SO many others that suffered to stay afloat and keep their people employed. My heart seemed to break daily in trying to listen, brainstorm, help, and support.

Our many supporting customers: That would take another chapter, so a general thank you will have to do. Thank you for sticking with us.

The various press outlets that picked up our story and amplified it: People were looking for a positive story through all the negatives. Somehow it was decided that we were one of those stories. We had our 15 minutes of fame. It was fun while it lasted. Thanks to: *Forbes Magazine, the Wall Street Journal, the Philadelphia Inquirer, 6ABC – Channel 6, the Northeast Times, KYW-News Radio, 1SEO's Lion's Den podcast, the Chamber of Commerce of Greater Philadelphia's Inspiring Stories, Montco Today, Chester County's Vista Today, the National Retail Federation's Small Business Spotlight,* and QVC and the Home Shopping Network — never in my wildest dreams, it all came out of the blue.

My publisher Book Baby, specifically Matt: You handled this *first-*time author's journey with TLC.

My editor Valerie. I am so glad I found you. Your attention to detail, coupled with your positive encouragement, got me through my three rewrites of the manuscript.

Jaws: I appreciate you taking the time to contribute the foreword in addition to participating in a number of my *firsts.*

LuAnn: My inspiration, while hitting cleanup as my beta reader. I'm fortunate to have been in the crowd that fateful December 2019 morning. Your honest feedback made me blow up my book and rewrite it a third time to hopefully make it a better story. Where did you come from? I'm indebted!

And so many others that I may have forgotten to mention: Forgive my declining memory.

FOREVER GRATEFUL!

With Much Love,

Keith

.   .   .

LIST OF 366 FIRSTS AND 10 CORE VALUES

The following are the full lists of the *firsts* I did this year – 366 of them! **I highlighted in BOLD the *firsts* that are featured in the book.** I just listed the balance to save you the boredom.

1. Jan-1	**Wednesday**	**Mummers Parade – Live**	
2. Jan-2	**Thursday**	**Daily Journal – Writing one**	
3. Jan-3	**Friday**	**Meditate**	
4. Jan-4	**Saturday**	**Drive the speed limit to work**	
5. Jan-5	**Sunday**	**Homemade pickles**	
6. Jan-6	**Monday**	**Tarot card reading**	
7. Jan-7	Tuesday	Call into a radio show	
8. Jan-8	**Wednesday**	**CPR certification class**	
9. Jan-9	**Thursday**	**Live portrait model drawing**	
10. Jan-10	**Friday**	**Visit a mosque – Attend an Islamic service**	
11. Jan-11	Saturday	Teeter machine	
12. Jan-12	Sunday	Welcome a new neighbor	
13. Jan-13	Monday	Online course – Drawing	
14. Jan-14	**Tuesday**	**Heart Ablation**	
15. Jan-15	**Wednesday**	**Tie a bow tie**	
16. Jan-16	**Thursday**	**Rushed to emergency room**	
17. Jan-17	**Friday**	**Overnight stay in the hospital**	
18. Jan-18	**Saturday**	**Listen to a podcast series**	

19. Jan-19	**Sunday**	**Binge-watch a series (*The Vietnam War*)**
20. Jan-20	Monday	Order from Amazon
21. Jan-21	Tuesday	Tweet
22. Jan-22	Wednesday	Play hooky and go to a movie by myself
23. Jan-23	**Thursday**	**Wear high heels**
24. Jan-24	Friday	Read to *first* grandson
25. Jan-25	Saturday	Video with Canon EOS Camera
26. Jan-26	**Sunday**	**Interview my mom for posterity**
27. Jan-27	Monday	Voice memo on iPhone
28. Jan-28	**Tuesday**	**Detail interior of car**
29. Jan-29	Wednesday	Try topical cannabinoid
30. Jan-30	Thursday	Wear CRAZY heart socks
31. Jan-31	**Friday**	**Lunch with daughter at her work**
32. Feb-1	Saturday	Order and eat Bangers & Mash
33. Feb-2	**Sunday**	**Attend a Jehovah Witness service**
34. Feb-3	Monday	BIG head as a birthday present
35. Feb-4	**Tuesday**	**iFLY Indoor Skydiving**
36. Feb-5	Wednesday	Retweet
37. Feb-6	Thursday	Drink a 5-hour energy drink
38. Feb-7	Friday	Meet White House IT Director
39. Feb-8	Saturday	Patch ripped leather in car
40. Feb-9	**Sunday**	**Attend a Mormon service**
41. Feb-10	Monday	Make a Venmo payment
42. Feb-11	**Tuesday**	**Work with my wife at her job**
43. Feb-12	**Wednesday**	**Medical marijuana caregiver card**
44. Feb-13	Thursday	A Woman of No Importance (play)
45. Feb-14	**Friday**	**Dispensary with caregiver card**

46. Feb-15	Saturday	**Race car at Las Vegas Motor Speedway**
47. Feb-16	Sunday	Descend 30 floors via stairs
48. Feb-17	Monday	Sleep on a couch in Vegas
49. Feb-18	TuesdayTry	Blue Chair Bay Coconut Rum
50. Feb-19	**Wednesday**	***Cher Live* in Vegas**
51. Feb-20	Thursday	Golf in Vegas
52. Feb-21	**Friday**	**Bake pot brownies for mom**
53. Feb-22	**Saturday**	**Home-brewed beer**
54. Feb-23	Sunday	Change *first* grandson's diaper
55. Feb-24	Monday	Change air filters at home
56. Feb-25	Tuesday	Perform plumbing at home
57. Feb-26	Wednesday	Eat pot brownies
58. Feb-27	Thursday	Hammock Beach Resort – Palm Coast, Florida
59. Feb-28	Friday	Ocean Course – Palm Coast, Florida
60. Feb-29	**Saturday**	**Wear golf knickers**
61. Mar-1	Sunday	Eat gator bites
62. Mar-2	Monday	Deplane for mechanical issue
63. Mar-3	Tuesday	Attend an AIM Mastermind event
64. Mar-4	Wednesday	Eat and drink a dirty cookie shot
65. Mar-5	Thursday	Austin, Texas – Best BBQ
66. Mar-6	**Friday**	**Dad's ashes in my golf bag**
67. Mar-7	Saturday	Take our dog Elliot on a new walking path
68. Mar-8	Sunday	Walk Riverwinds Nature Trail
69. Mar-9	**Monday**	**Business interruption claim**
70. Mar-10	Tuesday	Donate suits for Suit Drive
71. Mar-11	**Wednesday**	**Medical marijuana lozenges**
72. Mar-12	**Thursday**	**A pandemic (life changes)**

73. Mar-13	Friday	*The Best Man* (A Play)
74. Mar-14	Saturday	Axe throwing
75. Mar-15	Sunday	Global entry online renewal
76. Mar-16	Monday	Worried for the future of my business
77. Mar-17	Tuesday	No salary – Worked for free
78. Mar-18	Wednesday	COVID-19 exposure shut down my business
79. Mar-19	Thursday	Dealt with a threat to a life
80. Mar-20	Friday	Laid off staff @ 2:30: Part 1
81. Mar-20 heaven"	Friday	Hired back @ 4:30: Part 2 "Manna from
82. Mar-21	Saturday	Became a Call Center
83. Mar-22	Sunday	Gave up #1 son status
84. Mar-23	Monday	Purchased premade dinners
85. Mar-24	Tuesday	COVID-19 "Survival Guide"
86. Mar-25	Wednesday	Call from an employee's father
87. Mar-26	Thursday	A check for no reason other than to help me
88. Mar-27	Friday	Work on another business
89. Mar-28	Saturday	115 mph on I-95N to "why"
90. Mar-29	Sunday	Hacked – Asked for money
91. Mar-30	Monday	Use Slack (communication app)
92. Mar-31	Tuesday	Pep talk to industry members
93. Apr-1	Wednesday	Did NOT achieve a written goal
94. Apr-2	Thursday	Posted selfies of employees – My heroes
95. Apr-3	Friday	PPP Care Act loan filing
96. Apr-4	Saturday	Bible Study via Zoom
97. Apr-5	Sunday	Facebook post to LinkedIn
98. Apr-6	Monday	Article in *Forbes Magazine*

99. Apr-7   **Tuesday**   **Interviewed for Podcast**

100. Apr-8   **Wednesday**   **Passover Seder (via Zoom)**

101. Apr-9   **Thursday**   **PPP loan application accepted**

102. Apr-10   **Friday**   **Sent "pebble" poem product of gratitude**

103. Apr-11   **Saturday**   **Staff featured in the *Wall Street Journal***

104. Apr-12   Sunday   Family Easter Sunday via Zoom

105. Apr-13   Monday   Interviewed by 6ABC

106. Apr-14   Tuesday   Virtual Penn Relays

107. Apr-15   **Wednesday**   **Signed loan document via Zoom**

108. Apr-16   **Thursday**   **Cried on TV (*6ABC*)**

109. Apr-17   Friday   Called a "super hero"

110. Apr-18   **Saturday**   **Company Facebook page unpublished**

111. Apr-19   Sunday   Google Meets – Virtual tee time

112. Apr-20   **Monday**   **Worked through the night with no sleep**

113. Apr-21   **Tuesday**   **Saved 123 jobs – California unemployment calls**

114. Apr-22   **Wednesday**   **Lost 123 jobs – California unemployment calls**

115. Apr-23   Thursday   Wore a mask to Wawa

116. Apr-24   **Friday**   **Featured as Hero on Zoom meeting**

117. Apr-25   Saturday   Wrote to Mr. Zuckerberg's Facebook page

118. Apr-26   Sunday   Sales meeting on Sunday

119. Apr-27   **Monday**   **NRF's Small Business Spotlight**

119. Apr-28   **Tuesday**   **Cold-called for interview by KYW-Radio**

120. Apr-29   Wednesday   Contacted by a QVC producer

121. Apr-30   **Thursday**   **Called a book publisher**

122. May-1   **Friday**   **Wear tutu at board of directors**

Zoom meeting

123. May-2	Saturday	Took time to say *NO*
124. May-3	Sunday	Foam bumper golf
125. May-4	**Monday**	**NO machines running mid-day, mid-busy season**
126. May-5	**Tuesday**	**Margaritas at lunch at work during busy season**
127. May-6	Wednesday	Disinfectant wipes order
128. May-7	Thursday	Sold hand-held thermometers
129. May-8	Friday	Live on KYW-Radio
130. May-9	Saturday	Mascot – Honk for Mother's Day
131. May-10	Sunday	Ordered curbside pickup
132. May-11	**Monday**	***Twilight Zone* edition of the company newsletter**
133. May-12	Tuesday	Hired son – Full-time bookkeeper
134. May-13	**Wednesday**	**Started hand sanitizer business**
135. May-14	**Thursday**	**Signed two NDAs in a day**
136. May-15	Friday	Signed fourth NDA in a week
137. May-16	Saturday	Socially distanced dinner
138. May-17	Sunday	Spent a Sunday on collections
139. May-18	Monday	Applied vinyl on a sign
140. May-19	Tuesday	Lost call center jobs for NYC
141. May-20	Wednesday	Contact tracing calls prospecting
142. May-21	Thursday	Employees call for State of California
143. May-22	Friday	Sammy Sosa alcohol drink
144. May-23	Saturday	Spike's office safety S.O.S. kits
145. May-24	Sunday	Job hunted for my brother

146. May-25	Monday	Shot 38 on nine holes
147. May-26	Tuesday	Set up a Skype account
148. May-27	Wednesday	Mid-year staff thank you bonuses
149. May-28	Thursday	DHL office at airport
150. May-29	Friday	QVC and HSN Skype test
151. May-30	**Saturday**	**Canceled Nile River Cruise & Jerusalem trip**
152. May-31	**Sunday**	**Civil unrest in Center City, Philadelphia**
153. Jun-1	**Monday**	**Canceled industry group's summer meeting**
154. Jun-2	**Tuesday**	**QVC and HSN LIVE (9)**
155. Jun-3	**Wednesday**	**Slept overnight at work (10)**
156. Jun-4	Thursday	Met a fighter pilot
157. Jun-5	Friday	Personalized hand sanitizer
158. Jun-6	Saturday	Used Blue Jeans computer program
159. Jun-7	**Sunday**	**Wore pink tutu on golf course**
160. Jun-8	Monday	Zoom meeting on iPhone
161. Jun-9	Tuesday	Stopped praise from group
162. Jun-10	Wednesday	Shared screen in Zoom
163. Jun-11	Thursday	Learned ASANA program
164. Jun-12	Friday	Spoke to Facebook directly
165. Jun-13	Saturday	Employees quitting call centers
166. Jun-14	Sunday	Canceled City-to-Shore ride
167. Jun-15	Monday	Federal Reserve Main Street lending program
168. Jun-16	**Tuesday**	**A call like no other**
169. Jun-17	**Wednesday**	**Sing as front man to a band**
170. Jun-18	Thursday	Tipped gas attendant
171. Jun-19	Friday	Mobile machine product demo
172. Jun-20	Saturday	Employee tests positive for COVID-19

173. Jun-21	Sunday	Father's Day as Grumpa
174. Jun-22	Monday	Took a COVID-19 fast test
175. Jun-23	Tuesday	Used BrainToss app
176. Jun-24	Wednesday	Panama Jack Sidewalk Sale
177. Jun-25	**Thursday**	**Tailgate show for competitors**
178. Jun-26	Friday	Exported contacts from LinkedIn
179. Jun-27	**Saturday**	**Posted opinion on social media**
180. Jun-28	Sunday	Organized daughter's basement
181. Jun-29	Monday	"House call" as "Dr. Baldwin"
182. Jun-30	Tuesday	Facetime with grandson
183. Jul-1	**Wednesday**	**Fly a plane**
184. Jul-2	Thursday	Networking tailgate
185. Jul-3	Friday	Zoom retirement party call
186. Jul-4	Saturday	Camp Okanickon Trail hike
187. Jul-5	Sunday	Golf in three hours as a walker
188. Jul-6	**Monday**	**Questions for Conversations with a Black Man**
189. Jul-7	Tuesday	Endorse someone on LinkedIn
190. Jul-8	Wednesday	Convert CSV file to Excel
191. Jul-9	Thursday	Practice range on my way to work
192. Jul-10	**Friday**	**Listen to an audio book (*The Fire Next Time*)**
193. Jul-11	Saturday	Froze top row in Excel
194. Jul-12	Sunday	1st birthday with first grandchild
195. Jul-13	Monday	Emailed golf joke to golf group
196. Jul-14	Tuesday	PBE Zoom meeting
197. Jul-15	Wednesday	Live networking post-COVID-19
198. Jul-16	Thursday	Wear Sketchers

199. Jul-17	**Friday**	**Mooned friend on golf course**
200. Jul-18	Saturday	Medical marijuana lozenges with my old neighborhood friends
201. Jul-19	Sunday	Shot over 100 at Scotland Run
202. Jul-20	**Monday**	**Juggle**
203. Jul-21	Tuesday	Live in studio production
204. Jul-22	Wednesday	"Loved" a posting on LinkedIn
205. Jul-23	Thursday	YouTube Live event
206. Jul-24	**Friday**	**Play Pickle Ball**
207. Jul-25	Saturday	Walk railroad tracks at work
208. Jul-26	Sunday	Walk trail at Tacony-Palmyra Bridge
209. Jul-27	Monday	Phillies tickets moved to 2021
210. Jul-28	Tuesday	Added Google My Business photos
211. Jul-29	**Wednesday**	**Golf 18 holes with three clubs**
212. Jul-30	**Thursday**	**Father & Son fishing trip**
213. Jul-31	**Friday**	**Catch a King Salmon**
214. Aug-1	**Saturday**	**Kayak by myself**
215. Aug-2	Sunday	Eat chocolate-covered coffee beans
216. Aug-3	Monday	Call center for two states – California & New York
217. Aug-4	**Tuesday**	**Flood at one of the showrooms**
218. Aug-5	**Wednesday**	**A Seven-figure sale (sneeze guards)**
219. Aug-6	Thursday	Placed $300,000 on AMEX
220. Aug-7	Friday	Loaned employees out to keep them employed
221. Aug-8	**Saturday**	**Symphony Hall – Sirius 76**
222. Aug-9	**Sunday**	**Pandora Now – Sirius 3**
223. Aug-10	**Monday**	**PHISH Radio – Sirius 29**

224. Aug-11	**Tuesday**	**Hip Hop Nation – Sirius 44**	
225. Aug-12	Wednesday	Read *Charge of the Light Brigade*	
226. Aug-13	**Thursday**	**BPM (Beats Per Minute) – Sirius 51**	
227. Aug-14	**Friday**	**Bluegrass Junction – Sirius 62**	
228. Aug-15	**Saturdayen**	**Lighten – Sirius 65**	
229. Aug-16	**Sunday**	**Grandchild's first birthday party**	
230. Aug-17	**Monday**	**Real Jazz – Sirius 67**	
231. Aug-18	Tuesday	Member – Guest with my brother	
232. Aug-19	**Wednesday**	**BB King Bluesville – Sirius 74**	
233. Aug-20	**Thursday**	**Met Opera Radio – Sirius 75 (now 355)**	
234. Aug-21	**Friday**	**Joel Olsteen Radio – Sirius 128**	
235. Aug-22	Saturday	Political viewpoint via email	
236. Aug-23	**Sunday**	**Laugh USA – Sirius 98**	
237. Aug-24	Monday	Develop logo for my golf team	
238. Aug-25	**Tuesday**	**Rural Radio – Sirius 147**	
239. Aug-20	Wednesday	Business Radio – Sirius 123	
240. Aug-27	Thursday	Produce golf team merchandise	
241. Aug-28	Friday	Tee shot between marker and ball	
242. Aug-29	Saturday	Eat a prune	
243. Aug-30	Sunday	Wear mismatched socks	
244. Aug-31	**Monday**	**Sent invitation to fill a restaurant**	
245. Sep-1	Tuesday	PPP loan forgiveness sign up	
246. Sep-2	Wednesday	Dinner invite refusal due to COVID-19	
247. Sep-3	Thursday	Photo book of grandson's first year	
248. Sep-4	Friday	Massage chair during workday	
249. Sep-5	**Saturday**	**Horseshoe Bend Park hike**	
250. Sep-6	Sunday	Tried to drive to left side of lake on ninth hole	

251. Sep-7	Monday	Hit four consecutive 3 woods
252. Sep-8	**Tuesday**	**Filled a restaurant**
253. Sep-9	Wednesday	Paid for Larry Cohen's dinner
254. Sep-10	Thursday	Watched a movie on Prime
255. Sep-11	Friday	Friend drove cross country
256. Sep-12	Saturday	Parked Winnebago inside office
257. Sep-13	Sunday	Tried smelling salts
258. Sep-14	Monday	Received a virtual "shout out"
259. Sep-15	Tuesday	Asked Siri – Closest gun range
260. Sep-16	Wednesday	Painted a wine glass
261. Sep-17	**Thursday**	**Picked up a million-dollar check**
262. Sep-18	Friday	Walked backward around the block
263. Sep-19	Saturday	Walk on beach of the Delaware River
264. Sep-20	Sunday	Play a "Snell" named golf ball
265. Sep-21	Monday	Golf lesson on course
266. Sep-22	Tuesday	Went unsuccessfully to gun range to shoot
267. Sep-23	**Wednesday**	**Visit Vietnam War Memorial**
268. Sep-24	Thursday	COVID-19-inspired "Watch Party"
269. Sep-25	Friday	Used golf pushcart
270. Sep-26	Saturday	Took mom to her brother's home
271. Sep-27	Sunday	Three birdies in a round of golf
272. Sep-28	Monday	Solicited local competitors
273. Sep-29	Tuesday	Zoom call with mentor with Alzheimer's
274. Sep-30	Wednesday	Customer trade show as tailgate
275. Oct-1	Thursday	PPP loan forgiveness completed
276. Oct-2	**Friday**	**Acquired company due to COVID-19**
277. Oct-3	Saturday	Deschutes "Fresh Haze" beer

278. Oct-4   Sunday   Pocono Manor Golf Course

279. Oct-5   Monday   Drank pickle juice-infused vodka

280. Oct-6   Tuesday   Visited Sweet Valley, Pennsylvania

281. Oct-7   Wednesday   Birdied hole #16 at Riverwinds

282. Oct-8   Thursday   Ate a lemon for a charity challenge

283. Oct-9   Friday   Changed name on Zoom call

284. Oct-10   Saturday   Drove over the Manhattan Bridge

285. Oct-11   Sunday   Shot 39 on Scotland Run front nine

286. Oct-12   Monday   Watched *Collateral Beauty* movie

287. Oct-13   Tuesday   Contacted City Controller

288. Oct-14   Wednesday   Emailed and called Pennsylvania Senators

289. Oct-15   Thursday   Received first signed book of a new author

290. Oct-16   Friday   Rent abatement

291. Oct-17   Saturday   Trunk or Treat for Halloween

292. Oct-18   Sunday   Shot of whiskey at 7 a.m. golf match

293. Oct-19   Monday   Virtual cocktail tasting

294. Oct-20   Tuesday   Mail-in vote for President

295. Oct-21   Wednesday   Pedicure

296. Oct-22   Thursday   Skyline Drive, Virginia

297. Oct-23   Friday   Blue Ridge Parkway

298. Oct-24   Saturday   Stargazing app

299. Oct-25   Sunday   Visited Asheville, North Carolina

300. Oct-26   Monday   Play Farkle

301. Oct-27   Tuesday   Belgium gelato in a blue cone

302. Oct-28   Wednesday   Isle of Palms sunrise

303. Oct-29   Thursday   Lying next to live alligator on golf course

304. Oct-30   Friday   Wrote names on a seashell

305. Oct-31	Saturday	French press coffee
306. Nov-1	Sunday	Donation for pet charity
307. Nov-2	**Monday**	**Smoked a cigarette**
308. Nov-3	**Tuesday**	**Acupuncture**
309. Nov-4	Wednesday	Application to serve at a shelter
310. Nov-5	**Thursday**	**Virtual cooking class**
311. Nov-6	**Friday**	**Disc Golf (8)**
312. Nov-7	Saturday	First woman of color VP speech
313. Nov-8	Sunday	COVID-19 test to self
314. Nov-9	Monday	Golf without a glove
315. Nov-10	**Tuesday**	**Multiple staff test positive for COVID-19**
316. Nov-11	Wednesday	Used machine to apply custom medals
317. Nov-12	Thursday	Pick up dinner and "real" roses
318. Nov-13	Friday	Visit a Buddhist temple
319. Nov-14	Saturday	Reach out to a speech writer
320. Nov-15	Sunda	Drove left of lake on ninth hole
321. Nov-16	**Monday**	**Visit grandparents' gravesite**
322. Nov-17	**Tuesday**	**Call with Warren Buffett**
323. Nov-18	Wednesday	Business meeting at Top Golf
324. Nov-19	Thursday	Bernard Langer virtual interview
325. Nov-20	**Friday**	**Played hooky from work to play with my grandson**
326. Nov-21	Saturday	Hire speech/book coach
327. Nov-22	**Sunday**	**The opera – *Falstaff* (virtually)**
328. Nov-23	Monday	Quarantined
329. Nov-24	**Tuesday**	**COVID-19 test – Four-hour line**
330. Nov-25	Wednesday	Wrote prologue to my *first* book

331. Nov-26	Thursday	Communicated Thanksgiving gratitude and love
332. Nov-27	Friday	Visit gravesite of grandparents on mom's side
333. Nov-28	Saturday	Wrote outline for my *first* book
334. Nov-29	Sunday	Learn a magic trick
335. Nov-30	Monday	Draft of book cover
336. Dec-1	Tuesday	Attend a virtual trade show
337. Dec-2	Wednesday	Build a gingerbread house
338. Dec-3	**Thursday**	**Birding**
339. Dec-4	**Friday**	**Nitrile (medical) glove order**
340. Dec-5	**Saturday**	**Slept on the streets with the homeless**
341. Dec-6	Sunday	Laundromat
342. Dec-7	**Monday**	**Assemble bikes for charity**
343. Dec-8	**Tuesday**	**Watch a movie with subtitles**
344. Dec-9	**Wednesday**	**Guitar lesson**
345. Dec-10	Thursday	My Social Security statement
346. Dec-11	**Friday**	**Wrote a song – *Twenty-Twenty***
347. Dec-12	**Saturday**	**Free-form watercolor painting**
348. Dec-13	**Sunday**	**Perform a magic trick**
349. Dec-14	Monday	Wore wig for video birthday message
350. Dec-15	Tuesday	Make crab cakes from scratch
351. Dec-16	Wednesday	Tip jar for driving mom
352. Dec-1	7Thursday	Read Bible as an adult
353. Dec-18	**Friday**	**Wrote a speech**
354. Dec-19	**Saturday**	**Trap shooting**
355. Dec-20	Sunday	Research and pick a stock – AI
356. Dec-21	**Monday**	**Give money to homeless person at a stoplight**

357. Dec-22	Tuesday	Play a video game – FIFA
358. Dec-23	Wednesday	Wear an ugly Christmas sweater
359. Dec-24	Thursday	Gift-card-only Christmas presents
360. Dec-25	**Friday**	**Watch *It's a Wonderful Life***
361. Dec-26	**Saturday**	**Kwanzaa (learn about)**
362. Dec-27	**Sunday**	**Cast a spell**
363. Dec-28	Monday	Record my *first* speech
364. Dec-29	**Tuesday**	**Being blind (simulated)**
365. Dec-30	**Wednesday**	**Fly a drone**
366. Dec-31	**Thursday**	**Write a book (finish manuscript outline)**

*P.S. – **Looking back***: *The firsts had become a habit and there were still a number of them on my to-do list as my year of firsts wound down to an end. Out of my initial list of firsts, I did around half of them. What was I thinking when I listed juggling as a fast, same-day first? It wasn't. As you have seen, I came up with many more to fill in the blanks. A number of them I just could not do because of the pandemic or for other various life-gets-in-the-way reasons. Some of those that I did not get to I still want to do. When the world gets back to normal and comes off pause, I plan on continuing to do these firsts. I just may not pressure myself to do one every day. Following is a partial list of firsts yet to be done. I will hopefully get to them in 2021 and beyond:*

- Karaoke
- Shave head completely
- Try virtual reality
- Apply eye makeup
- Spend a day in a wheelchair
- Create and perform a rap song
- Tattoo (Henna? Real?)
- Make Limoncello
- Try psilocybin (magic mushrooms)

- TED Talk
- Kids interview me about my life
- Serve dinner at a shelter
- Walk to work
- Engrave holloware on computer
- Learn to edit a video
- Indoor rock climbing
- Skydive
- Visit Fenway Park
- Row on a river
- Drum lesson
- Attend a Yom Kippur service
- Mountain biking
- Wood carving
- Rebuild an engine
- Tailgate at a Penn State game
- Spin class
- Visit Jerusalem
- Travel down the Nile River
- Hot Yoga
- See a ballet (*Swan Lake*?)
- Eat a cricket
- Attend a poetry reading
- Do a mud run
- Snowboarding
- *First* with grandson – Take Luke to the zoo
- Participate in a Fantasy Football league
- Attend the Kentucky Derby
- Experience a jazz club
- Attend the Masters
- Experience a "silent" retreat

Experience and attend any religious services that I have not experienced (Quaker, Judaism, Hinduism, Shinto, Taoism, Baha'I, Confucianism, Jainism, Sikhism, Zoroastrianism, Atheism, Scientology, and Baptist).

I'm sure you can help me think of many other possible *firsts*. My brother once said to me: "I know a *first* you could do. You could run naked down the middle of the strip in Las Vegas." He cackled. I'm not looking for those types of *firsts*. My brother obviously has a warped sense of humor and has "issues." That is why I love him so much. I politely suggested he keep his suggestions to himself.

· · ·

OUR CORE VALUES

My company and I made it through the year utilizing our following 10 core values as our guiding light, our North Star. If you are looking to establish your own and have questions you can reach out to me at: keith@gospikes.com.

CARE: *Take care and pride in the quality of everything you touch and everything you do. Always ask yourself, "Is this my best work?" Everything you touch has your signature. Sign in bold ink that you care. Pay attention to the details and get them right — the* first *time. From the spelling of the client's name to the specific language we are placing on their awards, to the colors in their logo, details matter. Be a fanatic about accuracy. Do whatever it takes to meet and exceed the customer's needs.*

DEPENDABILITY: *Honor commitments and be dependable. There's no better way to earn people's trust than to be true to your word. Do what you say you're going to do, when you say you're going to do it. This includes being on time for appointments and abiding by our 24-hour rule for order entry, proofs, and returning customer calls and emails. Allow extra time by being organized for surprises and delays, and don't let these become excuses.*

Individual accountability for our team's success. "Dependability is THE Best Ability" — be there for your teammates.

RESPECT: *Assume positive intent. Work from the assumption that people are good, fair, and honest, and that the intent behind their actions is positive. Set aside your own judgment and preconceived notions. Always be professional. Give people the benefit of the doubt as well as respect. Give respect to others and expect respect in return.*

WIN-WIN: *Always create win-win solutions. It's a two-way street. Learn to think from others' perspectives. Discover what they need and find a way to help them meet those needs while fulfilling your own. Win-win solutions are always more effective and longer-lasting than win-lose solutions.*

FUN: *Keep things FUN. Remember that the world has bigger problems than the daily challenges that make up our work. Stuff happens. Keep perspective. Don't take things personally or take yourself too seriously. Laugh every day. Celebrate success. Catching people doing things right is more effective than catching them doing things wrong. Create and have fun while accomplishing goals.*

INTEGRITY: *Do the right thing — always. Demonstrate an unwavering commitment to doing the right thing in every action you take and in every decision, you make, even when no one is looking. Have integrity and always tell the truth. If you make a mistake, own up to it, apologize, make it right, and learn from it. We espouse greatness and back it up.*

YES: *Find a way to say "yes." Take personal responsibility for making things happen — somehow, someway. Respond to every situation by looking for how we can do it rather than explaining why it can't be done. Be resourceful and show initiative.*

HUSTLE: *Go the extra mile. Be willing to do whatever it takes to accomplish the job — plus a little bit more. HUSTLE. Take the next step to solve the problem, even if it means doing something that's not in your job description. Work* *quickly and efficiently. It's the extra mile that separates the average person from the superstar. Be a superstar.*

LEAN: *Be obsessive about organization. Regardless of the quality of your work, if you can't manage multiple issues, tasks, and promises, you won't be a superstar. Maintain a clean and orderly work area. Use an effective task management system for prioritizing and tracking outstanding issues and responsibilities. Attack the waste that creates downtime: defects, overproduction, waiting, non-utilized talent, transportation, inventory, motion, and extra processing. Work smarter, not harder.*

LEARN: *Look to continuously improve. Practice blameless problem solving. Apply your creativity, spirit, and enthusiasm to developing solutions rather than pointing fingers and dwelling on problems. Identify lessons learned and use those lessons to improve our processes so we don't make the same mistakes again. Get smarter with every mistake. LEARN from every experience. Regularly reevaluate every aspect of your job to find ways to improve. "Because we've always done it that way" is not a reason.*

CONTACT

If you have thoughts, comments, or seek more information I want to hear from you. If you have any feedback or questions concerning anything in this book please reach out to me at Keith@GoSpikes.com or visit me and my company at www.GoSpikes.com. You can also visit me via my author site www.KeithBaldwinFirsts.com

SERVICES INCLUDE:

- Keynote Speaking
- Executive Coaching
- Lending an ear to help

GIVING BACK:

In order to support my "Why" of *Saving a Job, Saves a Life*, a portion of the proceeds of this book will be donated to Baker Industries. Baker Industries' unique non-profit workforce development program provides essential work opportunity and training for over 200 vulnerable, hard to employ adults each year. Working from their two large production facilities, Baker successfully serve dozens of customers each day and demonstrate the capability and potential of individuals facing challenges when given a chance. Baker's program participants build work skills, self-esteem and hope in a caring environment that prepares them for sustained success in the workplace for these "returning citizens" in quest for a job.

For more information on Baker Industries please visit www.baker-industries.org